From New Deal
Banking Reform to
World War II
Inflation

From New Deal Banking Reform to World War II Inflation

MILTON FRIEDMAN

ANNA JACOBSON SCHWARTZ

A STUDY BY THE
NATIONAL BUREAU OF ECONOMIC RESEARCH, NEW YORK

PUBLISHED BY
PRINCETON UNIVERSITY PRESS, PRINCETON

This is a reprint of Chapters 8-10 of the authors' *A Monetary History of the United States, 1867-1960* (Princeton University Press for National Bureau of Economic Research, 1963). It includes certain other materials from that publication.

First PRINCETON PAPERBACK Edition 1980
Printed in the United States of America

RELATION OF THE DIRECTORS
TO THE WORK AND PUBLICATIONS
OF THE NATIONAL BUREAU OF ECONOMIC RESEARCH

RESOLVED, That (1) the object of the National Bureau of Economic Research is to ascertain and to present to the public important economic facts and their interpretation in a scientific and impartial manner. The Board of Directors is charged with the responsibility of ensuring that the work of the National Bureau is carried on in strict conformity with this object.

(2) The President of the National Bureau shall submit to the Board of Directors, or to its Executive Committee, for their formal adoption all specific proposals for research to be instituted.

(3) No research report shall be published until the President shall have submitted to each member of the Board the manuscript proposed for publication, and such information as will, in his opinion and in the opinion of the author, serve to determine the suitability of the report for publication in accordance with the principles of the National Bureau. Each manuscript shall contain a summary drawing attention to the nature and treatment of the problems studied, the character of the data and their utilization in the report, and the main conclusions reached.

(4) For each manuscript so submitted, a special committee of the Board shall be appointed by majority agreement of the President and Vice Presidents (or by the Executive Committee in case of inability to decide on the part of the President and Vice Presidents), consisting of three directors selected as nearly as may be one from each general division of the Board. The names of the special manuscript committee shall be stated to each Director when the manuscript is submitted to him. It shall be the duty of each member of the special manuscript committee to read the manuscript. If each member of the manuscript committee signifies his approval within thirty days of the transmittal of the manuscript, the report may be published. If at the end of that period any member of the manuscript committee withholds his approval, the President shall then notify each member of the Board, requesting approval or disapproval of publication, and thirty days additional shall be granted for this purpose. The manuscript shall then not be published unless at least a majority of the entire Board who shall have voted on the proposal within the time fixed for the receipt of votes shall have approved.

(5) No manuscript may be published, though approved by each member of the special manuscript committee, until forty-five days have elapsed from the transmittal of the report in manuscript form. The interval is allowed for the receipt of any memorandum of dissent or reservation, together with a brief statement of his reasons, that any member may wish to express; and such memorandum of dissent or reservation shall be published with the manuscript if he so desires. Publication does not, however, imply that each member of the Board has read the manuscript, or that either members of the Board in general or the special committee have passed on its validity in every detail.

(6) Publications of the National Bureau issued for informational purposes concerning the work of the Bureau and its staff, or issued to inform the public of activities of Bureau staff, and volumes issued as a result of various conferences involving the National Bureau shall contain a specific disclaimer noting that such publication has not passed through the normal review procedures required in this resolution. The Executive Committee of the Board is charged with review of all such publications from time to time to ensure that they do not take on the character of formal research reports of the National Bureau, requiring formal Board approval.

(7) Unless otherwise determined by the Board or exempted by the terms of paragraph 6, a copy of this resolution shall be printed in each National Bureau publication.

(Resolution adopted October 25, 1926,
as revised February 6, 1933, February 24, 1941, and April 20, 1968)

Contents

Experience in controversies such as these brings out the impossibility of learning anything from facts till they are examined and interpreted by reason; and teaches that the most reckless and treacherous of all theorists is he who professes to let facts and figures speak for themselves, who keeps in the background the part he has played, perhaps unconsciously, in selecting and grouping them, and in suggesting the argument post hoc ergo propter hoc.

ALFRED MARSHALL

From New Deal
Banking Reform to
World War II
Inflation

CHAPTER 1

New Deal Changes in the Banking Structure and Monetary Standard

THE New Deal period offers a striking contrast in monetary and banking matters. On the one hand, monetary policy was accorded little importance in affecting the course of economic affairs and the policy actually followed was hesitant and almost entirely passive. On the other hand, the foundations of the American financial structure and the character of the monetary standard were profoundly modified. Both developments were direct outgrowths of the dramatic experiences of the preceding years. The apparent failure of monetary policy to stem the depression led to the relegation of money to a minor role in affecting the course of economic events. At the same time, the collapse of the banking system produced a demand for remedial legislation that led to the enactment of federal deposit insurance, to changes in the powers of the Federal Reserve System, and to closer regulation of banks and other financial institutions. The depressed state of the economy, the large preceding fall in prices and, despite those conditions, the poor competitive position of our exports thanks to the depreciation of the pound and other currencies, all combined with the New Deal atmosphere to foster experimentation with the monetary standard. The experiments involved temporary departure from gold, a period of flexible and depreciating exchange rates, silver purchases, subsequent nominal return to gold at a higher price for gold, and drastic changes in the terms and conditions under which gold could be held and obtained by private parties.

This chapter describes the changes that were made in the banking structure (section 1) and in the monetary standard (section 2). The next chapter discusses the monetary policies followed during the New Deal period.

1. *Changes in the Banking Structure*

Three kinds of legislative measures were enacted after the 1933 banking panic: emergency measures designed to reopen closed banks and to strengthen banks permitted to open; measures that effected a more lasting alteration in the commercial banking structure—the most important being federal deposit insurance—and, more generally, in the financial structure; measures that altered the structure and powers of the Federal Reserve System. In addition, the banking system was affected in important ways by the reaction of the banks themselves, independently of legislation, to their experiences during the prior contraction.

EMERGENCY MEASURES

We have already had occasion to refer to the Emergency Banking Act of March 9, 1933. Title I of the act approved and confirmed the action taken by President Roosevelt in proclaiming a nationwide bank holiday from March 6 to March 9, inclusive, under the wartime measure of October 6, 1917, which conferred broad powers over banking and currency upon the President of the United States.[1] Title I, further, amended the wartime measure to empower the President in time of national emergency to regulate or prohibit the payment of deposits by all banking institutions. During the period of emergency proclaimed by the President, member banks were forbidden to transact any banking business unless authorized by the Secretary of the Treasury with the approval of the President.

Title II of the act provided for the reopening and operation on a restricted basis of certain national banks with impaired assets, which under existing laws would have been placed in receivership and liquidated. Conservators were to be appointed for those banks by the Comptroller of the Currency. The Comptroller could direct the conservators to make available for immediate withdrawal amounts of existing deposits he deemed it safe to release; and the conservators, subject to his approval, could receive new deposits, available for immediate withdrawal without restriction and segregated from other liabilities of the bank. The conservators were also to be charged with the duty of preparing plans of reorganization, subject to the Comptroller's approval, which could be put into effect with the consent of 75 per cent of a bank's depositors and other creditors or of two-thirds of the stockholders.

Title III provided for issues of nonassessable preferred stock by national banks to be sold to the general public, or the Reconstruction Finance Corporation (RFC), which might also buy similar issues from state banks.

Title IV provided for emergency issues of Federal Reserve Bank notes up to the face value of direct obligations of the United States deposited as security, or up to 90 per cent of the estimated value of eligible paper and bankers' acceptances acquired under the provisions of the Emergency Banking Act. After the emergency recognized by the Presidential proclamation of March 6, 1933, had terminated, Federal Reserve Bank notes could be issued only on the security of direct obligations of the United States. Over $200 million of Federal Reserve Bank notes were issued

---

[1] By a proclamation issued on Dec. 30, 1933, the President relinquished jurisdiction over nonmember banks assumed by the federal government at the time of his proclamation of a banking holiday.

in 1933. Thereafter until the war, they were retired as fast as returned from circulation. The liability for those notes was assumed by the Treasury in March 1935.

Under Title IV, Federal Reserve Banks were also authorized, until March 3, 1934, to make advances in exceptional and exigent circumstances to member banks on their own notes on the security of any acceptable assets. That provision superseded the one regarding advances to member banks in the Glass-Steagall Act (see Chapter 7, footnote 26). The provision was extended by Presidential proclamation until March 3, 1935, when it expired. The provision adopted in the Banking Act of 1935 omitted the requirement that advances be made only in exceptional and exigent circumstances and to member banks whose other means of obtaining accommodation from Federal Reserve Banks were exhausted (see below, pp. 447–448).

Opening of Banks

Under the authority of the Emergency Banking Act, President Roosevelt issued a proclamation on March 9 continuing the banking holiday, and an executive order on March 10 empowering the Secretary of the Treasury to issue licenses to member banks to reopen. Every member bank was directed to make application for a license to the Federal Reserve Bank of its district, which would serve as an agent of the Secretary in granting licenses. The executive order also empowered state banking authorities to reopen their sound banks that were not members of the Federal Reserve System. Another executive order dated March 18 granted state banking authorities permission to appoint conservators for unlicensed state member banks when consistent with state law.

In a statement to the press on March 11 and a radio address on March 12, the President announced the program for reopening licensed banks on March 13, 14, and 15. Member banks licensed by the Secretary of the Treasury as well as nonmember banks licensed by state banking authorities "opened for normal business on an unrestricted basis, except so far as affected by legal contracts between the banks and depositors with respect to withdrawals or notice of withdrawals"[2] on March 13, in the twelve Federal Reserve Bank cities; on March 14, in some 250 cities having active, recognized clearing house associations; and on March 15, elsewhere.

Effect on Number and Deposits of Banks

At the turn of the year, two months before the banking holiday, there had been nearly 17,800 commercial banks in operation, by the definition of banks then in use (Table 13). When the banking holiday was ter-

---

[2] Statement by the Secretary of the Treasury to the superintendent of banks of each state, Mar. 11, 1933, *Federal Reserve Bulletin,* Mar. 1933, p. 128.

TABLE 13
NUMBER AND DEPOSITS OF COMMERCIAL BANKS BEFORE
AND AFTER BANKING HOLIDAY

Definition of Banks and Class of Banks	Number (1)	Deposits (billions of dollars)		Ratio (3) ÷ (2) (4)
		Adjusted Demand Plus Time, Seasonally Adjusted (2)	Total Demand Plus Time, Unadjusted for Seasonal (3)	
As defined in:		DEC. 31, 1932		
All-Bank Statistics				
1. Active commercial banks	18,074	29.2	36.1	1.24
2. Not classified as banks by 1932 definition	278	1.0		
Federal Reserve Bulletin, 1932				
3. Active commercial banks	17,796	28.2		
		MAR. 15, 1933		
4. Suspended, merged, or liquidated between Dec. 31, 1932, and Mar. 15, 1933	447		0.2	
5. Total commercial banks (line 3 minus line 4)	17,349			
6. Licensed	11,878	23.3	27.4	1.18
7. Unlicensed	5,430	3.4	4.0	
8. Licensed plus unlicensed (line 6 plus line 7)	17,308	26.7	31.4	
9. Discrepancy (line 5 minus line 8)	41			

NOTE: Where reported figures are not available, estimates are shown only for items useful in deriving line 8, as described in source notes.

SOURCE, BY LINE

1.   Col. 1: Interpolation between June 1932 and June 1933 figures, shown in *All-Bank Statistics*, p. 37; the interpolation was based on June and Dec. 1932 and June 1933 figures on number of banks in *Banking and Monetary Statistics*, p. 19. The difference between the latter and former series at June dates was interpolated along a straight line and added to the Dec. figure in *ibid*.
    Col. 2: Table A-1.
    Col. 3: Interpolation between June 1932 and June 1933 figures, shown in *All-Bank Statistics*, p. 36; the interpolation was based on June and Dec. 1932 and June 1933 figures on deposits of banks in *Banking and Monetary Statistics*, p. 19. The ratio of the Dec. figure to its own inter-June straight-line trend value was multiplied by the straight-line trend value computed at the end of Dec. between the June figures in *All-Bank Statistics*.
2.   Col. 1: Line 1 minus line 3.
    Col. 2: The excess of demand deposits adjusted plus time deposits for June dates, 1932–33, in *All-Bank Statistics* (pp. 60 and 36), over the corresponding sums in *Banking and Monetary Statistics* (p. 34) was obtained; an estimate of the excess was interpolated for Dec. along a straight line. An estimate was then added for deposits

(continued)

NOTES to TABLE 13 (continued)

in commercial banks included in the *Banking and Monetary Statistics* series but not included in the *Federal Reserve Bulletin* (*FRB*) series for 1932 (referred to in the table as defined in *FRB*, 1932,). *FRB* in 1932 did not show adjusted deposits, so only a comparison of total deposits excluding interbank deposits in this source (Dec. 1933, p. 746) and in *Banking and Monetary Statistics* (p. 19) is possible. A rough conversion to adjusted deposits was made of excess of total deposits in *ibid.* over the *FRB* figure, and added to the excess of adjusted deposits in *All-Bank Statistics* over the series in *Banking and Monetary Statistics*.

3. Col. 1: *FRB*, Dec. 1933, p. 746.
   Col. 2: Line 1 minus line 2.
4. Cols. 1, 3: *FRB*, Sept. 1937, p. 867.
6. Col. 1: Sum of figures for licensed member banks on Mar. 15, 1933 (*FRB*, June 1935, p. 404), and for licensed nonmember banks on Mar. 22, 1933 (*Annual Report* of the Secretary of the Treasury, 1933, p. 24).
   Col. 2: Figure for end of Mar. from Table A-1: (a) adjusted to Mar. 15, by multiplying by ratio of total deposits of licensed member banks on Mar. 15 to corresponding figure for Mar. 29 (25,554/25,850, *FRB*, June 1935, p. 404 and Apr. 1933, p. 216); and (b) adjusted to 1932 definition of banks by subtracting line 2, col. 2, reduced 10 per cent for assumed change in deposits, Dec. 31, 1932–Mar. 15, 1933.
   Col. 3: Sum of figures for licensed member banks on Mar. 15, 1933 (*FRB*, June 1935, p. 404), for licensed nonmember banks on Apr. 12, 1933 (*FRB*), minus an estimate of the deposits in nonmember banks that were licensed between Mar. 15 and Apr. 12. The figures are deposits as of Dec. 31, 1932, scaled down 10 per cent for assumed change in deposits, Dec. 31, 1932–Mar. 15, 1933.
7. Cols. 1, 3: Derived as the sum of:

	Number	Deposits ($ millions)
(a) Unlicensed member banks on Mar. 15, 1933 (*Federal Reserve Bulletin*)	1,621	2,867
(b) Unlicensed nonmember banks on Apr. 12, 1933 (*FRB*)	2,959	1,321
(c) Fall in unlicensed nonmember banks, Mar. 15–Apr. 12, 1933	850	325
	5,430	4,513

For item c, the changes, Mar. 15–Apr. 12, 1933, were estimated as follows:

	Number
(1) Licensed nonmember banks, Mar. 22 (*Annual Report*, Treasury, 1933, p. 24)	6,800
(2) Licensed nonmember banks, Apr. 12 (*FRB*, June 1935, p. 404)	7,392
(3) Liquidations of licensed and unlicensed nonmember banks, Mar. 16–Apr. 30 (*FRB*, Apr. 1934, p. 251)	258
Change in number, (2) + (3) − (1)	850

We had no information on deposits corresponding to numbers shown above. We arbitrarily assumed that the change in deposits in licensed nonmember banks, Mar. 22–Apr. 12, 1933, on a per-bank basis, approximated the change in deposits of licensed member banks, on a per-bank basis, Mar. 15–Apr. 12, 1933. The ratio for member banks between those two dates was 105.0. We used 104.0 for nonmember banks, multiplied average deposits on Apr. 12 by this ratio to get the

(continued)

average on Mar. 22, and multiplied again by the number of licensed nonmember banks to get estimated deposits in licensed nonmember banks on Mar. 22.

		Deposits ($ millions)
(1)	Licensed nonmember banks, Mar. 22 (as above)	4,803
(2)	Licensed nonmember banks, Apr. 12 (*FRB*, June 1935, p. 404)	5,020
(3)	Liquidations of licensed and unlicensed nonmember banks, Mar. 16–Apr. 30 (*FRB*, Apr. 1934, p. 251)	108
	Change in deposits, (2) + (3) − (1)	325

The figure for number of banks needed no further adjustment. That for deposits needed to be reduced $161 million to correct for overstatement of deposits in non-member banks; and by $321 million, for overstatement of deposits in member banks. The deposits of nonmember banks on Apr. 12, 1933, and of member banks on Mar. 15, 1933, are the deposits those banks had on Dec. 31, 1932. We have a measure of the overstatement for nonmember banks on June 30, 1933: data on number of and deposits in unlicensed member and nonmember banks in *Federal Reserve Bulletin*, June 1935, p. 404, where member bank deposits are the deposits those banks held on June 30, 1933, and nonmember bank deposits are the deposits those banks held on Dec. 31, 1932. These figures may be compared with the data in *All-Bank Statistics*, p. 72 (6 mutual savings banks with estimated $7 million in deposits have been deducted to obtain all commercial bank figures), which presumably show actual June 30, 1933, nonmember as well as member bank figures. The Dec. 1932 data for nonmember banks overstate deposits on June 30, 1933, by 12.2 per cent. Applying this percentage to line b, above, yields $161 million.

The measure of the overstatement for member banks is also based on an end-of-June 1933 comparison. For June 28, 1933, deposits in unlicensed member banks are the deposits those banks had on Dec. 31, 1932 (*FRB*, July 1933, p. 453). For June 30, 1933, we have actual deposits in those banks on this date (*FRB*, June 1935, p. 404). There is an 11.2 percentage difference between the two sets of figures. Applying this percentage to line a, above, yields $321 million.

7. Col. 2: Entry for unlicensed in col. 3 divided by ratio, line 6, col. 4.

9. Col. 1: Line 3 minus the sum of lines 4 and 8. Any of the components, lines 4, 6, and 7, may contribute to the discrepancy of 41 banks, based on the total shown in line 3. (In *Banking and Monetary Statistics*, p. 19, the total figure is 17,802, presumably because of the addition of certain private banks that did not report to state banking authorities and of institutions earlier not classified as commercial banks.) Line 4, for example, gives revised figures. Earlier sources showed the number of suspended banks, Jan. 1–Mar. 15, 1933, as 462 (see *Federal Reserve Bulletin*, Apr. 1934, p. 251). If 15 banks were excluded from the number of suspensions by the later source because they were reopened by June 30, 1933 (banks not licensed after the holiday were not considered suspensions if reopened by that date), our total of active banks in Dec. 1932 derived from lines 4, 6, and 7 would be too small by that number. Both lines 6 and 7 are partly estimated. The use of Mar. 22 figures for licensed nonmembers may slightly exaggerate the total for all banks in line 6. The figure for unlicensed nonmember banks included in line 7 was obtained indirectly and may well be too small not only by the discrepancy of 41 but also by a larger number, if line 6 is an overstatement.

minated, only 17,300 remained to be recorded in the statistics, and fewer than 12,000 of those were licensed to open and do business. The more than 5,000 unlicensed banks were left in a state of limbo, to be either reopened later—the fate of some 3,000—or to be closed for good and either liquidated or consolidated with other banks—the fate of over 2,000

TABLE 14

DISPOSITION BY DECEMBER 31, 1936, OF COMMERCIAL BANKS NOT LICENSED TO OPEN AT
TERMINATION OF BANKING HOLIDAY, MARCH 15, 1933
(deposits in millions of dollars)

| | | Change in Number of Banks | | | Deposits in Banks | Change in Deposits in Banks | | |
Date	Number Still Unlicensed (1)	Total (2)	Licensed to Reopen (3)	Suspended, Liquidated, or Merged (4)	Still Unlicensed[a] (5)	Total (6)	Licensed to Reopen (7)	Suspended, Liquidated, or Merged (8)
1933								
Mar. 15	5,430				4,031			
June 30	3,078	2,352	1,964	388	2,200	1,831	642	1,189
Dec. 30	1,769	1,309	576	733	1.025	1,175	496	679
1934								
June 30[b]	622	1,147	477	670	346	679	225	454
Dec. 26	190	432	174	258	96	250	79	171
1936								
Dec. 31	0	190	107	83	0	96	67	29
				.				
Total Mar. 15, 1933, to Dec. 31, 1936		5,430	3,298	2,132		4,031	1,509	2,522

[a] Deposits are unadjusted for interbank deposits, float, or seasonal.

[b] For nonmember banks, June 27, 1934.

SOURCE, BY COLUMN

(1, 5)   Sums of data for member and nonmember banks.

        Mar. 15, 1933: Unrounded figures from notes to Table 13, line 7, col. 1.
June 30, 1933: *All-Bank Statistics*, p. 72 (6 mutual savings banks with estimated
$7 million in deposits deducted to obtain all unlicensed commercial bank
figures). Other dates: *Federal Reserve Bulletin*, Jan. 1935, p. 62. Zero is shown
for Dec. 31, 1936, although there were still 10 unlicensed banks, with $1,748,000
deposits, neither granted licenses to reopen nor placed in liquidation or receivership on this date (*FRB*, Sept. 1937,,p. 867). These banks are treated here
as if they were in receivership by this date.

    (2)   Change in col. 1.

    (3)   Col. 2 minus col. 4.

(4, 8)   *Annual Report* of the Comptroller of the Currency, 1934, pp. 785–790; 1935,
pp. 807–808. Figure for Dec. 31, 1936, is a residual obtained by subtracting
sum of data through Dec. 30, 1934, from total for period through Dec. 31,
1936, in *FRB*, Sept. 1937, p. 867.

    (6)   Change in col. 5.

    (7)   Col. 6 minus col. 8. Deposits in banks granted licenses, July 1, 1933, to Dec. 31,
1936· (*FRB*), amounted to $716 million compared with total of $867 million
shown here.

(Table 14). The changes in deposits were only slightly less drastic. From December 1932 to March 15, 1933, deposits in banks open for business fell by one-sixth. Seventy per cent of the decline was accounted for by the deposits on the books of banks not licensed to open, yet not finally disposed of (Table 13, lines 3–7, col. 2).

The banks licensed to open operated generally without restrictions, though in some cases legal contracts were in effect limiting withdrawals by depositors to a specified fraction of the amounts due them.[3] Many of the unlicensed banks, in their turn, were open for a limited range of business, with conservators authorized to receive new deposits subject to the order of the depositor and segregated from other funds. The line between licensed and unlicensed banks was therefore less sharp in practice than in the records.

Fate of Unlicensed Banks

Table 14 shows what happened to the unlicensed banks over the next several years. By the end of June 1933 over 2,300 of the banks, holding nearly half the total restricted deposits, had been disposed of—nearly 2,000 banks were licensed to reopen, 388 closed. However, the closed banks had decidedly the larger volume of deposits, and this was to remain true for the rest of the period as well, so that the three-fifths of the banks ultimately reopened held only three-eighths of the deposits.

The RFC played a major role in the restoration of the banking system as it had in the futile attempts to shore it up before the banking holiday. It invested a total of over $1 billion in bank capital—one-third of the total capital of all banks in the United States in 1933—and purchased capital issues of 6,139 banks, or almost one-half the number of banks.[4] In addition, it made loans to open banks for distribution to de-

---

[3] "Deposits in licensed banks the payment of which has been deferred beyond the time originally contemplated" amounted to $103 million in June 1933, $55 million in June 1934, and were apparently zero in June 1935 (sums of national and nonnational bank data from Comptroller of the Currency, *Annual Report,* 1933, pp. 420, 629; 1934, pp. 523, 755).

[4] The RFC was authorized to buy preferred stock and capital notes and debentures of banks by the Emergency Banking Act and an amendment to it. Most of the banks in which it invested were those originally permitted to resume operations only on a limited withdrawal basis (Jesse H. Jones [with Edward Angly], *Fifty Billion Dollars,* New York, Macmillan, 1951, p. 21). To avoid the suggestion that RFC investment signified a bank's weakness, some stronger banks which did not actually need new capital were asked to sell the Corporation a modest amount of preferred stock or capital notes. According to Jones, fewer than twenty of the more than six thousand banks into which the RFC put capital actually had no need of it (p. 34). The capital was invested on the understanding that it would be retired out of about one-half the net earnings of the banks after payment of dividends or interest on RFC capital. RFC investment permitted the banks to charge off losses. Approximately 51 per cent of its investment had been retired by February 1939 (Reconstruction Finance Corporation, *Seven-Year Report to the*

positors of $187 million and to closed banks of over $900 million, on the
security of the best assets of those institutions. The loans, made after the
banking panic, were in addition to loans of $951 million to open banks
and of $80 million to closed banks made before the banking panic.[5] In
aggregate, 5,816 open banks and 2,773 closed banks obtained RFC loans
totaling more than $2 billion. RFC and other federal authorities doubtless
also played a role in fostering bank mergers, particularly purchase by
larger banks of smaller banks with doubtful portfolios, that served further
to reduce the number of individual banks and, hopefully, to strengthen
their solvency.

Effects on Money Stock Measures

The banking holiday and its aftermath make our recorded figures on
the money stock even less reliable than for other times as indicators of
some consistent economic magnitude meriting the label money. Before
the banking holiday, many banks had imposed restrictions on the use of
deposits in an attempt to avoid suspension. Those deposits are counted in
full in the recorded money stock. On the other hand, after the holiday,
both restricted and unrestricted deposits in unlicensed banks are excluded
completely from the recorded money stock.[6] The shift in treatment, which
can hardly correspond to a shift in economic significance, is the major
factor behind the sharp decline in the recorded figures in March 1933.
Consistent accounting would require exclusion of restricted deposits
throughout or their inclusion throughout. Criteria of economic significance
would call for including in the money stock a fraction of restricted
deposits, the fraction fluctuating over time. Any one of these courses
would eliminate the discontinuous drop in our series in March 1933 and
yield a milder decline before March and a milder rise thereafter.

Unfortunately, there is no adequate statistical basis for estimating

---

President and the Congress of the U.S., February 2, 1932, to February 1, 1939,
p. 5).
[5] RFC, *Seven-Year Report*, pp. 4, 6, for total loans. For RFC loans from Feb. 2,
1932, to Mar. 3, 1933, see RFC, *Summaries of the Activities of the RFC and Its
Condition as of December 31, 1935*, GPO, Jan. 1936, p. 14. Loans for distribution
to depositors in closed banks were relatively small before the banking holiday because the original RFC Act limited their aggregate amount to $200 million. An
amendment June 14, 1933, removed the limit. Loans to going banks were relatively small after the banking holiday because they were superseded by RFC
capital purchases.
[6] The restricted deposits in licensed banks referred to in footnote 3 above are
included in Table A-1. Figures on unrestricted deposits in unlicensed banks are
available only for national banks at call dates June 1933–Dec. 1934 (Comptroller
of the Currency, *Annual Report*, 1933, p. 649; 1934, p. 776; 1935, p. 806). The
largest amount of unrestricted deposits recorded was $77 million in June 1933,
8 per cent of frozen deposits. The absolute amount declined along with frozen
deposits in unlicensed banks, the ratio of the first to the second remaining in the
neighborhood of a tenth.

restricted deposits before March 1933;[7] hence they cannot easily be excluded. Table 15 and Chart 34 therefore bridge the discontinuity at that month by *including* restricted deposits throughout to derive an alternative estimate of the stock of money similar in construction before and after the holiday. This alternative estimate is compared with the estimate in our basic tables.

Neither of these two estimates is economically ideal. The alternative estimate may be viewed as setting an upper limit to the "ideal" estimate of the money stock, and our money stock figures in Table A-1 as setting a lower limit. We have noted that the figures in Table A-1 are not continuous from February to March 1933, since the figures for February include restricted deposits and the figures for March exclude them. That is why a dotted line is used on Chart 34 in connecting the values for February and March. The alternative estimate at the end of March, however, is also not strictly continuous with the end-of-February figure, so a dotted line again is used in connecting the two figures. At the end of March, depositors in unlicensed banks, for which neither a conservator nor a receiver had been appointed, had reason to regard deposits in such

---

[7] See *Federal Reserve Bulletin,* Dec. 1937, p. 1206, for a discussion of the extent of the restriction of withdrawals before the banking holiday.

The placing of restrictions on deposit withdrawals, a practice that had been used in 1931 in the East North Central States, became more prevalent in 1932 as a measure to cope with the steady withdrawal of funds. These restrictions on deposit withdrawals were usually imposed through 'depositors' agreements' deferring withdrawal of varying percentages of deposits over periods of time ranging up to five years, certain percentages of deposits to be released at the end of the first year and additional percentages at the end of the succeeding years. New business was conducted on an unrestricted basis. Unfortunately, comprehensive figures are not available to show the number of banks that obtained deposit deferment agreements, or the amount of deposits involved in such deferment agreements, but from what information is available it appears that the practice was followed in a number of States during 1931 and 1932.

Another type of bank moratoria that became common during this period, particularly in the East North Central States, was the reorganization of banks through the waiver or surrender of a portion of deposits by the depositors. This was accomplished in some cases through outright contributions by certain of the depositors, but usually there was a segregation of assets for the benefit of waiving depositors under a trust agreement, with a right in the bank to substitute assets during a period of time running generally from two to five years. Figures are not available at present to show the losses sustained by depositors through this type of reorganization of distressed banks. . . .

Many banks in a number of places had closed temporarily in 1932 under special 'banking holidays' declared by civil authorities. The first of a series of State-wide banking holidays was declared in Nevada at the beginning of November, 1932. Though originally for a 12-day period, it was subsequently extended. Early in 1933 more local bank holidays were declared by city authorities and many existing ones were extended, in order to permit banks to obtain deposit deferment or waiver agreements and to afford banks an opportunity to raise funds and make adjustments necessary to enable them to continue to meet their obligations.

TABLE 15

ALTERNATIVE MONEY STOCK ESTIMATES, MARCH 1933–JUNE 1935
(amounts in millions of dollars)

Date	Ratio of Total Deposits, Unlicensed to Licensed Banks (1)	Commercial Bank Deposits Adjusted (2)	Unlicensed Bank Deposits Adjusted (3)	Commercial Bank (Licensed and Unlicensed) Deposits Adjusted (4)	Currency Held by the Public (5)	Currency Plus Commercial Bank (Licensed and Unlicensed) Deposits Adjusted (6)	Recorded Money Stock (7)
1933							
Mar. 29	13.49	24,461	3,300	27,761	5,509	33,270	29,970
Apr. 12	12.84						
May 3	10.96	24,545	2,690	27,235	5,202	32,437	29,747
May 31	8.87	25,081	2,225	27,306	5,019	32,325	30,100
June 28	7.18	25,138	1,805	26,943	4,949	31,892	30,087
June 30	7.07						
Aug. 2	6.30	25,274	1,592	26,866	4,886	31,752	30,160
Aug. 30	5.71	25,342	1,447	26,789	4,850	31,639	30,192
Sept. 27	5.17	25,431	1,315	26,746	4,830	31,576	30,261
Oct. 25	4.69						
Nov. 1	4.50	25,584	1,151	26,735	4,803	31,538	30,387
Nov. 29	3.82	25,719	982	26,701	4,844	31,545	30,563
Dec. 30	3.18						
1934							
Jan. 3	3.10	25,968	805	26,773	4,839	31,612	30,807
Jan. 31	2.58	26,463	683	27,146	4,491	31,637	30,954
Feb. 28	2.15	27,101	583	27,684	4,513	32,197	31,614
Mar. 5	2.08						
Mar. 28	1.78	27,690	493	28,183	4,550	32,733	32,240
May 2	1.41	28,015	395	28,410	4,556	32,966	32,571
May 30	1.17	28,232	330	28,562	4,566	33,128	32,798
June 27	0.97	28,489	276	28,765	4,584	33,349	33,073
June 30	0.95						
July 25	0.80						
Aug. 1	0.77	28,957	223	29,180	4,609	33,789	33,566

Date	Col. 1	Col. 2	Col. 3	Col. 4	Col. 5	Col. 6	Col. 7
Aug. 22	0.70	29,606	198	29,804	4,628	34,432	34,234
Aug. 29	0.67						
Sept. 26	0.57						
Oct. 3	0.53	29,470	156	29,626	4,627	34,253	34,097
Oct. 31	0.38	30,155	115	30,270	4,590	34,860	34,745
Nov. 28	0.34	30,547	104	30,651	4,631	35,282	35,178
Dec. 26	0.26						
1935							
Jan. 2	0.25	30,502	76	30,578	4,559	35,137	35,061
Jan. 30	0.20	31,414	63	31,477	4,621	36,098	36,035
Feb. 27	0.18	32,065	58	32,123	4,700	36,823	36,765
Mar. 27	0.14						
Apr. 3	0.13	32,103	42	32,145	4,714	36,859	36,817
Apr. 24	0.12						
May 1	0.12	32,669	39	32,708	4,708	37,416	37,377
May 29	0.11	32,866	36	32,902	4,715	37,617	37,581
June 30		33,341	0	33,341	4,708	38,049	38,049

SOURCE, BY COLUMN

(1) At italicized dates, data for licensed and unlicensed banks are available. Ratios for dates not in italics, corresponding to the Wed. nearest end of month in Table A-1, were interpolated on a straight line between logarithms of the ratios at italicized dates.

Data for licensed and unlicensed banks are sums for member and nonmember banks. For member banks, see *Federal Reserve Bulletin*, Apr. 1933, p. 216; and Sept. 1934–June 1935 issues. For nonmember banks: Mar. 29, 1933, estimated as in Table 13, lines 6 and 7, col. 3; Apr. 12, 1933, June 30, 1933 (licensed), and subsequent italicized dates: *FRB*, Sept. 1934–June 1935 issues; June 30, 1933 (unlicensed), *All-Bank Statistics*, p. 72.

Original figures for Mar. 29, and Apr. 12, 1933, are deposits held by the designated licensed and unlicensed banks on Dec. 31, 1932. No adjustment for shrinkage in deposits after Dec. 1932 was made on the assumption that col. 1 would not be affected. Figures for unlicensed banks and for licensed member banks on June 30, 1933, are as of that date; original figures for licensed nonmember banks are deposits held by those banks on Dec. 31, 1932; these figures were reduced 10 per cent for comparability with data for other banks on this date. Figures for member banks on Oct. 25, 1933, are as of that date; for nonmember banks the deposits held by those banks on Dec. 31, 1932; figures for licensed nonmembers were reduced 10 per cent, for unlicensed nonmembers 12.2 per cent for comparability with member bank data. Thereafter figures were assumed to be on a current basis.

Table A-1.

(2, 5, 7)
(3) Col. 1 times col. 2.
(4) Col. 2 plus col. 3.
(6) Col. 4 plus col. 5

CHART 34

Alternative Money Stock Estimates, February 1933–June 1935

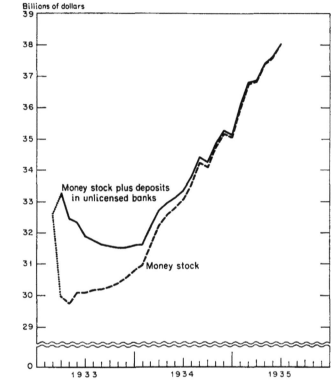

Billions of dollars

Money stock plus deposits in unlicensed banks

Money stock

SOURCE: Table 15, cols. 6 and 7, and Table A-1, col. 8.

banks as less akin to cash then they had been before the banking holiday, even though restricted then. The attempt to achieve continuity with February by including all deposits in unlicensed banks in March figures accordingly overstates the money stock even on the concept implicit in the estimates for the end of February.[8] And that concept itself overstates

[8] The figures for currency held by the public in the alternative estimate also involve an overstatement. Table A-1 treats vault cash in unlicensed banks, beginning Mar. 1933, as currency held by the public because unlicensed banks are not counted as banks. We estimate the amount of vault cash in unlicensed banks to have been about $50 million at the end of that month, and to have declined thereafter along with the reduction in deposits in unlicensed banks. Strictly, the alternative estimate of money stock including deposits in unlicensed banks should exclude from currency held by the public the vault cash in those banks.

the money stock by treating $1 of restricted deposits as strictly on a par with $1 of unrestricted deposits.

Another defect in our figures traceable to the bank holiday is their exclusion of perhaps as much as $1 billion of currency substitutes introduced in communities bereft of banking facilities before, during, and immediately after the panic.[9] To the extent currency substitutes were used because restricted deposits were unavailable to depositors, the error of their exclusion from Table A-1 before the panic is offset by the error of the inclusion of restricted deposits. To the extent they were so used after the panic, currency substitutes should be added to Table A-1, since unlicensed bank deposits are not included in that table, but not to the alternative estimates in Table 15 or Chart 34, since these include unlicensed bank deposits. To the extent currency substitutes came into use to replace deposits in failed banks and the reduction of deposits in open banks, i.e., to enable the public to raise the ratio of currency to deposits, both Table A-1 and Table 15 should include them. There seems no way now, however, of estimating the changing amounts of these currency substitutes in 1932 and 1933.

Finally, we note two minor defects in the series in Table A-1: the figures exclude unrestricted deposits in unlicensed banks; the figures for commercial bank deposits are probably too low for February 1933 and too high for March 1933.[10]

None of the several experiments we have made to take these various defects into account has been sufficiently illuminating to add much to the simple statement that an "ideal" estimate would be somewhere between the two curves in Chart 34. Almost any such intermediate curve which is plausible, in the sense that it is consistent with our qualitative knowledge of other defects and also divides the space between the two limits in proportions that do not vary erratically from month to month, implies that economic recovery in the half-year after the panic owed nothing to monetary expansion; the apparent rise in the stock of money is simply a statistical fiction. The emergency revival of the banking system contributed to recovery by restoring confidence in the monetary and economic system and thereby inducing the public to reduce money balances

[9] See Chap. 7, footnote 32.

[10] For the information available on the amount of unrestricted deposits in unlicensed banks, see footnote 6 above.

As to the second defect, the reason is that no published figures are available between the middle of Feb. and the middle of Apr. for the interpolators used to estimate nonmember bank deposits between call dates. End-of-Feb. and end-of-Mar. interpolators were obtained along a straight line between the Feb. and Apr. figures for the interpolators. This problem does not arise with the monthly member bank figures, since the gaps in this series were filled on the basis of weekly reporting member bank figures which are available throughout for Wednesdays nearest the end of the month. See our forthcoming companion volume, "Trends and Cycles in the Stock of Money in the United States, 1867–1960," a National Bureau study.

relative to income (to raise velocity) rather than by producing a growth in the stock of money.

Federal Insurance of Bank Deposits

Federal insurance of bank deposits was the most important structural change in the banking system to result from the 1933 panic, and, indeed in our view, the structural change most conducive to monetary stability since state bank note issues were taxed out of existence immediately after the Civil War. Individual states had experimented with systems of deposit insurance and numerous proposals for federal deposit insurance had been introduced into the U.S. Congress over many years. A bill providing for deposit insurance was passed by the House of Representatives in 1932 under the sponsorship of Representative Henry B Steagall, chairman of the House Banking and Currency Committee, but killed in the Senate because of intense opposition by Senator Carter Glass, an influential member of the Senate Banking and Currency Committee. Glass favored merely a liquidating corporation to advance to depositors in failed banks the estimated amount of their ultimate recovery. In 1933, Steagall and Glass agreed to combine the two proposals and incorporate them in the Banking Act of 1933. The resulting section of the act provided for a permanent deposit insurance plan with very extensive coverage to become effective July 1, 1934.[11]

It is a nice example of how institutions are developed and shaped that the actual plan which first became effective on January 1, 1934, resulted from an amendment to the Banking Act of 1933 introduced by a Senator from the minority party and at least initially opposed by President Roosevelt.[12] It was opposed also by leading bankers and by some ranking

[11] FDIC, *Annual Report,* 1950, pp. 63–67. We have also been greatly helped by a letter from Clark Warburton, which summarized the detailed origins of federal deposit insurance. See also Chap. 7, footnote 27, above.

[12] Jones (*Fifty Billion Dollars,* pp. 45–46) asserts that President Roosevelt opposed deposit insurance and requested Congress to reject the Vandenberg amendment. See also Arthur M. Schlesinger, Jr., *The Coming of the New Deal,* Boston, Houghton Mifflin, 1959, p. 443; B. N. Timmons, *Jesse H. Jones,* New York, Holt, 1956, pp. 184, 195.

Carter H. Golembe comments:

. . . it was the only important piece of legislation during the New Deal's famous 'one hundred days' which was neither requested nor supported by the new administration.

Deposit insurance was purely a creature of Congress. For almost fifty years members had been attempting to secure legislation to this end, without success; while in individual states the record of experimentation with bank-obligation insurance systems dated back more than a century. The adoption of nation-wide deposit insurance in 1933 was made possible by the times, by the perseverance

individuals in the Federal Reserve System.[13] The amendment, introduced by Senator Arthur Vandenberg, provided for a temporary system of deposit insurance, pending the adoption on July 1, 1934, of the permanent system. The period of operation of the temporary plan was extended to July 1, 1935, by an amendment in 1934 and to August 31, 1935, by a Congressional resolution signed by the President. On August 23, 1935, a permanent system in roughly its present form became effective under the provisions of Title I of the Banking Act of 1935.

The Banking Act of 1933 neither abolished nor reduced the powers of any existing government body concerned with banking. It simply superimposed an additional agency, the Federal Deposit Insurance Corporation, whose functions both supplemented and duplicated those of existing agencies. Under the terms of the act, all banks that were members of the Federal Reserve System were required to have their deposits insured by the FDIC; nonmember banks could be admitted to insurance upon application to and approval by the Corporation. Insurance was initially (January 1, 1934) limited to a maximum of $2,500 of deposits for each depositor; the limit was raised to $5,000 on July 1, 1934, and to $10,000 on September 21, 1950.[14] Insured banks were required in return to pay

of the Chairman of the House Committee on Banking and Currency [Henry B. Steagall], and by the fact that the legislation attracted support from two groups which formerly had divergent aims and interests—those who were determined to end destruction of circulating medium due to bank failures and those who sought to preserve the existing banking structure ("The Deposit Insurance Legislation of 1933," *Political Science Quarterly,* June 1960, pp. 181–182).

[13] Golembe, "Deposit Insurance Legislation," p. 198, footnote 23. At meetings of the board of directors of the New York Federal Reserve Bank in 1933, strong opposition to deposit insurance was expressed by Harrison, Eugene Black, then governor of the Federal Reserve Board, and members of the New York board. The chief alternative proposed was RFC loans under liberalized lending authority, possibly combined with Federal Reserve loans to member banks under sect. 10(b), the Reserve System to be guaranteed against loss on such loans by the federal government. Also proposed was a relaxation of requirements for membership by banks in the Reserve System. The alternative makes clear that opposition was not so much to the assumption by government of ultimate responsibility for deposits as to the by-passing of the Reserve System and the establishment of a potential competitor (George L. Harrison Papers on the Federal Reserve System, Columbia University Library, Harrison, Notes, Vol. III, Apr. 10, May 25, June 1, 1933, pp. 153–156, 197–200, 205–206; for a full description of the Papers, see Chap. 5, footnote 41 and the accompanying text).

[14] Despite the impression conveyed by these limits, protection of the circulating medium rather than protection of the small depositor against loss was the overriding concern of the legislators in establishing deposit insurance, as in earlier attempts to introduce it. In support of this contention, Golembe cites the fact that "under the original insurance plan, slated to go into operation on June 30, 1934, insurance coverage was to apply to all types of deposit accounts, with maximum limits for each depositor which were fairly generous . . . . Only in the temporary plan, designed to operate for six months, was coverage restricted to $2,500 for each depositor. However, the original plan never did go into effect. After several extensions of the temporary plan, during the course of which coverage

premiums calculated as a percentage of their deposits[15] and, if not members of the Federal Reserve System, to submit to examination by the FDIC. The Corporation had the right to examine national and state member banks only if it obtained the written consent either of the Comptroller of the Currency or of the Board of Governors of the Federal Reserve System. In 1950, however, the FDIC was empowered to make special examinations of member banks at its own discretion. Member banks are therefore in principle subject to examination by three agencies: the Federal Reserve System; the Comptroller of the Currency, if national banks, or their state banking commissions, if state banks; and the FDIC. Nonmember insured banks may be examined by two agencies: their state banking commissions and the FDIC. In practice, of course, agreements have been worked out among the different agencies to minimize duplicate examination.[16]

Insurance first became effective on January 1, 1934. Within six months, nearly 14,000 of the nation's 15,348 commercial banks, accounting for

---

was raised to $5,000 for each depositor . . . it was found that this provided full coverage for more than 98 per cent of the depositors." Moreover, FDIC procedures in helping a distressed insured bank, which have the effect of protecting all deposits, and the immediate payment of insured deposits rather than payment over time in the form of receivers' dividends, suggest that protection of the circulating medium from the consequences of bank failures was the primary function of deposit insurance (Golembe, "The Deposit Insurance Legislation," pp. 193–194).

[15] The premium for members of the Temporary Deposit Insurance Fund was ½ of 1 per cent of deposits eligible for insurance. Only one-half the premium was ever paid, and part of that half which was unused at the close of the temporary fund was returned to the banks. Under the permanent system, the premium was changed to $\frac{1}{12}$ of 1 per cent of total deposits, payable semiannually. The Federal Deposit Insurance Act of Sept. 21, 1950, again changed the base for deposit insurance assessment. Each semiannual assessment computation is now based on the average of reports on two dates instead of the daily average for the six-months' period; also, in determining the assessment base, other items besides cash items are deductible from deposits. In addition, the act provided that three-fifths of the premium payments by insured banks in excess of the Corporation's operating expenses, losses, and additions to the insurance fund to cover anticipated losses during the calendar year are to be credited pro rata to the banks to be applied in the following year as part payment for premiums which become due in that year. An amendment, dated July 14, 1960, raised the fraction to two-thirds.

[16] In addition numerous clearing house associations also exercise a degree of supervision over their member banks. The variety of supervisory agreements has been a perennial source of concern to the supervising bodies themselves, and one of their important activities has been coordination of examination and standards (see Board of Governors of the Federal Reserve System, *Annual Report*, 1938, pp. 11–18; and FDIC, *Annual Report*, 1938, pp. 61–79). See also Clark Warburton, "Co-ordination of Monetary, Bank Supervisory, and Loan Agencies of the Federal Government," *Journal of Finance*, June 1950, pp. 161–166. Warburton argues, correctly in our view, that the Board of Governors should be relieved of such duties as the regular examination of member banks, which should be concentrated in the agencies concerned with the affairs of individual banks, such as the Comptroller of the Currency, the state banking commissions, and the FDIC.

some 97 per cent of all commercial bank deposits, were covered by insurance. The number of uninsured commercial banks has since declined to under 400, and their deposits now amount to less than 1 per cent of total deposits in all commercial banks. Mutual savings banks, which were also eligible for insurance, found it much less attractive. In mid-1934 only 66 out of 565 banks, accounting for only a bit over one-tenth of all mutual savings deposits, were insured. The coverage of mutual savings banks rose slowly until World War II, then accelerated, so that by the end of 1945, 192 out of 542 banks accounting for two-thirds of all deposits were insured, and by the end of 1960, 325 out of 515 accounting for 87 per cent of all deposits.[17]

Federal deposit insurance has been accompanied by a dramatic change in commercial bank failures and in losses borne by depositors in banks that fail (Table 16). From 1921 through 1933, every year requires at least three digits to record the number of banks that suspended; from 1934 on, two digits suffice, and from 1943 through 1960, one digit, for both insured and noninsured banks. For the thirteen-year period 1921 to 1933, losses borne by depositors averaged $146 million a year or 45 cents per $100 of adjusted deposits in all commercial banks. For the twenty-seven years since, losses have averaged $706,000 a year, or less than two-tenths of 1 cent per $100 of adjusted deposits in all commercial banks; moreover, over half the total losses during the twenty-seven years occurred in the very first year of the period and were mostly a heritage of the pre-FDIC period.

Technically, only deposits not exceeding a specified sum (since 1950, $10,000) are insured. In 1960, insured deposits amounted to only 57 per cent of all deposits of insured banks. In practice, however, the near-absence of bank failures recorded in Table 16 means that all deposits are effectively insured. The reduction in failures is not of course attributable to any correspondingly drastic improvement in the quality of bank officials or in the effectiveness of the supervisory authorities; nor is it attributable to the addition of still another examination agency, though the addition

[17] The wartime increase is attributable to the admission to membership of 125 New York State mutual savings banks on July 1, 1943. They and others had withdrawn from the temporary deposit insurance plan in June 1934. They wanted a premium rate that recognized the lower factor of risk in insuring savings banks and, in addition, believed that the savings banks' own insurance agency could safeguard depositors better than any national agency. In New York the mutual savings banks created their own insurance fund on July 1, 1934. Mutual savings banks in two New England states also organized statewide insurance plans. The New York plan and the arguments for it were abandoned in favor of membership in the FDIC in 1943. It was then held that in a real emergency statewide protection would not be strong enough and federal assistance would be required (A. A. Berle, *The Bank that Banks Built: The Story of Savings Banks Trust Company, 1933–1958*, New York, Harper, 1959, pp. 65, 71–73). See also FDIC, *Annual Report*, 1960, pp. 91, 93.

TABLE 16
COMMERCIAL BANK SUSPENSIONS, 1921–60
PART I. BEFORE FDIC

Year	Number of Suspensions (1)	Deposits (2)	Losses Borne by Depositors (3)	Losses to Depositors per $100 of Deposits Adjusted in All Commercial Banks (dollars) (4)
		(thousands of dollars)		
1921	506	172,806	59,967	0.21
1922	366	91,182	38,223	0.13
1923	646	149,601	62,142	0.19
1924	775	210,150	79,381	0.23
1925	617	166,937	60,799	0.16
1926	975	260,153	83,066	0.21
1927	669	199,332	60,681	0.15
1928	498	142,386	43,813	0.10
1929	659	230,643	76,659	0.18
1930	1,350	837,096	237,359	0.57
1931	2,293	1,690,232	390,476	1.01
1932	1,453	706,187	168,302	0.57
1933	4,000	3,596,708	540,396	2.15

PART II. AFTER FDIC

ALL COMMERCIAL BANKS

Year	Number of Suspensions	Deposits	Losses Borne by Depositors	Losses per $100
1934	61	37,332	6,502	0.02282
1935	31	13,902	600	0.00180
1936	72	28,100	185	0.00049
1937	82	33,877	155	0 00039
1938	80	58,243	293	0.00076
1939	71	158,627	1,374	0.00329
1940	48	142,787	57	0.00012
1941	17	29,797	33	0.00006
1942	23	19,517	20	0.00003
1943	5	12,525	13	0.00002
1944	2	1,915	4	0.0
1945	1	5,695	0	0.0
1946	2	494	0	0.0
1947	6	7,207	0	0.0
1948	3	10,674	0	0.0
1949	8	8,027	69	0.00006
1950	5	5,555	0	0.0
1951	5	6,097	394	0.00031
1952	4	3,313	0	0.0
1953	3	18,652	70	0.00005
1954	4	2,948	407	0.00028
1955	5	11,953	8	0.00001
1956	3	11,689	178	0.00011
1957	2	2,418	0	0.0
1958	9	10,413	277	0.00016
1959	3	2,595	46	0.00003
1960	2	7,990	546	0.00031

(continued)

TABLE 16 (concluded)
PART II. AFTER FDIC

BREAKDOWN OF COMMERCIAL BANKS, BY INSURED STATUS

	Insured Banks			Noninsured Banks		
Year	Number of Suspensions	Deposits	Losses Borne by Depositors	Number of Suspensions	Deposits[a]	Losses Borne by Depositors[b]
		(thousands of dollars)			(thousands of dollars)	
	(1)	(2)	(3)	(1)	(2)	(3)
1934	9	1,968	19	52	35,364	6,483
1935	25	13,319	415	6	583	185
1936	69	27,508	171	3	592	14
1937	75	33,349	110	7	528	45
1938	73	57,205	33	7	1,038	260
1939	59	156,188	936	12	2,439	438
1940	43	142,429	31	5	358	26
1941	15	29,718	33	2	79	0
1942	20	19,186	5	3	331	15
1943	5	12,525	13	0	0	0
1944	2	1,915	4	0	0	0
1945	1	5,695	0	0	0	0
1946	1	347	0	1	147	0
1947	5	7,040	0	1	167	n.a.
1948	3	10,674	0	0	0	0
1949	4	5,475	0	4	2,552	69
1950	4	5,513	0	1	42	0
1951	2	3,408	0	3	2,689	394
1952	3	3,170	0	1	143	0
1953	2	18,262	0	1	390	70
1954	2	998	0	2	1,950	407
1955	5	11,953	8	0	0	0
1956	2	11,329	62	1	360	116
1957	1	1,163	0	1	1,255	n.a.
1958	4	8,240	55	5	2,173	222
1959	3	2,595	46	0	0	0
1960	1	6,955	289	1	1,035	257

SOURCE, BY COLUMN

PART I

(1-3) Unpublished estimates, Division of Research and Statistics, FDIC, used with permission of the Corporation. Number and deposits slightly revised, by FDIC, from *Federal Reserve Bulletin*, Sept. 1937, pp. 868, 873. Losses estimated by FDIC by applying to the deposits the appropriate loss percentages derived from samples (see FDIC, *Annual Report*, 1934, pp. 84, 86; 1940, pp. 70-73).

(4) Col. 3 divided by June commercial bank deposits in Table A-1.

PART II

All Commercial Banks

(1-3) Sum of corresponding cols. for insured and noninsured banks.

(4) Col. 3 divided by June commercial bank deposits in Table A-1.

Insured Banks

(1-3) FDIC, *Annual Report*, 1958, pp. 5, 27-28; 1959, p. 5; 1960, p. 5. The banks counted are those requiring disbursements by the FDIC. Two mutual savings

(continued)

Notes to Table 16 (concluded)
banks included in the published figures were deducted by us (*ibid.*, 1938, pp. 250, 256, and 1939, p. 216).

Noninsured Banks

(1–3) Unpublished estimates, Division of Research and Statistics, FDIC; for cols. 1 and 2, the estimates are revisions of figures given in FDIC, *Annual Report*, 1960, p. 181, and sources listed there.

ᵃ Deposits of noninsured suspended banks are missing in the following years for the following numbers of banks: 1938, 1; 1939, 2; 1941, 1; and 1954, 1.

ᵇ Losses borne by depositors for the following numbers of noninsured suspended banks are missing in the years marked "n.a." and in the additional years listed below.

Year	Banks	Deposits ($000's)
1934	6	341
1938	1	n.a.
1939	2	n.a.
1940	2	12
1941	1	n.a.
1942	1	101
1951	1	1,600
1954	1	n.a.
1958	3	454

n.a. = not available.

of the FDIC apparently meant closer supervision and examination of insured state banks. Rather, it reflects, in the main, two other factors. First, "bad" banks, though perhaps no less frequent than before, are seldom permitted to fail if they are insured; instead, they are reorganized under new management or merged with a good bank, with the FDIC assuming responsibility for losses in connection with depreciated assets. Second, the knowledge on the part of small depositors that they will be able to realize on their deposits even if the bank should experience financial difficulties prevents the failure of one bank from producing "runs" on other banks that in turn may force "sound" banks to suspend. Deposit insurance is thus a form of insurance that tends to reduce the contingency insured against.

Adopted as a result of the widespread losses imposed by bank failures in the early 1930's, federal deposit insurance, to 1960 at least, has succeeded in achieving what had been a major objective of banking reform for at least a century, namely, the prevention of banking panics. Such panics arose out of or were greatly intensified by a loss of confidence in the ability of banks to convert deposits into currency and a consequent desire on the part of the public to increase the fraction of its money held in the form of currency. The resulting runs on banks could be met in a fractional reserve system only if confidence were restored at an early stage. Otherwise, they inevitably brought restriction of convertibility of deposits into currency.

As we have seen, the Aldrich-Vreeland Act and then the Federal Reserve System were both attempts to solve this problem by enabling banks to convert their assets into additional high-powered money for use in meeting the demands of their depositors for currency. The aim was to make it possible for runs or their equivalent, once begun, to be met without forcing banks either to suspend business individually or, by concerted action, to restrict the conversion of deposits into currency. The Aldrich-Vreeland Act succeeded on the one occasion it was used, the outbreak of World War I. The Federal Reserve System failed in the early 1930's though, as we have seen, proper use of its powers could have averted the panic. As these powers were in fact used, however, the existence of the System served only to postpone repeatedly the final crisis, which, when it finally came, was more severe and far-reaching than any earlier panic.

Federal deposit insurance attempts to solve the problem by removing the initial reason for runs—loss of confidence in the ability to convert deposits into currency. While there have been substantial changes since 1934 in the ratio of currency to deposits (see Chapters 9 to 11 below), there have been no radical changes in short periods like those before 1934, always the invariable hallmark of a liquidity crisis and a banking panic. And it is hard to believe that any are likely to occur in the foreseeable future.

True, if for any reason there should be a substantial and long-continued decline in the stock of money, such as occurred from 1929 to 1933, the effects on the value of bank assets would very likely cause so many banks to become insolvent as to exhaust existing reserve funds of the FDIC. However, the greater part of the 1929–33 decline in the stock of money was not independent of the initial bank failures. It was rather a consequence of them, because of their effect on the deposit-currency ratio and the failure of the Reserve System to offset the fall in the ratio by a sufficient increase in high-powered money. Had federal deposit insurance been in existence in 1930, it would very likely have prevented the initial fall in the deposit-currency ratio in late 1930 and hence the tragic sequence of events that fall set in train, including the drastic decline in the money stock. It may be that, today, a radical change in the deposit-currency ratio would evoke a different and more suitable response from the monetary authorities, so that, even in the absence of federal deposit insurance, a banking panic, once begun, would not be permitted to cumulate. The existence of federal deposit insurance greatly reduces, if it does not eliminate, the need to rely on such a response.

As we have seen in earlier chapters, banking panics have occurred only during severe contractions and have greatly intensified such contractions, if indeed they have not been the primary factor converting what would otherwise have been mild contractions into severe ones. That is why we regard federal deposit insurance as so important a change in our banking structure and as contributing so greatly to monetary stability—in practice far more than the establishment of the Federal Reserve System.[18]

Other Changes

The other changes in the commercial and savings banking structure during the New Deal period are much less far reaching than the establishment of deposit insurance and can be noted summarily.

Conditions of membership in the Federal Reserve System were modified to make permissible the admission of Morris Plan and mutual savings banks. Rules governing the establishment of branch banks were somewhat liberalized, and double liability on stock of national banks was eliminated. Investment affiliates of commercial banks were prohibited, and interlocking directorates between commercial banks and investment companies restricted.

National bank notes were converted into a Treasury obligation and arrangements made to retire them from circulation. The provision for issuing them terminated on August 1, 1935, with the redemption of the two remaining issues of U.S. bonds bearing the circulation privilege.[19] The volume in circulation had declined to $650 million by August 1935. It has been declining steadily ever since; even so, at the end of 1960, the volume listed as still in circulation was $55 million.[20]

[18] See Milton Friedman, "Why the American Economy is Depression-Proof," *Nationalekonomiska Föreningens,* sammantrade den 28 April 1954, pp. 59–60. To avoid misunderstanding, we should note explicitly that deposit insurance is but one of several ways in which a panic-proof banking system could have been achieved. Our comments are not intended to suggest that some other method might not have been preferable to deposit insurance. For an alternative method, see Friedman, *A Program for Monetary Stability,* New York, Fordham University Press, 1960, pp. 65–76.

[19] Each national bank transferred to the Treasury the liability for its circulating notes by depositing enough funds with it over and above the 5 per cent redemption fund already held by the Treasury to cover its notes outstanding. Those deposits reduced member bank reserves, but the funds disbursed by the Treasury to redeem the called bonds restored reserves. Since 1935, as national bank notes have returned from circulation, Federal Reserve Banks have shipped them to the Treasury for retirement. Payment for these notes is made to the Federal Reserve Banks by a charge against the Treasury's account. The Treasury replenishes its account by depositing with the Reserve Banks gold certificate credits which it set aside for this purpose, drawn from part of the profit accruing to the government upon the devaluation of the dollar (see footnote 53, below).

[20] This sum includes the amount that has been lost or destroyed as well as notes that are in numismatic collections and notes that are still in use as currency. To judge from the rate at which the sum outstanding has been declining, it seems likely that perhaps half the sum outstanding will sooner or later be offered for retirement. If we ignore amounts held in numismatic collections, this implies that

Banks were prohibited by law or regulation from paying interest on demand deposits and from paying rates of interest on time deposits higher than those specified by the Board of Governors of the Federal Reserve System for member banks and by the FDIC for insured non-member banks. Member banks were also prohibited from acting as agents of nonbank lenders in placing funds in the form of security loans in the stock market.[21]

Throughout American banking history, the view has recurrently been expressed that payment of interest on deposits led to "excessive" competition among banks, and "forced" them to reduce reserves to an undesirably low level and to engage in unduly risky investment and lending policies because of the necessity of earning income to pay the interest. The suggestion had frequently been made that the payment of interest be prohibited.[22] The prohibition was finally adopted for demand deposits in

something like $30 million of national bank notes has been lost or destroyed. Though large in absolute amount, the annual rate of loss implied is rather small. For the 97 years from 1864 through 1960, the average amount of national bank notes in circulation was $369 million. The conjectured sum lost or destroyed is roughly 10 per cent of this average or roughly one-tenth of 1 per cent per year.

These estimates imply that paper currency is lost or destroyed at the rate of $1 per year for each $1,000.

[21] In addition, the Banking Act of 1933 made member banks subject to severe reprisal for undue use of bank credit "for the speculative carrying of or trading in securities, real estate, or commodities, or for any other purposes inconsistent with the maintenance of sound credit conditions." The Reserve Banks were authorized to suspend uncooperative banks "from the use of the credit facilities of the Federal Reserve System." The Federal Reserve Board was authorized to fix for each district "the percentage of individual bank capital and surplus which may be represented by loans secured by stock or bond collateral." If, despite an official warning to curtail them, such loans by member banks were increased, Reserve Bank 90-day advances to the offending banks on their own notes became due immediately, and the banks might be suspended from rediscount privileges.

[22] L. W. Mints, *A History of Banking Theory*, University of Chicago Press, 1945, pp. 141, 185, 209, 234–235. The suggestion predated the establishment of the Federal Reserve System—when there was no general distinction between demand and time deposits—and the arguments advanced related particularly to payment of interest on bankers' balances which were, for the most part at least, withdrawable on demand. In 1933, during the discussions leading to the Banking Act of 1933, the arguments were restated against demand deposits generally, whether or not they were bankers' balances. A quotation from O. M. W. Sprague (*History of Crises Under the National Banking System*, National Monetary Commission, 1910, p. 21) provides a good summary of the general stand against payment of interest on deposits:

> The interest-paying banks were unable to maintain large reserves and at the same time realize a profit from the use of the funds thus attracted. Particularly was this the case when the accumulation of such funds was only temporary. The extra supply of money to be lent forced down rates, and, as rates fell, more and more had to be lent by the banks in order even to equal the interest which they had contracted to pay.

The argument is of course a standard one made by private groups seeking "cartel" powers: e.g., one of the arguments used in the 1930's in justifying control

member banks—in the Banking Act of 1933—and for demand deposits in other insured banks—in the Banking Act of 1935—partly because of the greater willingness after 1933 to legislate with respect to economic matters, partly because of the view—in our opinion, largely erroneous—that the banking difficulties of the early 1930's derived in considerable measure from the stock market boom and the participation of banks in the boom as direct lenders and as agents for others.[23]

One consequence of the prohibition of payment of interest on demand deposits has been a marked decline in the importance of interbank deposits—the demand deposits on which the payment of interest had been most widespread and at the highest rates. For member banks, balances at domestic banks were 76 per cent of deposits at Federal Reserve Banks at the end of 1933. They had fallen to 49 per cent by the end of 1937 and to 28 per cent by 1948. They have since risen to about 50 per cent. Beyond this, the prohibition had no great effect until recent years. The

---

over entry into medicine was that physicians whose incomes were "unduly" low would be driven to engage in "unethical" practices. See, for example, A. D. Bevain, "The Overcrowding of the Medical Profession," *Journal of the Association of Medical Colleges*, Nov. 1936, pp. 377–384; and Milton Friedman and Simon Kuznets, *Income from Independent Professional Practice*, New York, NBER, 1945, p. 12 and references there cited in footnote 18.

The payment or nonpayment of interest on demand deposits does not alter in any way the incentive to use assets so as to yield the largest return, as judged by the banker, where return is defined to include nonmonetary as well as monetary elements. The prohibition of payment of interest is simply a government enforced price-fixing agreement. If the prohibition were effective, if it initially increased returns to existing banks, and if entry into the banking industry were free, the effects would be the usual open cartel effects: more banks than would otherwise exist, each operating at partial capacity and competing away the initial extra returns until the returns to skill and capital invested in banking were the same as in other fields. Since entry is not free, thanks to the need to get a franchise from a government authority, the results would likely be intermediate between those just described and the results to be expected if entry were prohibited entirely: a higher market value of the stock of banks, and roughly the competitive return to skill and per dollar of market value of capital.

Of course, all this assumes that the prohibition is not evaded as, of course, it can be at least partly by altering the amount of services given to depositors.

[23] After the prohibition of the payment of interest on demand deposits was in effect, another reason favoring the prohibition was discovered. Under the temporary deposit insurance plan, banks were assessed on insured deposits only; under the proposed permanent plan, on total deposits. City banks complained that under the permanent plan, their assessments would subsidize small country banks, since total deposits of city banks were considerably larger than their insured deposits while total deposits of country banks were not much more than their insured deposits. It was then noted that the reduction in expenses as a result of the prohibition of the payment of interest on demand deposits—expenses mainly borne by city banks —served as an offset to their assessments for deposit insurance (*Banking Act of 1935,* Hearings before a subcommittee of the Senate Committee on Banking and Currency on S. 1715, 74th Cong., 1st sess., 1935, part 1, pp. 29–30; part 2, pp. 433, 490–492).

rate of earnings on bank assets was so low during the 1930's and 1940's that banks were led to impose service charges on depositors, that is, the rate of interest on demand deposits was essentially negative, so that the fixed price for demand deposits was, as it were, above the market price for demand deposits. Competition has taken the form of changes in these service charges and of the provision of special services to depositors.

The limitation of rates of interest paid on time deposits,[24] though initially welcomed by commercial banks, has more recently been a hindrance to them in the competition for these deposits with alternative institutions, particularly savings banks and savings and loan associations, which pay higher rates (see Chapter 12). These rates, too, have for much of the time been ineffective. Discontinuous changes in them after they have become effective have produced sizable perturbations in the rate of change of commercial bank time deposits.

The reduction in interbank deposits plus the prohibition of banks' acting as agents of nonbank lenders in placing funds on the stock market contributed to the sharp decline in security loans by banks and the dwindling in importance of the call-loan market as a means of investing secondary reserves.

CHANGES IN THE STRUCTURE AND POWERS OF THE FEDERAL RESERVE SYSTEM

The Banking Act of 1935 changed the name of the Federal Reserve Board to the Board of Governors of the Federal Reserve System; reconstituted the Board by eliminating ex officio members; raised the salaries and lengthened the terms of the Board members; and reorganized the Federal Open Market Committee to consist of the seven members of the Board plus five representatives of the Federal Reserve Banks, instead of the twelve heads of the Banks, as under the Banking Act of 1933.[25] In addi-

---

[24] Regulation Q of the Board of Governors regulating interest rates on time deposits provides that where state banking authorities have fixed maximum interest rates payable on time deposits at figures lower than those set by the Board of Governors, the lower state figures become the maximum which can be paid by member banks located in those states.

[25] The change in name was the final seal on the transfer of effective power from the Banks to the Board. Heretofore, the chief executive officers of the Banks had been governors, the title generally assigned to the operative head of central banks. Only the executive head of the Board had also been a governor and addressed as such. The other members were simply members of the Board and were addressed without title. Henceforth, the members of the Board were governors in formal title as in fact and the executive heads of the Banks were presidents.

According to Marriner Eccles, it was at Senator Glass' insistence that the Secretary of the Treasury as an ex officio member was dropped: " 'When I was Secretary of Treasury,' Glass said, . . . 'I had considerable influence with the action of the Board, and I . . . have suspected . . . that frequently since the Secretary of the Treasury had too much influence upon the Board, and I do not

tion, it completed a step begun in the Banking Act of 1933 by eliminating the power of Banks to buy and sell government securities for their own account except with the explicit permission or at the direction of the Federal Open Market Committee.[26] These measures recognized and

---

think he ought to be there'" (*Beckoning Frontiers*, New York, Knopf, 1951, p. 216 n.). Eccles says Senator Glass had no objection to the ex officio membership of the Comptroller of the Currency, but Secretary of the Treasury Morgenthau was piqued that a subordinate in his department and not he would serve on the Board so, to mollify him, the Comptroller was also dropped. As we shall see in Chapters 10 and 11 and as we saw in Chapter 5, the Treasury does not need actual representation on the Board of Governors to exercise considerable influence upon its actions.

The chief executive officer of each Federal Reserve Bank was designated for the first time in the Banking Act of 1935 as the president, formerly called governor, rather than the chairman of the board of directors who is also known as the Federal Reserve agent. The election of each Bank's president and first vice-president by the board of directors is subject to the approval of the Board of Governors. Since 1942, the five representatives of the Reserve Banks chosen annually to serve on the Federal Open Market Committee must be either Reserve Bank presidents or vice-presidents. The role of the Federal Reserve agents, who supervise the issue of Federal Reserve notes, has been greatly reduced since the Banking Act of 1935.

[26] The regulations governing the Federal Open Market Committee (FOMC)—organized under the Banking Act of 1933 and composed of all the Reserve Bank governors—gave the Banks permission to purchase government securities for their own account, subject to certain restrictions, in an emergency involving individual banking institutions (Federal Reserve Board, *Annual Report* for 1933, p. 302). Harrison tried but failed to persuade the FOMC organized under the Banking Act of 1935 to adopt a similar provision. On the first vote, his motion was passed 6 to 5, with all the Bank presidents and one member of the Board voting in favor (there were only six Board members at the time; a seven-man Board was not appointed until 1955). The motion finally lost by a tie vote, for the Board member changed his vote on the ground that the motion—which he still favored—ought not prevail without a larger affirmative margin (Harrison, Miscellaneous, Vol. IV, letter, dated Jan. 19, 1937, Harrison to Eccles; also Harrison, Open Market, Vol. IV, minutes of meeting, Jan. 26, 1937).

The by-laws of the FOMC under the Banking Act of 1935 also provided that members representing Banks did not serve as representatives of the particular Banks that elected them nor were they to be instructed by those Banks. Eccles said that "the open market committee should be composed entirely as a public body and . . . the banks should participate only through an advisory committee, the banks not knowing what was to be done but having a chance to be heard through a committee" (Harrison, Notes, Vol. VII, July 16, 1936; also Vol. VII, Mar. 5, 1936).

Presidents of Banks serving on the FOMC were prohibited by its by-laws from divulging to their directors actions taken at a FOMC meeting. Eccles said that "it would not be proper for directors of the Federal reserve banks affiliated with organizations owning Government securities to have any information which might benefit the organization with which they are associated" (*ibid.*, Vol. VII, July 16, 1936). He disclaimed the idea that any of the directors would take advantage of their situation, but "there is a good deal of talk in Congress about just that sort of thing." Harrison deplored the "throttling of officers and directors of reserve banks by the Board of Governors of the Federal Reserve System" (*ibid.*, Nov. 12, 1936).

consolidated the trend of power within the System away from the Federal Reserve Banks and toward Washington. In the same direction was the provision requiring the Board and the Federal Open Market Committee to keep and publish a complete record of all actions taken and of the considerations underlying the actions.

The broadening of the powers of the System was of greater significance than the change in its structure. The Board and the Banks naturally attributed the System's failure to stem the 1929–33 contraction and to prevent the banking panic to its inadequate powers rather than to the use it made of the powers it had. It both requested additional powers and was urged to accept them. The first measure along these lines preceded the panic: the Glass-Steagall Act, discussed earlier, which broadened acceptable collateral for Federal Reserve notes and permitted emergency advances to member banks on any asset. Other provisions of the Banking Act of 1935, all extending the System's powers, are:

(1) Enlargement of the Board's power to alter reserve requirements. First granted in 1933 by the Thomas Amendment to the Agricultural Adjustment Act of 1933 as an emergency power to be exercised only with permission of the President, the emergency power was replaced by a permanent grant of authority, not dependent on Presidential permission, to change reserve requirements between the minimum percentages specified in the act of June 1917 and twice those percentages.[27] A further change in reserve requirements prescribed reserves against government deposits. Country banks, in particular, benefited by a provision permitting "due from" items to be deducted from gross demand deposits instead of solely from "due to" items.

(2) Broadening of the lending powers of the Banks. The section of the Glass-Steagall Act which had allowed emergency advances was liberalized and made permanent. It authorized a Reserve Bank to make advances to

[27] In Aug. 1948 Congress granted the Board temporary power, terminating June 30, 1949, to raise the maximum percentages permitted under the Banking Act of 1935 by 4 points on demand deposits, by 1½ points on time deposits.

In July 1959 the Board was authorized to treat vault cash as part of a member bank's reserves. In Dec. 1959 central reserve and reserve city banks with vault cash holdings greater than 2 per cent of their demand deposits and country banks with vault cash holdings greater than 4 per cent of their demand deposits were given permission to count the excess as reserves. Effective Aug. 25, 1960, the percentage was changed to 2½ per cent for country banks and, effective Sept. 1, 1960, to 1 per cent for reserve city and central reserve city banks. Since Nov. 1960 all vault cash has been counted as part of a member bank's reserves.

Under the law passed in July 1959, the Board was also required to eliminate the central reserve city classification within three years. By Dec. 1, 1960, there was no longer any differential between central reserve and reserve city reserve requirements, and the central reserve city classification that had come into existence nearly a hundred years earlier passed into history.

The Board's authority to allow individual banks in central reserve and reserve cities to carry lower reserves was also broadened in July 1959.

its member banks on any satisfactory security whenever desired, subject only to the rules of the Board. The theory of eligibility as the basis for Federal Reserve credit was thus laid to rest.

(3) Empowering the Board to set a maximum limit to interest rates paid by member banks on time deposits. Granted by the Banking Act of 1933, that power was reaffirmed by the Banking Act of 1935 which gave the same power to the Federal Deposit Insurance Corporation with regard to insured nonmember banks.

(4) Granting of power to the Board to regulate credit advanced by bankers and brokers to their customers for purchasing and carrying registered securities. With this power, granted by the Securities Exchange Act of 1934, the Board has since set margin requirements for loans granted by member and nonmember banks on stocks (Regulation U), and by members of national security exchanges on stocks and bonds (Regulation T).[28] This grant of power was the final outcome of the concern of the Board with stock market speculation in the late twenties and of its attempt to use "direct pressure" to discriminate between stock market and other uses of credit. It was the precursor of other powers directed at the control of particular uses of credit—in particular, control over credit extended for the purchase of consumer goods and for real estate construction, both of which proved to be temporary powers. We shall have occasion to refer to credit controls later (see below, Chapters 9 and 10).

The additional powers, like the powers already possessed by the System, can be divided into three categories: those whose main role is to enable the Board to control the *quantity of money*—we may call these the instruments of monetary policy; those whose main role is to enable the Board to control the *price and use of credit*—we may call these the instruments of credit policy;[29] and those whose main role is to enable the Board to supervise the operations of · banks—we may call these the instruments of *bank supervision*. Of course, as our use of the word "main" suggests, there is no hard and fast line between them, and each power may have effects on the quantity of money, the price and use of credit, and the operations of banks. Open market operations and rediscounting were the

[28] Originally margin requirements were applied only against "long" security transactions. On Nov. 1, 1937, the Board included short sales within the scope of margin regulation, with margin for short sales set at 50 per cent, for long reduced from 55 to 40 per cent. Since the war, margin requirements have been uniform for both long and short sales. Up to Apr. 1, 1936, variable percentage margins were set, the margin requirement rising within limits set with each increase in the price of the security. Since then, margin requirements have been a fixed percentage of the price.

[29] Warburton refers to the same distinction, terming it one between "monetary control" and "loan control" (see "Monetary Control under the Federal Reserve Act," *Political Science Quarterly,* Dec. 1946, pp. 513–516).

chief initial monetary powers; the banking measures under consideration added power to vary reserve requirements. Eligibility requirements were the chief initial credit powers; the powers added in this class included control of security credit and, for a time later on, consumer and real estate credit; in addition, the granting of authority to Reserve Banks to make advances to member banks on any satisfactory security rendered the initial eligibility requirements largely irrelevant. Bank examination, requirements for admission to the Federal Reserve System, and, in terms of initial views about their role, reserve requirements were the chief initial supervisory powers; the added powers included control over interest rates on time deposits, control over the percentage of bank capital and surplus that could be represented by security loans, and the policing of the prohibition of the payment of interest on demand deposits.

POLICIES OF BANKS

The banks that survived the holocaust of the early thirties probably differed from those that went under. In addition, and very likely much more important, they undoubtedly drew from the experience lessons that affected their future behavior. For both reasons, the banks that survived understandably placed far greater weight on liquidity than the banks in existence in 1929.

The pressure for liquidity is, as we shall see, the best explanation for two notable changes in the composition of bank assets. The changes are: first, a sharp rise in the fraction held in the form of cash assets (cash in vault, items in process of collection, and balances at other banks including Reserve Banks), a change commented on earlier (Chapter 7, section 2) in connection with the emergence of "excess" reserves in 1932; second, a sharp rise in investments relative to loans.

In 1929, cash assets amounted to 14 per cent of total assets, and loans were more than two and one-half times investments (Table 17). By mid-1933, cash assets had risen to 18 per cent of total assets along with a shrinkage of more than one-third in total assets, and there is little doubt that only the frozen condition of banks prevented the percentage from being still higher. At the same time loans were only slightly larger than investments. Moreover, the investments had shifted in composition, from less than 40 per cent in the form of U.S. government securities in 1929 to over 50 per cent in 1933[30] and, judging from member bank data, from nearly three-quarters of U.S. securities in the form of bonds, generally longer term, to only a bit over one-half in this form (Table 18). Those moves were all in the direction of increasing the fraction of its assets that an individual bank could convert into cash at short notice and with small capital loss—these were properties of its assets whose importance had been

[30] *All-Bank Statistics,* p. 35.

TABLE 17

COMPOSITION OF ASSETS OF COMMERCIAL BANKS, SELECTED DATES, 1929–60

Date[a]	Assets (billions of dollars)					Percentage of Total Assets in:				Ratio of Loans to Investments (10)
	Loans (1)	Investments (2)	Cash Assets (3)	Other (4)	Total (5)	Loans (6)	Investments (7)	Cash Assets (8)	Other (9)	
1929	36.1	13.7	9.0	3.6	62.4	57.9	22.0	14.4	5.8	2.6
1933	16.5	14.1	7.4	2.6	40.5	40.7	34.8	18.3	6.4	1.2
1934	15.7	17.1	9.6	2.5	45.0	34.9	38.0	21.3	5.6	0.9
1935	15.0	19 7	11.8	2.4	48.9	30.7	40.3	24.1	4.9	0.8
1936	15.6	23.1	14.5	2.4	55.6	28.1	41.5	26.1	4.3	0.7
1937	17.5	22.1	15.0	2.3	56.9	30.8	38.8	26.4	4.0	0.8
1938	16.1	21.1	16.8	2.2	56 2	28.6	37.5	29.9	3.9	0.8
1939	16.4	23.0	19.9	2.2	61.4	26.7	37.5	32.4	3.6	0.7
1940	17.4	23 8	24.6	2.0	67.8	25.7	35.1	36.3	2.9	0.7
1941	20 3	27 3	25.8	1.9	75.4	26.9	36.2	34.2	2.5	0.7
1945	23.7	90.9	30.2	1.5	146.2	16.2	62.2	20.7	1.0	0.3
1948	39.9	74.0	34.2	1.8	149.8	26.6	49.4	22.8	1.2	0.5
1957	91.0	73.5	40 0	3.9	208.4	43.7	35.3	19.2	1.9	1.2
1958	95.6	84 3	43 5	4.4	227.8	42.0	37.0	19.1	1.9	1.1
1959	103.4	82.7	42.9	4.7	233.7	44.2	35.4	18.4	2.0	1.3
1960	115.3	74 8	47 1	5.3	242 5	47.5	30.8	19.4	2.2	1.5

[a] June 30 or nearest available call date.

SOURCE: Cols. 1–5, from *All-Bank Statistics*, pp. 34–35; and *Federal Reserve Bulletin*.

TABLE 18
CHIEF KINDS OF UNITED STATES GOVERNMENT DIRECT OBLIGATIONS HELD BY MEMBER BANKS, 1928–41

End of:	Member Bank Holdings (millions of dollars)				Per Cent of Total Member Bank Holdings in:			Holdings as Per Cent of Total Amounts Outside Federal Reserve Banks			
	Total (1)	Bills and Certificates (2)	Notes (3)	Treasury and Liberty Bonds (4)	Bills and Certificates (5)	Notes (6)	Treasury and Liberty Bonds (7)	Total (8)	Bills and Certificates (9)	Notes (10)	Treasury and Liberty Bonds (11)
Dec. 1928	4,312	554	729	3,028	12.85	16.91	70.22	28.0	29.4	32.7	26.8
June 1929	4,155	446	704	3,005	10.73	16.94	72.32	27.6	28.3	32.7	26.6
June 1930	4,061	259	463	3,340	6.38	11.40	82.25	29.4	22.2	33.6	29.7
June 1931	5,343	901	403	4,039	16.86	7.54	75.59	36.1	47.4	94.8	32.4
June 1932	5,628	962	503	4,163	17.09	8.94	73.97	34.6	42.5	50.8	32.0
June 1933	6,887	1,113	2,049	3,725	16.16	29.75	54.09	36.2	50.2	53.4	28.7
June 1934	9,137	1,427	2,871	4,838	15.62	31.42	52.95	40.0	65.5	52.9	31.8
June 1935	9,871	1,099	4,314	4,458	11.13	43.70	45.16	41.7	75.9	50.7	32.5
June 1936	11,721	1,266	5,161	5,295	10.80	44.03	45.18	41.2	73.0	52.2	31.4
June 1937	10,870	821	4,361	5,689	7.55	40.12	52.34	35.8	48.9	46.2	29.6
June 1938	10,215	316	3,653	6,246	3.09	35.76	61.15	34.5	63.3	45.8	29.6
June 1939	10,946	441	2,720	7,786	4.03	24.85	71.13	35.1	52.2	44.8	32.0
June 1940	11,600	797	2,543	8,261	6.87	21.92	71.22	36.5	61.2	48.4	32.8
June 1941	14,238	1,127	2,631	10,481	7.92	18.48	73.61	40.3	70.3	53.9	36.3

NOTE: Details do not necessarily add to totals because of rounding.

SOURCE, BY COLUMN

(1) Sum of cols. 2–4.
(2–4) *Banking and Monetary Statistics*, p. 77.
(8) Holdings of the Federal Reserve Banks were deducted from the total of the 4 kinds of debt outstanding (*ibid.*, pp. 332, 343, 375, 509–510). All bonds held by the Federal Reserve Banks were treated as Treasury or Liberty bonds. Col. 1 was expressed as a percentage of the difference.
(9–11) Procedure similar to that for col. 8, except that in 1929–31, no June breakdown of Federal Reserve holdings was available. The percentage distribution of the 4 kinds of debt in June 1929 and 1930 was assumed the same as on the preceding Dec. 31 and in June 1931 the same as on the following Dec. 31.

impressed on commercial bankers by the experiences of the preceding few years.

As total assets increased sharply after 1933, bankers took the opportunity offered by the increase to strengthen their cash position and to expand investments, and among them, governments, more rapidly than loans. By 1940, cash assets had mounted to 36 per cent of total assets (Table 17). Loans were only about 70 per cent of investments and about 70 per cent of investments were in the form of U.S. government securities.

Unfortunately, there are no adequate data on the maturity distribution of bank investments. Beginning in late 1928, data are available on the distribution of government security holdings of all member banks among three categories: bills and certificates of indebtedness; notes; and bonds (see Table 18). The first category had a maturity of less than one year when issued, the second, of one to five years, and the third, of more than five years. However, depending on the particular security, the remaining maturity, *when purchased* or held, might be quite different from the original maturity. A bond, for example, might have a remaining maturity when purchased or held of less than a year and so be comparable in maturity to bills. In consequence, the distribution of security holdings among the indicated categories is at best a very rough index of their distribution by maturity.

The data show a decided shift in the composition of the security holdings of banks after 1928 and 1929. In 1928, 1929, and 1930, bonds constituted about 70 to 80 per cent of the total of U.S. securities held by member banks, the balance being distributed somewhat more in notes than in bills and certificates. In 1931 and 1932, bonds remained about 75 per cent of the total, but about two-thirds of the remainder was in the form of bills and certificates and one-third in notes, suggesting that under the pressure of successive liquidity crises banks shifted into shorter-term securities. After 1932, the fraction in the form of bonds fell steadily to 54 and 53 per cent in June of 1933 and 1934, 45 per cent in June of 1935 and 1936. True, after 1932, notes rose sharply relative to bills and certificates, from one-third of the three combined in 1932 to two-thirds in 1933 and 1934 and to four-fifths in 1935 and 1936. However, that shift was largely a result of a limited supply of bills and certificates. Member banks held close to 50 per cent of the bills and certificates outside the Federal Reserve Banks from 1931 to 1933, and around 70 per cent from 1934 to 1936. They held roughly 50 per cent of the notes from 1932 to 1936 and around one-third of the bonds. By contrast, in 1928 banks held about 30 per cent each of the bills and certificates and of the notes outside the Federal Reserve System and about a quarter of the bonds. The banks had absorbed so much larger a fraction of the bills, certificates, and notes outside the Federal Reserve System than of the bonds that banks had become the dominant factor in the market for these short-term obligations.

No doubt changes in the demand for loans and in the supply of investments, and the large increase in available reserves produced by the gold inflows—all of which constituted changes in the supply of assets for banks to hold—played a role in the shifts in asset composition. However, the major factor was not those but rather a shift in the liquidity preferences of commercial banks, that is, a change in the demand by banks for assets, which is to say, in the portfolio composition they sought to attain for any given structure of yields. The inflow of gold—the most dramatic force operating on the supply side—in the first instance increased the cash assets of the banking system. But the banks were individually free to convert the additional assets into other forms, and collectively of course that conversion would have been and was reflected in a rise in the stock of money and in the total assets of banks. Such reactions on the part of banks could therefore have offset in full, as they did in part, the effect of the gold inflow on the *ratio* of cash assets to total assets. There was, of course, some lag in the reactions of banks, and no doubt the lag made cash assets somewhat larger relative to total assets during the periods of steady gold inflow than they otherwise would have been. Such a lag cannot, however, account for the continued increase in the ratio of cash assets to total assets, since there was no corresponding increase in the rate of gold inflow. Moreover, such a lag cannot explain the shifting composition of noncash assets.

The behavior of rates of interest is decisive evidence that the shifting composition of noncash assets cannot be explained by changes in the supply of assets available for banks to hold but only by changes in liquidity preferences on the part of the banks. Suppose the shifts in bank portfolios had reflected mainly shifts in supply without a change in the preferences of banks for different kinds of assets. The assets whose *relative* importance in the portfolio increased should then also have been the ones on which the yield rose in comparison with the yield on other assets, since the issuers of such assets would have had to raise their yield to induce banks to hold them in increased amount.[31] In fact, the structure of

---

[31] The wording is deliberately vague about how the yields should be compared, whether in terms of the ratio of yields or the absolute difference between them (spread). It is an open question, about which there is no general agreement, which is the more relevant for judging changes in the relative attractiveness of assets. In our view, this question cannot be given a single answer; sometimes the one and sometimes the other will be the more relevant, though on the whole, for our present purpose, the spread seems preferable. Fortunately, however, for the episode under discussion, it makes no difference how the question is answered. Except for cash assets (see footnote 32), the major movements in the spread and in the relative yield were in the same direction.

CHART 35   **37**

Changing Relations Among Interest Yields, 1928–39

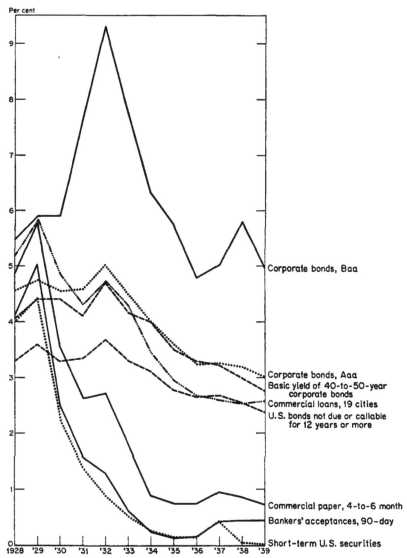

Per cent

Corporate bonds, Baa

Corporate bonds, Aaa
Basic yield of 40-to-50-year
    corporate bonds
Commercial loans, 19 cities
U.S. bonds not due or callable
    for 12 years or more

Commercial paper, 4-to-6 month

Bankers' acceptances, 90-day

Short-term U.S. securities

SOURCE: Baa and Aaa corporate bonds, commercial loans, bankers' acceptances, *Banking and Monetary Statistics*, pp. 448, 464, 468. Commercial loan rate, annual averages; for 1939 based on Jan.-Feb. only; monthly data unavailable thereafter on a comparable basis. Basic yield of 40- to 50-year corporate bonds, *Historical Statistics*, 1960, p. 657, Series X-347. U.S. government bonds, *Federal Reserve Bulletin*, Dec. 1938, p. 1045; Feb. 1940, p. 139. Commercial paper, *Historical Statistics*, 1949, p. 346, averaged annually. Short-term U.S. government securities, *FRB*, May 1945, p. 483: 3- to 6-month certificates and notes, 1928–30; 3- to 9-month Treasury bills, 1931–42.

interest rates moved the other way for assets other than cash assets.[32] Rates charged on customer loans and yields on long-term government bonds were low after 1933 by earlier standards, and customer rates had fallen more than long-term bond yields; however, rates on short-term commercial paper, bankers' acceptances, and short-term U.S. securities— the kinds of assets whose relative importance in bank portfolios had increased most—were lower still by those standards (see Chart 35).[33] Among corporate bonds, yields on lower-grade bonds had fallen decidedly less from 1929 to 1936 than yields on high-grade bonds had, again suggesting a shift of preference toward the more certain. The most notable change in the structure of rates of return from before to after the 1929–33 contraction was the sharp widening in spread among assets differing in the degree of confidence the holder could attach to their convertibility into a known cash sum at need and on short notice. It follows that the initial supposition that the change in bank portfolios reflected mainly shifts in the supply of assets is untenable. The change must have reflected shifts in demand by banks and others for different kinds of assets.[34] Moreover, the change in the distribution of government

[32] The argument from interest rates alone, which is decisive for other assets, is not decisive for cash assets. It does not, of course, follow that there was no shift in preferences for cash assets comparable to that for the other assets that rose in relative importance in bank portfolios. On the contrary, we argue below that there was such a shift, and that it reinforced a change in conditions of supply to produce a much larger rise in the relative importance of cash assets in bank portfolios than would otherwise have occurred.

For the cash assets of Table 17, the yield fell from a minor positive amount, because of interest paid on interbank balances, to zero. The ratio of the yield on other assets to the yield on cash assets therefore rose from a finite amount to infinity. However, the spread between other yields and the yield on cash assets as a whole undoubtedly fell. For an unduplicated cash total for the banking system as a whole, i.e., high-powered money holdings, the yield was zero throughout, so the ratio of yields remained unchanged, while the spread fell. The change in conditions of supply therefore fostered a rise in the fraction of assets held in the form of cash assets.

[33] It should be noted that the customer loan rate is not, like all the other rates in Chart 35, a market rate, and may for that reason be subject to a wider margin of error. In addition, other dimensions of the loan, such as collateral conditions, the size of the compensating balance borrowers are required to hold, and so on, may vary more than for market rates.

[34] The increased demand for short- relative to long-term securities was no doubt partly motivated by a belief that rates of interest were likely to rise in the future. That expectation would make long securities less attractive than short at the same rate, or at a difference in rates that prevailed earlier when such expectations were not held. David Meiselman argues persuasively that the whole of the change in spread between one-year and longer rates on corporate bonds can be explained by the shift in relative demand arising from such expectation effects (see his The Term Structure of Interest Rates, Englewood Cliffs, N.J., Prentice-Hall, 1962). Meiselman does not consider in detail rates for periods of less than a year, which play a crucial role in our analysis.

These expectation effects do not, of course, explain the widening of the spread between more and less risky investments of the same maturity; that must have

securities of varying maturity between banks and other holders could only have occurred because the change in bank preferences for liquidity was greater than any corresponding change in the preferences of other holders.

The evidence furnished by interest rates is confirmed by a study by C. O. Hardy and Jacob Viner of the availability of bank credit in the Chicago Federal Reserve District during the period from the bank holiday to September 1, 1934. The study, based mainly on interviews with bankers and brokers, was undertaken "to find out so far as possible whether, and to what extent, the small volume of bank loans was due to the desire of banks to retain or attain liquidity, to the attitude of examining officials, to the unwillingness of businessmen to assume the risk of borrowing to maintain or expand their operations, or to the impairment of the capital of many businessmen by losses incurred during the depression which made

---

reflected a shift of preference toward the less risky for other reasons. As the next sentence in the text indicates, they can explain the change in distribution of government securities among banks and others only if banks had different expectations from those of others, believing that rates would rise more rapidly in the rather short-term future than others thought they would.

While Meiselman's conclusion may be entirely justified for rates for periods of a year or longer and while its being the correct explanation for rates for shorter periods would not seriously affect the conclusions stated in the text—since they do not depend on the reason for the shift in preferences—we do not believe that his conclusion can be extended to the rates for very short periods with which we are most concerned. As we have seen, banks came to play a dominant role in the market for some of these assets, and the behavior of the corresponding rates therefore hinges critically on shifts in banks' preferences. The evidence we adduce below to explain the notable increase in bank cash assets strongly supports the view that the 1929–33 experience led banks to attach a much greater value than formerly to assets that could be converted into known cash sums at need and at short notice for reasons other than the belief that interest rates would rise. Their experience, more trying than that of other asset holders, must have impressed them with their greater need to hedge against uncertainty; and the structure of their liabilities meant that such hedging required them to shift to shorter-term securities, as they did.

A shift in bank preferences for reasons other than expectations about future rates therefore explains in a simple and straightforward manner (1) the very great increase in spread for very short-term relative not only to long-term but also to one-year rates; (2) the sharp shift in composition of bank portfolios; (3) the shift in the distribution of government securities among holders; and (4) the behavior of "excess reserves." The expectations hypothesis can then supplement this explanation for banks and be the major explanation for longer rates and other holders.

In more recent work on the cyclical behavior of the term structure of interest rates, Reuben Kessel has found that combining the expectations hypothesis with liquidity considerations gives a more satisfactory explanation of the empirical evidence than either gives alone for maturities both shorter and longer than one year. While the finding does not demonstrate that *shifts* in liquidity preference played the role we assign to them, it perhaps makes that interpretation more plausible than it would otherwise be (see his forthcoming "The Cyclical Behavior of the Term Structure of Interest Rates," an NBER study, in preparation).

them poor banking risks." The authors concluded: "That there exists a genuine unsatisfied demand for credit on the part of solvent borrowers, many of whom could make economically sound use of working capital . . . That one of the most serious aspects of this unsatisfied demand is the pressure for liquidation of old working-capital loans, even sound ones. That this pressure is partly due to a determination on the part of bankers to avoid a recurrence of the errors to which they attribute much of the responsibility for the recent wave of bank failures . . . ."[35]

The increased fraction of bank assets held in the form of cash assets, unlike the increased fraction held in short-term investments, can be partly explained by supply considerations. As noted, a lagged reaction to the gold inflow may have contributed to the increase. More important, because longer lasting, rates of interest in general fell, which made cash assets more attractive compared to other assets (or, equivalently, less costly in terms of income sacrificed). Moreover, the shift in preferences depressed particularly the yields on short-term highly liquid assets, fostering still more the shift into cash. For example, the yield on Treasury bills averaged 0.515 per cent per year in 1933, 0.256 in 1934, 0.137 in 1935, and 0.143 in 1936. After rising to 0.447 in 1937 in response to the doubling of reserve requirements (see Chapter 9 below), it fell to 0.053 in 1938, 0.023 in 1939, and 0.014 in 1940. At those yields it was hardly worthwhile to hold bills instead of cash. In consequence, while the ratio of government securities to total assets for all banks reached its peak in 1936, the ratio of cash assets to total assets continued rising until 1940.

While supply considerations explain part of the shift into cash assets, they cannot explain the whole of the shift, which was motivated also by the same desire for liquidity as the shift into investments. To begin with, cash assets were acquired along with investments to satisfy that desire; after 1936, the acquisition of cash assets became the most convenient and least costly way to achieve the desired liquidity. Indirect confirmation of these propositions is furnished by the evidence from interest rates that the shift into investments reflected a change in the liquidity preferences of banks. Such a change could clearly be expected also to affect cash assets since those assets fulfill par excellence the end desired in holding short-term investments—convertibility into known sums at need and on short notice. In addition, there are a number of other bits of evidence that together are fairly decisive.

Perhaps the most striking of these is a comparison between Canadian and United States experience made by George R. Morrison.[36] Canada's

---

[35] *Report on the Availability of Bank Credit in the Seventh Federal Reserve District*, submitted to the Secretary of the Treasury, GPO, 1935, pp. 3 and VI.

[36] In "Liquidity Preferences of Commercial Banks," unpublished Ph.D. dissertation, University of Chicago, 1962.

cyclical experience was almost the same as that of the United States from 1929 to 1939, except that it was spared any bank failures or widespread runs on banks. Rates of interest moved in much the same way as in the United States—to be expected from the close link between the financial markets in the two countries. Canadian banks increased their cash assets relative to their deposits, but by a very much smaller proportion than did U.S. banks.

A second bit of evidence comes from Morrison's examination of the relation in the United States between cash assets and interest rates before 1929 and after 1939. On the basis of both earlier and later experience, the increase in cash assets in the 1930's was much larger than the increase that might have been expected to be produced by the decline in yields alone.

Our analysis of the reaction of member banks to the doubling of reserve requirements in 1936 and 1937 is still another bit of evidence that they had accumulated cash assets because their demand for liquidity had risen. When the rise in reserve requirements immobilized the accumulated cash, they proceeded rather promptly to accumulate additional cash for liquidity purposes (see the more detailed discussion in Chapter 9).[37]

The form taken by the increase in cash assets was doubtless affected by the prohibition of payment of interest on demand deposits. Had the prohibition not existed, more of the growth of cash assets might have taken the form of balances at other commercial banks rather than at Federal Reserve Banks. As it was, there was no incentive to hold at other commercial banks balances desired for their liquidity. How great this effect was is by no means clear. The low yield on short-term assets would have meant a low rate of interest offered for interbank balances and perhaps even a zero rate of interest, in which case the result would have been the same.

The shift in liquidity preferences of banks was destined to be temporary. To judge by the experience of earlier episodes,[38] the passage of time without any extensive series of bank failures would have dulled the fears of bank managers, leading them to set a lower premium on liquidity. In any case, the establishment of FDIC, which was accompanied by a dramatic reduction in the rate of bank failures, provided additional assurance against the occurrence of "runs" of the kind that had produced the shift in liquidity preferences. Such assurance, while by no means clear at the start of FDIC, eventually became increasingly clear, but still it took

[37] See also Phillip Cagan's forthcoming monograph on determinants and effects of changes in the money stock in the United States since 1875, a National Bureau study, Chap. 5.

[38] See Chap. 2, sect. 4; Chap. 3, sect. 3; and Chap. 4, sect. 6. Also see Cagan's forthcoming study referred to in the preceding footnote, and Morrison's study referred to in footnote 36, above.

time for banks to adapt their behavior to that new fact It is therefore not surprising that the ratio of cash assets to total assets continued rising until 1940.

Though the ratio of cash assets to total assets fell drastically during the war and remained at an even lower level thereafter, it has remained above its 1929 level (Table 17, col. 8). The reason is not a continued higher preference on the part of banks for cash assets but rather a rise in reserve requirements. Banks have no choice about the form of their required reserves. That fraction of their assets has to be kept as cash assets—indeed, until 1959, as deposit balances at the Federal Reserve System—and, as they found out at great cost in 1930–33, can not be drawn upon for emergencies without precipitating suspension. A change in a bank's cash ratio as a result of a change in reserve requirements is, therefore, a different phenomenon from a change as a result of a shift in asset preference.

Aggregate data on required reserves are available only for member banks. Accordingly, Table 19, which eliminates required reserves from both the numerator and denominator of the cash ratio, is restricted to member banks. In 1929, member banks held 11.3 per cent of their assets in excess of required reserves in the form of cash in vault, cash items in the process of collection, and balances at banks (commercial and Federal Reserve) in excess of required reserves. That ratio rose steadily from 1933 to 1936, then fell as a result of the doubling of reserve requirements in 1936–37, then resumed its rise to a peak of nearly 30 per cent in 1940. By 1945 it was back to roughly its 1929 level, and it has fluctuated around that level since, whereas the ratio of all cash assets to total assets (column 3) has fluctuated around a level several percentage points higher than the 1929 level.

Unlike the cash ratio, the ratio of investments to loans continued to rise during the war. Although it has fallen since, it is still about twice its 1929 level. However, the divergent behavior of the cash ratio and the investment-loan ratio does not imply that the effect of the increased preference for liquidity on the demand for investments lasted longer than its effect on the demand for cash. Just as the demand for both categories expanded together from 1932 to 1940, so the demand for both could have declined together subsequently, since the divergent behavior of the actual ratios can be readily explained by differences on the supply side. During the war there was a rapid increase in the supply of government securities, and probably also a decrease in the relative demand for bank loans because many firms were financed by federal government funds. As is consistent with this interpretation, the spread in yield between highly liquid and less liquid bank assets narrowed, if anything, during the war—to an especially striking extent if government bonds whose

TABLE 19
RELATION OF CASH ASSETS TO REQUIRED RESERVES AND TOTAL ASSETS,
MEMBER BANKS, SELECTED DATES, 1929–60
(dollars in billions)

Date[a]	Total Assets (1)	Cash Assets (2)	Cash Assets as Percentage of Total Assets (3)	Required Reserves (4)	Required Reserves as Percentage of Total Assets (5)	Cash Assets in Excess of Required Reserves as Percentage of Total Assets in Excess of Required Reserves (6)
1929	45.5	7.2	15.8	2 3	5.1	11.3
1933	33.0	6 2	18.8	1 8	5.5	14.1
1934	37.4	8.2	21.9	2 1	5.6	17 3
1935	40 7	10.1	24 8	2 6	6 4	19.7
1936	46.5	12.5	26.9	2 9	6.2	22.0
1937	47.5	13.0	27.4	6 0	12.6	16.9
1938	47.1	14.8	31.4	5 1	10.8	23.1
1939	51.9	17.6	33.9	5 9.	11 4	25.4
1940	57.8	21.8	37.7	6.9	11 9	29.3
1941	64 9	22.7	35.0	7.8	12 0	26.1
1945	126.4	25.8	20.4	13.3	10 5	11.1
1948	127.3	30.3	23.8	16.7	13.1	12.3
1957	176.5	35 3	20.0	18.3	10 4	10.7
1958	194.0	38.5	19.8	18.3	9.4	11.5
1959	197.3	37 9	19.2	18.0	9.1	11.1
1960	204 2	41.9	20.5	17 7	8.7	13.0

[a] June 30 or nearest available call date.

SOURCE, BY COLUMN

(1) *Banking and Monetary Statistics*, pp. 72 and 74, and *Member Bank Call Report*.
(2) The sum of reserves at Federal Reserve Banks, cash in vault, balances at domestic and foreign banks, and cash items in process of collection, from same source as for col. 1.
(3) Col. 2 divided by col. 1.
(4) 1929–41: *Banking and Monetary Statistics*, pp. 395–396.
   1945–59: *Member Bank Call Report*.
   1960: Average for week ending June 15, 1960, from *Federal Reserve Bulletin*, Dec. 1960, p. 1350.
(5) Col. 4 divided by col. 1.
(6) Computed from cols. 1, 2, and 4.

prices were pegged by the Federal Reserve are regarded as highly liquid assets. After the war, the supply of government securities remained high, and an increasing proportion of business firms found it possible to raise funds they required on the open market. The spread of rates of return continued to narrow through 1960. Supply conditions had reverted somewhat by that time, but not fully, to prewar conditions, hence the investment-loan ratio remained above its 1929 level.

It should be noted that our interpretation of the changes in the composition of bank assets and, in particular, of the emergence of a large volume of "excess reserves" in the 1930's runs sharply counter to an interpretation that is widely held[39]—and one that was also implicit in Federal Reserve policy in the 1930's and has been to a lesser degree since. According to that interpretation, excess reserves were primarily unneeded surplus funds held by banks, proof of easy-money conditions and of a lack of private demand for credit. Banks were, as it were, in metastable equilibrium. Additional funds acquired by banks were in the main simply added to cash balances; additional demands on banks were met by reducing balances. There was no unique desired structure of assets, corresponding to given rates of return on assets, disturbance of which would prompt banks to seek to restore that same structure; they would be content to retain the new one. On this view, changes in reserve requirements had no effect, so long as they did not absorb all excess reserves either for all banks or for any significant group of banks.[40] This was the view explicitly presented by the Board of Governors in connection with the doubling of reserve requirements in 1936–37.[41] As we have already implied and as we

[39] Woodlief Thomas, "Monetary Controls," *Banking Studies*, Board of Governors of the Federal Reserve System, 1941, reprinted 1947, pp. 341–342; Allan Sproul, "Changing Concepts of Central Banking," *Money, Trade, and Economic Growth*, in Honor of J. H. Williams, New York, Macmillan, 1951, pp. 297–298; R. A. Gordon, *Business Fluctuations*, New York, Harper, 1952, pp. 398–399. An interpretation essentially identical with ours is presented by Paul A. Samuelson, "Fiscal Policy and Income Determination," *Quarterly Journal of Economics*, Aug. 1942, p. 594.

[40] See Board of Governors of the Federal Reserve System, *Annual Report*, 1936, p. 15; 1937, p. 2; E. A. Goldenweiser, *Monetary Management*, New York, McGraw-Hill, 1949, pp. 57–59; and *idem, American Monetary Policy*, New York, McGraw-Hill, 1951, pp. 175–182.

[41] Opinions expressed within the System were less dogmatic and unqualified than official justifications for the actions taken were, though their general tenor was the same.

A series of memoranda dealing with excess reserves, prepared at the Federal Reserve Bank of New York from 1934 on, apparently provided the initial intellectual basis for doubling reserve requirements (see Chap. 9, sect. 4). These memoranda, as well as statements by Bank officials to the New York board of directors, the FOMC, and the Board of Governors, present essentially the view outlined above, when they deal with the specific subject of the large accumulation of excess reserves and the measures that should be taken to deal with them. For example, a memorandum, dated Nov. 7, 1935, "Plans for Credit Control," states, "Had there been no gold inflow the excess reserves created by the Reserve System

point out in more detail in Chapter 9 in discussing the 1937–38 contraction, the reaction to the doubling of requirements contradicts the official view and supports our interpretation.

2. *Changes in the Monetary Standard*

GOLD POLICY

President Roosevelt's proclamation of a bank holiday on March 6, 1933, also prohibited banks from paying out gold or dealing in foreign exchange during the bank holiday. The Emergency Banking Act of March 9, 1933, which confirmed and extended the March 6 proclamation, granted the President emergency powers over banking transactions and over foreign exchange dealings and gold and currency movements. The next day, March 10, the President issued an executive order extending the restrictions on gold and foreign exchange dealings beyond the banking holiday proper and, in effect, prohibiting gold payments by banking and non-banking institutions alike, unless permitted by the Secretary of the Treasury under license. The order also narrowly limited foreign exchange dealings. Those measures were a precursor to nearly a year of tinkering with the monetary standard which culminated in the most far-reaching alteration in its legal structure since the departure from gold during the Civil War and subsequent resumption in 1879.[42]

Despite the effective suspension of gold payments, the price of gold,

---

would now have been entirely absorbed by the increase in the required reserves [as a result of deposit expansion]"—a statement implying that deposit expansion would have been identical even if the reserves had increased at a much slower rate (Harrison, Notes, Vol. VI; also Harrison, Special, no. 9, p. 2). At the same time, this view is occasionally qualified by the recognition that the same level of excess reserves may have different effects on the willingness of member banks to expand their earning assets, and in different contexts statements are made that go even further in the direction of our intepretation. For example, President Harrison suggested, in commenting on the first rise in reserve requirements in 1936, that it "lessened to some extent the pressure upon banks to invest their surplus funds," i.e., that it had a contractionary effect (Harrison, Open Market, Vol. IV, unrevised minutes of meeting, Nov. 19, 1936). The explicit reconciliation of the two strands in System opinion rested on a distinction of magnitude.

The conclusion we draw from perusal of the Harrison Papers is that the officers of the New York Bank quite explicitly recognized the changed liquidity preferences of banks and the desirability of excess reserves to meet them from 1930 to 1934 or 1935 (see Chap. 7, sect. 5), but they could not accept excess reserves so large in magnitude as those that accumulated thereafter as a reflection of such changed preferences, hence were led to the view that they had no constructive effects.

[42] For a detailed chronology and description of the steps taken during the year, see J. D. Paris, *Monetary Policies of the United States, 1932–1938,* New York, Columbia University Press, 1938, pp. 12–32 and 118–120. For a different kind of description of the same events, see F. A. Pearson, W. I. Myers, and A. R. Gans, "Warren as Presidential Adviser," *Farm Economics,* New York State College of Agriculture, Cornell University, No. 211, Dec. 1957.

or the rate of exchange between the dollar and currencies like the French franc that remained rigidly linked to gold, hovered around "par" for over a month. *The suspension was presumably regarded as part of the banking emergency and hence expected to be temporary;* foreign exchange transactions were strictly controlled and limited; the administration made no official announcement that it proposed to permit the dollar to depreciate or be devalued; and after some weeks, several licenses to export gold were granted. Moreover, the technical gold position was sufficiently strong so that there was little doubt the preceding gold parity could have been maintained if desired; the ratio of the gold stock to the total stock of money was higher than at any time since 1914.

One important step, unprecedented in the United States, was taken during this period. On April 5, an executive order forbade the "hoarding" of gold and required all holders of gold, including member banks, to deliver their holdings of gold coin, bullion, or certificates to Federal Reserve Banks on or before May 1 except for rare coins, reasonable amounts for use in industry and the arts, and a maximum of $100 per person in gold coin and gold certificates.[43] The gold coin and gold certificates were exchanged for other currency or deposits at face value, and the bullion was paid for at the legal price of $20.67 per fine ounce. The "nationalization" of gold outside Federal Reserve Banks was later completed by an order of the Secretary of the Treasury, dated December 28, 1933, excepting only rare coins and a few other minor items from the requirement that all gold coin, gold bullion, and gold certificates be delivered to the Treasurer of the United States at face value corresponding to the legal price of $20.67 per fine ounce. The expiration date for the surrender of gold was later set as January 17, 1934,[44] when the market price of gold was in the neighborhood of $33 per fine ounce.[45]

---

[43] *Federal Reserve Bulletin,* Apr. 1933, pp. 213–214.

[44] *FRB,* Feb. 1934, p. 80.

[45] Pearson, Myers, and Gans, "Warren," p. 5647. The amount of gold coin and gold certificates outside the Treasury and the Federal Reserve Banks at the end of Feb. 1933 was estimated by contemporary Federal Reserve statistics to be $1,220 million, of which $571 million was in coin and $649 million in certificates (*FRB,* Feb. 1934, p. 95). These statistics show the amount of gold coin outside the Treasury and Federal Reserve as falling to $367 million at the end of Mar. 1933 (before the first executive order requiring the transfer of gold coin), to $335 million at the end of Apr., then declining gradually to $311 million at the end of Dec. and to $287 million at the end of Jan. 1934 (*ibid.*). The gold coin then outstanding was dropped from the monthly circulation statement as of Jan. 31, 1934. It was assumed that that amount had mainly been lost, destroyed, exported without record, or was in numismatic collections, although some unknown amount remained illegally in private hands. Since the amount turned in to the Treasury at $20.67 an ounce between June 1934 and June 1960 totaled less than $12 million, it might be concluded that the amount of gold coin outstanding after Jan. 1934 was not significant.

The experience with national bank notes analyzed in footnote 20, however, in-

An executive order of April 20, 1933, extending and revising the gold embargo, and comments by the President at his news conference the preceding day ended the period of stability in the price of gold. The President made it clear that the administration intended to permit the dollar to depreciate in terms of foreign currencies as a means of achieving a rise in domestic prices. The order applied the restrictions on foreign exchange transactions not only to banks licensed under the executive

---

dicates that losses could have accounted for only a small part of the $287 million still outstanding at the end of Jan. 1934. Whatever losses there were presumably occurred during the period from 1907 to 1933, since in 1907 the Director of the Mint presented revised estimates of gold coin in circulation which took into account probable losses from 1873 to 1907. The average amount of gold coin reported as in circulation from 1907 through 1933 was $490 million. The rate of loss of gold coin would presumably be substantially less than that of national bank notes. Even the rate of loss for national bank notes of roughly $1 per $1,000 per year would have meant a loss of only $12.7 million over the 26-year period.

Could unrecorded gold exports have accounted for most of the $287 million of gold coin not surrendered by the public by the end of Jan. 1934? We think not. The two main channels for export of gold without record before 1934 were immigrant remittances and travel expenditures. To estimate the probable size of such exports, we applied to the balance of payments figures for those items, 1907–33, the ratio of the gold correction for 1873–1900 to similar balance of payments figures for those years. The estimate so obtained is $80 million, but it may well be an overstatement: (1) the gold correction for the earlier period is only in part —although probably in major part—attributable to unrecorded exports; (2) travel expenditures for the earlier period are limited to passengers' transportation and travel expenses, while for the period since 1907 they also include import freight payments.

If the estimates of gold lost and gold exported without record are added to the gold coin returned to the Treasury since 1934, we are still far short of accounting for even half of the $287 million. We therefore concluded that in Jan. 1934 the bulk of the $287 million was retained illegally in private hands. For this reason we restored to the gold stock and gold circulation the $287 million which the Federal Reserve subtracted for 1914–33 from the figures as originally published. Since gold coin has not been a component of the money stock since Jan. 31, 1934, our series exclude the $287 million since that date.

Until July 14, 1954, it was lawful for U.S. citizens to hold as rare coin only two coins of each specimen minted. A regulation of the Secretary of the Treasury (*Federal Register*, XIX, No. 135, July 14, 1954, p. 4331) removed any limit on the possession of gold coin minted before Apr. 5, 1933, designating all such coins as of numismatic value.

Although it has been illegal since 1933 for the public to hold gold certificates, amounts outstanding were not dropped from the monthly circulation statement after Jan. 1934, as they were for gold coin. There has, however, been a substantial decline in gold certificates from the total of $178 million recorded as outstanding at the end of Jan. 1934. At the end of 1960 only $30 million was still reported in circulation, most of which probably may not be returned to the Treasury. Application of the loss rate for national bank notes to the average amount of gold certificates in circulation from 1880 through 1933 yields a probable loss of $24 million over the 53-year period. However, in all likelihood this is an overestimate, since gold certificates were surely subject to a decidedly smaller rate of loss. This judgment is based on the fact that, compared with national bank notes, gold certificates were of higher denominations, and a larger proportion of the amounts outstanding was held in bank vaults.

order of March 10, but also to all persons dealing in foreign exchange. On the same day, the Thomas amendment to the Agricultural Adjustment Act was offered in Congress. The amendment, enacted into law on May 12, and explicitly directed at achieving a price rise through expansion of the money stock, contained a provision authorizing the President to reduce the gold content of the dollar to as low as 50 per cent of its former weight. The dollar price of gold immediately started rising, which is to say that so also did the dollar price of foreign currencies, including both those like the French franc that remained on gold and those like the pound sterling that had gone off gold at an earlier date. In the next three months, the market price of gold rose to $30 an ounce, and thereafter fluctuated erratically between a low of about $27 and a high of nearly $35 until January 30, 1934, when the Gold Reserve Act was passed.[46] During that period, the United States had a floating exchange rate determined in the market from day to day, as in the period from 1862 to 1879. However, there was considerably greater government interference in the market. On September 8, 1933, an official gold price, to be fixed daily at the estimated world market figure less shipping and insurance cost, was established. The Treasury agreed to buy gold at that price to give American gold miners a price as high as they could have obtained by export in the absence of the export embargo.

Starting in October, the government intervened actively to raise the price of gold. The Reconstruction Finance Corporation was authorized to buy newly mined domestic gold from October 25 on, and a few days later, through the agency of the Federal Reserve Banks, to buy gold abroad. The purchase price was raised almost daily. For a time, the large scale of RFC purchases abroad made the announced price for newly-mined domestic gold the effective market price. From the end of November, however, until the end of January 1934, the announced price exceeded the market price abroad.[47]

The aim of the gold policy was to raise the price level of commodities, particularly farm products and raw materials, which sustained the greatest relative decline during the preceding years of deflation. That aim was pursued simultaneously through other New Deal measures, of which the National Recovery Administration's promulgation of "codes" and the Agricultural Adjustment Administration's production controls were the most notable. It was not pursued, as we have seen, through any substantial increase in the quantity of money, though the Thomas amendment provided the legal basis for an increase even without the concurrence of the Federal Reserve System. Most farm products and raw materials exported by the United States had a world market in which this country,

[46] See Pearson, Myers, and Gans, "Warren," pp. 5636, 5645–5647.
[47] Pearson, Myers, and Gans, "Warren," p. 5646.

while sometimes important as both supplier and purchaser, was seldom dominant. The prices of such commodities in foreign currencies were determined by world demand and supply and were affected by events in the United States only insofar as these, in turn, affected the amounts supplied and demanded by the United States. Even then, such prices were affected much less than in proportion to the changes in U.S. sales and purchases. Hence, the decline in the foreign exchange value of the dollar meant a roughly proportional rise in the dollar price of such commodities, which is, of course, what did happen to the dollar prices of cotton, petroleum products, leaf tobacco, wheat, and similar items. The aim of the gold policy to raise prices of farm products and raw materials was therefore largely achieved.

The decline in the foreign exchange value of the dollar was initially a product of speculative sale of dollars in the expectation of devaluation—a short-term capital outflow. The decline was sustained by shifts in the demand (by which, as always, we mean demand schedules) for imports and supply (again, supply schedules) of exports produced by the cessation of internal deflation. The resolution of the banking panic and restoration of confidence in the monetary system were accompanied by an increase in velocity, a higher rate of spending, and rising prices. As a result, prices rose in the United States relative to prices in other countries. If the exchange value of the dollar had not fallen, the price rise would have discouraged exports and encouraged imports. Those forces were subsequently reinforced by U.S. purchase of gold at home and abroad.

U.S. purchase of domestic gold involved a reduction in the supply of goods for export, since gold is a potential export good, and hence a reduction in the demand for dollars by holders of other currencies (to buy the domestically produced gold). The purchase of foreign gold involved an increase in the demand for goods for import (namely, gold) and hence in the supply of dollars offered in exchange for foreign currencies (to buy foreign gold). The combined effect was to create a potential deficit in the U.S. balance of payments at the former exchange rate. Given a flexible rate, the potential deficit was closed by a depreciation of the dollar sufficient to generate, through an increase in exports or a decline in imports or a movement of speculative funds, an amount of foreign currencies exceeding the amount demanded for other purposes by enough to pay for the gold.

These effects depended very little on the fact that gold was the commodity purchased. Given a floating exchange rate, essentially the same effects on the dollar prices of internationally traded goods would have followed from the same dollar volume of government purchase of wheat or perfume or foreign-owned art masterpieces, or from the economically equivalent program, adopted after World War II, of building up stockpiles of foreign-produced strategic goods. Of course, had one of these other commodities been used as the vehicle for the purchase program, gold would have been one of the class of domestically produced goods, export of which was stimulated by the U.S. depreciation of the dollar, and one of the class of foreign-produced goods, import of which was discouraged by the depreciation. Consequently, the hypothetical alternative purchase program would have tended to make the net inflow of gold less or the net outflow of gold more than it otherwise would have been. As it was, the use of gold as the vehicle necessarily meant an accumulation of gold, just as the use of wheat or perfume or foreign-owned masterpieces would have meant an accumulation of that commodity.

The choice of gold as the vehicle did have an important effect on the impact of the program on foreign countries. In the first place—and a corresponding effect would be present for any particular commodity— the program had a special impact on gold-producing countries. In the second place—and this effect would be present only for a commodity serving as the basis of a monetary standard—it had a special impact on gold-standard countries. Being committed to sell gold at a fixed price in terms of their own currency, those countries necessarily experienced pressure on their gold reserves, which in turn necessitated either abandonment of the gold standard or internal deflationary pressure. Entirely aside from the changes in the *relative* demands and supplies of goods they imported or exported arising out of the gold-purchase program, those countries were placed in the position of having to adjust their whole nominal price level.[48]

---

[48] It may help to put this point somewhat differently in terms of a particular example. Suppose the purchase program had been for French perfumes. Then, given the French internal monetary position, the price of such perfumes in francs would rise, the price in francs of other French exports would tend to fall (since the depreciation of the dollar would make them more expensive to Americans in dollars and hence reduce the quantity demanded at the former franc price), and the price in francs of goods imported into France from the U.S. would also tend to fall (since the depreciation of the dollar would reduce the franc equivalent of the former dollar price). Nothing can be said about the remaining prices: some might remain constant, some fall and some rise, depending on their substitutability in consumption and production for other exports and imports.

Now let the purchase program be for gold, either a program to spend a fixed number of dollars per month for gold, or to buy a fixed number of ounces per month at the market price in dollars, or to buy whatever number of ounces would be offered at a fixed dollar price higher than the prior market price, or any combination of these programs. Let France be on a gold standard and be the only country on a gold standard. Suppose, first, that France takes whatever measures are necessary to preserve her gold reserves intact and hence to force all U.S. gold purchases to be made elsewhere. This could occur through a general deflation of all French prices sufficient to make the depreciation of the dollar vis-à-vis the franc enough greater than its depreciation vis-à-vis other (nongold-standard) currencies so that the fixed franc price for gold, times the dollar price of the franc, yields a dollar price of gold above (or just equal to) the market price of gold in other

The device used to achieve a decline in the exchange value of the dollar—borrowing funds (through the issue of RFC securities) to purchase gold—was not unprecedented. The identical device was incorporated in the Resumption Act and employed before 1879 but that time for precisely the opposite purpose: to promote a rise in the exchange value of the dollar. In discussing that episode, we pointed out that the mechanical as opposed to the psychological effects of the accumulation of a gold reserve rendered resumption more rather than less difficult. The reasons are precisely those just given to explain why the gold purchases contributed to the decline in the exchange value of the dollar. In the one case as in the other, it is doubtful that the device was nearly so important as the less dramatic forces that were at work beneath the surface, but this is clearer in the 1879 episode when the device worked against the objective than it is in the 1933 episode when it fostered the objective.

A major obstacle to using gold as a vehicle for lowering the exchange value of the dollar and thereby raising prices was the existence of the so-called gold clause in many government and private obligations and in private contracts. That clause, whose use dated back to the greenback period after the Civil War, required payment either in gold proper, or in a nominal amount of currency equal to the value of a specified weight of gold. It was designed precisely to protect lenders and others against currency depreciation. The clause, if honored, would have multiplied the nominal obligations of the federal government and of many private borrowers for interest and principal of debt by the ratio of the new price of gold to the old price of gold. Also it would have reduced the stimulating

---

currencies, times the price of those currencies in dollars. It would then be cheaper for the U.S. to buy gold in those other countries than to acquire it from France at the fixed franc price. France would have avoided a reduction of her gold reserve at the cost of undergoing a general deflation. However, even if we ignore the costs of the deflationary process, this involves a greater adjustment than is appropriate. At the lower nominal price level in France, the former gold reserves would now have a greater value in terms of goods and services. Hence, it would be appropriate for France to make part of the adjustment through a reduction in gold reserves measured in ounces of gold.

This final point makes clear how the adjustment would tend to occur if all countries except the U.S. were on a gold standard. The extra gold demanded by the U.S. would be provided both from new production and by a reduction in reserves that would otherwise have been held, matched by a reduction in the price level in terms of gold in the rest of the world.

For the United States, the primary effect of the existence of some gold-standard countries or of all other countries' adherence to the gold standard would be a change in the magnitude of the depreciation of the dollar in terms of foreign currency, since the depreciation would have to be enough to offset not only the change in "real" demands and supplies produced by the purchase program but also the decline in the general level of prices in terms of gold in the rest of the world. If the program selected provided for spending a fixed number of dollars per month on gold, there would be a secondary effect arising out of the fact that the same number of dollars expended would buy different quantities of gold.

effects on private activity of the reduction in the ratio of debt to income which, it was hoped, would result from currency depreciation. Accordingly, a joint resolution was introduced into Congress on May 6 and passed on June 5, 1933, abrogating the gold clause in all public and private contracts, past and future. In February 1935, the Supreme Court, by a five-to-four decision, in effect upheld the constitutionality of that resolution.[49]

At the outset, the gold policy was one of two mutually inconsistent policies with respect to the monetary standard simultaneously pursued by President Roosevelt. The other was the organization of a World Monetary and Economic Conference which convened in London, June 1933. President Hoover had set in train the arrangements for the convocation of the conference in May 1932, and it was originally scheduled to be held in January 1933. The aim of the conference was to achieve cooperative action on international economic problems, and hopes were high that it would produce an agreement stabilizing foreign exchange arrangements. But the conference was nearly a complete failure. One reason was that, while it was in process, the President apparently decided definitely to adopt the path of currency depreciation. He sent a message to the conference on July 2, 1933, which dissociated the United States from any attempt to achieve what was described as a "temporary and probably an artificial stability in foreign exchange on the part of a few large countries" and was termed a "specious fallacy."[50] The message was at the time given much of the public blame for the failure of the conference. However, whatever the President might have said and however consistent U.S. policy might have been, it seems dubious that the economic preconditions existed for a viable exchange stabilization agreement. The fundamental difficulties were the probable incompatibility of the exchange rates of the sterling bloc and of the nations that still remained on gold, and the unwillingness at the time of the gold-bloc countries to change their gold parities.

The period of a variable price for gold came to an end on January 31, 1934, when the President, under the authority of the Gold Reserve Act passed the day before, specified a fixed buying and selling price of $35 an ounce for gold, thereby devaluing the gold dollar to 59.06 per cent of its former weight. Under the terms of the act, title to all gold coin and bullion was to be vested in the United States; all gold coins were to be withdrawn from circulation and melted into bullion and further gold

[49] The Court upheld the right of Congress to abrogate the gold clause in private, state, and city obligations, but not in those of the U.S. government. The Court, however, denied the claim of a plaintiff for a judgment for $16,931.25 in legal tender currency on his U.S. government bond of $10,000, on the ground that he had not shown any loss whatever in relation to purchasing power.

[50] Message reproduced in Paris, *Monetary Policies,* pp. 166–167.

coinage was to be discontinued; the Secretary of the Treasury was to control all dealings in gold; and the President was authorized to fix the weight of the gold dollar at any level between 50 and 60 per cent of its prior legal weight.[51]

Since the Treasury had formerly valued its own gold holdings at $20.67 an ounce and paid only that price for the gold it acquired from private individuals, commercial banks, and the Federal Reserve System, it realized a large "paper" profit from the revaluation of the dollar; which is to say, the Treasury could print additional paper money entitled "gold certificates" to a nominal value of nearly $3 billion without acquiring additional gold and yet conform to the legal requirement that it hold a specified weight of gold (now less than before) for each dollar printed. Those gold certificates could not legally be held by private individuals, but they could be held by Federal Reserve Banks. Accordingly, to realize its "profits," the Treasury had to turn over gold certificates to the Federal Reserve System, receiving in return a deposit credit that it could convert into Federal Reserve notes or pay out by check. Stripped of its legal trappings, the economic effect was identical with a simple grant of authority to the Treasury to print and to put in circulation nearly $3 billion of fiat currency in addition to the $3 billion in greenbacks already explicitly authorized by the Thomas Amendment to the Agricultural Adjustment Act.[52]

[51] The President requested the legislation in a message to Congress on Jan. 15, 1934. He recommended vesting title to all gold in the United States in the government for three reasons: (1) to end use of gold as a means of payment; (2) to limit transfer of gold bullion to settlement of international balances; (3) and to give the government ownership of any added dollar value of the country's gold stock as a result of a decrease in the gold content of the dollar.

On the same day an executive order regulating transactions in foreign exchange reaffirmed the regulations in the order of Apr. 20, 1933, requiring a Treasury license for every transaction in foreign exchange, for transfer of credit between banks in and outside the United States, and for export of any legal tender currency from the United States. But the order specifically excluded from the license requirement foreign exchange transactions for usual business purposes, for reasonable travel expenses, for fulfillment of contracts in existence before Mar. 9, 1933, and for transfers of credit between banks in the Continental United States and banks in its possessions. The authority of the Treasury and its agent, the Federal Reserve Banks, to require complete information on every foreign exchange transaction was reaffirmed, as was the Treasury's power to prohibit types of transactions not approved.

On Jan. 16, 1934, the function of buying gold of domestic origin was transferred from the RFC to the Federal Reserve Banks. The weight of the gold dollar, as fixed in the Presidential proclamation of Jan. 31, 1934, was 15.238+ grains of standard gold 0.900 fine (or 13.714+ grains of pure gold), which is 59.06 per cent of the weight of the old gold dollar fixed at 25.8 grains of standard gold 0.900 fine (or 23.22 grains of pure gold). An ounce troy equals 480 grains. The new price of gold, $35, is obtained by dividing 480 by 13.714+, as the old price, $20.67, is obtained by dividing 480 by 23.22.

[52] The legal trappings do raise a problem in getting an economically meaning-

Of the paper profit, $2 billion was assigned to a stabilization fund set up under the control of the Secretary of the Treasury and authorized to deal in gold, foreign exchange, securities, and other credit instruments for the purpose of stabilizing the exchange value of the dollar.[53]

Since February 1, 1934, the official price of gold has remained fixed at $35 an ounce. In this sense, that date marked the return to a gold standard. But the gold standard to which the United States returned was very different, both domestically and internationally, from the one it had left less than a year earlier. The Mint has since bought all gold offered to it at the price of $35 an ounce but sells only for the purpose of foreign payment. As noted, the holding of gold coin and bullion is forbidden to private individuals in the United States, except for use in industry and the arts and for numismatic holdings, and gold no longer circulates domestically. The Federal Reserve continues to have a gold reserve requirement, but the state of the reserve has not been a direct influence on policy at any time since 1933, though it has threatened to become one since a sharp decline in the U.S. gold stock began in 1958. For example, when, in 1945, the System was approaching the then existing requirement (40 per cent for notes and 35 per cent for deposits), the law was changed to require a uniform 25 per cent.

Fixed buying and selling prices for gold have no longer been the major reliance for maintaining rigid exchange rates with other currencies, even those of countries nominally on gold. Instead, a new central bank organ was created, the stabilization fund, with powers to engage in open market purchase and sale of foreign exchange and nonmonetary gold to influence exchange rates. During the late thirties, most of the so-called gold-bloc countries finally left gold, and nominally floating exchange rates with government speculation through stabilization funds became the rule.

---

ful breakdown of high-powered money, by assets of the monetary authorities. One division that seems economically significant is between commodity money (the monetary gold stock) and fiduciary money (the balance). So long as the price of gold is unchanged, this division is fairly clear and meaningful. The change in the price, however, raises difficulties. If all the gold is revalued at the new price, the arithmetic makes the increase in price appear as a sudden rise in the commodity component of high-powered money and a decline in the fiduciary component. Economically, there is no such change. Hence our gold stock figures, in the breakdown of high-powered money, by assets of the monetary authorities, are expressed at cost, which means that the paper profits are kept as part of the fiduciary component of high-powered money, but subsequent acquisitions at the higher price are included in full in the commodity component. See also Chap. 5, above, pp. 209–212.

[53] Of the balance of the paper profit, $645 million was used for the redemption of national bank notes, which simply substituted one form of fiduciary currency for another; $27 million was transferred to the Federal Reserve Banks for making industrial loans; $2 million was charged off to losses in melting gold coins; and $141 million remained in the General Fund cash balance (see Paris, *Monetary Policies*, p. 29).

During the war, many countries fixed "official" exchange rates but sought to maintain them by extensive control over foreign exchange transactions, imitating the devices developed by Schacht for Germany in the 1930's, rather than by free purchase or sale at fixed prices of either gold or foreign exchange. Since then, an even wider variety of actual arrangements has coexisted.

Perhaps the best description of the role of gold in the United States since 1934 is that, rather than being the basis of the monetary system, it is a commodity whose price is officially supported in the same way as the price of wheat, for example, has been under various agricultural programs. The major differences are that the support price for agricultural products is paid only to domestic producers, the gold-support price to foreign as well as domestic; the agricultural products accumulated are freely sold at the support prices to anyone, the gold only to certain foreign purchasers and not to any domestic ones. In consequence, the gold program has set a floor under the world price of gold in terms of dollars.

The substitution in January 1934 of a fixed price for gold, rather than a variable price as under the earlier purchase program, meant that the number of dollars spent on gold was no longer under the direct control of U.S. authorities. Having fixed the price, they were committed to buy all that was offered. But the effects of such purchases were the same as under the earlier program. For the United States, the purchases meant an increase in the dollar value of other exports relative to the dollar value of imports, thanks to a rise in prices of internationally traded goods relative to domestic goods through the combined effect of changes in exchange rates and in domestic price levels of the various countries. For gold-producing countries, the purchases meant an increased price for one of their products, hence an expansion in the gold industry relative to other industries and a rise in income. For gold-standard countries, the price fixed for gold by the United States determined the rate of exchange between their currencies and dollars. They either had to adjust their internal price level to that new rate—in the process presumably disposing of some of their reserves as measured in ounces of gold—or to change their own fixed price for gold. For all gold-standard and gold-producing countries except the United States and for nongold-standard and nongold-producing countries, the gold purchases meant a reshuffling of international trade in response to a decreased U.S. demand for products other than gold, and an increased demand for such products by gold-producing countries; the program meant an increased supply of products from the United States and a decreased supply from gold-producing countries. Finally, international trade had to adjust to measures adopted by gold-standard countries to meet loss of their reserves.

The price fixed for gold initially overvalued the product, of course,

and therefore stimulated a rapid increase in production and a rapid accumulation of government stocks. Production in the United States including its possessions rose from less than 2.6 million ounces in 1933 to 6
million in 1940; in the world, from 25 million ounces in 1933 to 41
million in 1940. The rise in prices of other commodities and services since
1940 has lowered the relative price of gold and reduced U.S. gold output
(1960) below its 1933 level, though world output still exceeds the level
of that year. The gold stock in the Treasury rose from 200 million ounces
when the support price was fixed in early 1934 to 630 million ounces by
the end of 1940, a rise that was 1¾ times as much as aggregate world
output during the intervening period. The gold stock declined somewhat
during the war, then rose to an all-time high in 1949. By the end of 1960
it had fallen again to about 510 million ounces, still about 2½ times its
level when the fixed price was established.

In purchasing gold, as in purchasing agricultural or other commodities,
the U.S. government can be said to have three proximate sources of
funds:[54] tax receipts, borrowing, or creation of money.[55] The one difference is that the support program for other commodities (excepting silver,
for which see below) carries with it no authorization to create money,
whereas the support program for gold does, thereby automatically providing the financial means for its continuance. Treasury deposits at Federal
Reserve Banks can be increased through gold purchases by gold certificate
credits equal to the amount of gold purchased times the official price of
gold. Except for a minor handling charge (¼ of 1 per cent), this has
also been, in practice, the amount the Treasury spent by drawing a check
on its deposits in acquiring gold. Gold purchases are usually financed in
this way; hence, increases in the gold stockpile produce no automatic
budgetary pressure. The link between gold purchases and Treasury
authorization to create high-powered money is, of course, the main
remnant of the historical role of gold, and still serves to give gold some
special monetary significance. The one important occasion when a different method of finance was used was in 1937, when the Treasury
"sterilized" gold by paying for gold with funds raised through security
issues (see Chapter 9, section 3).

It is easier to describe the gold policy of the United States since 1934
than it is to describe the resulting monetary standard of the United States.

[54] The word proximate is intended as a warning of the oversimplification involved in associating particular expenditures with particular receipts.
[55] It might be more meaningful to describe the two latter as borrowing in
interest-bearing form and borrowing in noninterest-bearing form. More fundamentally still, money creation may itself be either borrowing (if prices are not
raised thereby) or taxation (if prices are raised). See Friedman, "Discussion of
the Inflationary Gap," *Essays in Positive Economics*, University of Chicago Press,
1955, p. 257; also, above, Chap. 2, footnote 64, and Chap. 5, footnote 35.

It is not a gold standard in the sense that the volume of gold or the maintenance of the nominal value of gold at a fixed price can be said to determine directly or even at several removes the volume of money. It is conventional to term it—as President Roosevelt did—a managed standard, but that simply evades the difficult problems of definition. It is clearly a fiduciary rather than a commodity standard, but it is not possible to specify briefly who manages its quantity and on what principles. The Federal Reserve System, the Treasury, and still other agencies have affected its quantity by their actions in accordance with a wide variety of objectives. In principle, the Federal Reserve System has the power to make the quantity of money anything it wishes, within broad limits, but it has seldom stated its objectives in those terms. It has sometimes, as when it supported bond prices, explicitly relinquished its control. And it clearly is not unaffected in its actions by gold flows. So long as the exchange rate between the dollar and other currencies is kept fixed, the behavior of relative stocks of money in various countries must be close to what would be produced by gold standards yielding the same exchange rates, even though the mechanism may be quite different. Perhaps a "discretionary fiduciary standard" is the best simple term to characterize the monetary standard which has evolved. If it is vague and ambiguous, so is the standard it denotes.

The rise in the dollar price of gold-bloc currencies was at first much greater than that of currencies not linked to gold. From January 1933 to September 1934 the rise was 70 per cent for the currencies of France, Switzerland, Belgium, the Netherlands, and Italy, and less than 50 per cent for the pound sterling. The gold-standard currencies therefore appreciated not only relative to the dollar but also relative to other currencies. The differential appreciation measured the special impact of our gold price-support program on the position of the gold-standard countries. The fact that they lost gold meant that they bore, as it were, a larger part of the effect of the expansion of U.S. exports and contraction of U.S. imports other than gold than other countries did, and thereby cushioned the initial impact on those other countries.

As we have seen, had nothing else intervened, the gold-standard countries would have had to reduce their internal price levels relative to those of other countries in order to stay on gold, which is to say, in order to render something like the new structure of exchange rates consistent with no pressure on the balance of payments. In fact, something else did intervene, but it intensified rather than eased the problem of the gold-standard countries. Gold purchases under the fixed price-support program coincided with a flight of capital to the United States from Europe largely induced by political changes: first, the rise to power of Hitler in Germany which led to a large-scale attempt to transfer capital out of Germany, particularly by Jews; then the increasing fears of war which led to a flight of capital from France, Britain, and other European countries.

Since the flight of capital constituted an increased demand for dollars, its effects on exchange rates and on U.S. trade in commodities and services other than gold were in precisely the opposite direction to those of the gold price-support program and tended to offset them.[56] There was simultaneously an increased offer of dollars for gold on the part of the U.S. government and an increased demand on the part of foreigners for dollars to hold. By trading assets held abroad for gold and transferring the gold to the U.S. Treasury, foreigners could acquire dollars and the Treasury could acquire gold without in any way affecting the rest of the U.S. balance of payments. To the extent that such offsetting occurred, the gold program did not affect U.S. trade currents and the relative prices of internationally traded goods in the United States in ways described earlier. Since such changes in trade currents and relative prices tended to reduce the amount of gold offered for sale to the United States at its fixed price, the capital inflow meant that this country acquired a larger amount of gold at $35 an ounce than it otherwise would have. Hence, while the capital inflow and the gold price-support program had opposite effects on U.S. exchange rates and on U.S. trade in commodities and services other than gold, both tended to raise its gold stock.

For gold-standard countries that were themselves subject to a capital

[56] If the U.S. had continued its floating exchange-rate policy of 1933 and had fixed no firm price at which it was willing to buy the world's gold, the capital flight would have produced an appreciation of the U.S. dollar relative to other currencies, which would have discouraged exports from the U.S. and encouraged imports into the U.S. That outcome would have produced the unfavorable balance of trade required as the physical side of the capital import—and incidentally, would have worked against one of the domestic objectives of New Deal policy, namely, to raise exports relative to imports as a means of stimulating employment. If, instead, the U.S. and other countries involved had all been on a gold standard of the nineteenth century variety, the attempt to transfer capital to the U.S. would have increased gold reserves in this country, even without a rise in the dollar price of gold, and decreased gold reserves abroad; it would have increased proportionately the money stock in the U.S. and thereby have promoted a rise in domestic prices and income; and it would have decreased the money stock abroad and thereby have promoted a fall in prices and income in foreign countries. These changes would have tended to produce precisely the same shift in relative prices and the same unfavorable balance of trade as the appreciation of the dollar under the hypothetical floating exchange rates would have done.

To avoid misunderstanding, we should record explicitly that the actual working out of the adjustment might be—and in our opinion would be—very different under floating and rigid rates for reasons that are outlined in a different connection in Friedman, "The Case for Flexible Exchange Rates," *Essays in Positive Economics*, pp. 157–203. Nevertheless, the character of the adjustment required would be identical; the difference—and in some contexts an essential difference— is the efficiency of the mechanism of adjustment.

outflow—that is, for all the important so-called gold-bloc countries that had remained on gold after 1933—the capital outflow reinforced rather than offset the effect of the gold price-support program. It required an additional reduction in internal price levels beyond that called for by the support program. Exports had to be still larger relative to imports if they were to finance the capital outflow without a continued outflow of gold.

The deflation that would have been required by the combined effect of the U.S. gold price-support program and the capital outflow was more than the gold-bloc countries were willing to undergo, as perhaps the effect of either alone might also have been. Accordingly, in the fall of 1936, France and Switzerland devalued their currencies in conjunction with a tripartite agreement between the United States, France, and Great Britain. Other gold-bloc countries either followed suit or abandoned the gold standard.

There is no direct way to separate the opposite effects on U.S. international trade of the capital flight and the gold-price support program; one can only record their combined effect on international trade together, of course, with the effect of still other factors, such as the changing level of business activity. On the whole, however, Table 20, which summarizes the combined effect, suggests that the gold price-support program was quantitatively more important than the flight of capital in its effects on U.S. international trade for the years 1934–39 as a whole. The evidence is, however, somewhat mixed, and this conclusion must therefore be regarded as highly tentative.

The chief ambiguity in the evidence is in the balance-of-payments figures in the first two parts of the table. As we have seen, the gold price-support program alone would have tended to produce an increase in the U.S. balance of trade in commodities and services other than gold, through either exchange rate changes, or changes in international prices sufficient to lower U.S. prices relative to foreign prices when both were expressed in a common currency.[57] The capital inflow alone would have acted in the opposite direction. Because of errors in balance of payments figures, it is by no means clear what actually happened. Lines 1 and 5 give the balance of trade estimated directly from figures on imports and exports, line 1 in absolute amounts, line 5 as a percentage of national income to adjust for both price changes and changes in the size of the economy. To judge from these statistics, the balance of trade was substantially lower for 1934–39 as a whole than for the decade of the twenties, and a trifle lower than for the depression years 1930–33. Lines 2 and 6 give the balance of trade as estimated indirectly from figures on capital and gold movements; the difference between the estimates in line 1 and line 2 is

[57] Note that this is consistent with a rise in the absolute level of U.S. prices if the exchange value of the dollar depreciates.

the item labeled "errors and omissions" in the official figures published on the balance of payments. These errors and omissions are sufficiently large to reverse the direction of difference. Lines 2 and 6 show the balance of trade as noticeably larger in 1934–39 than in either the twenties or 1930–33 (in line 2, the balance of trade is equal to that in the twenties, but since prices were lower, it was decidedly larger in real terms). Lines 1 and 5 imply that capital flows were quantitatively more important; lines 2 and 6, that the gold-purchase program was more important.

We are inclined to put more weight on the evidence from lines 2 and 6 than on that from lines 1 and 5, for two reasons. First, an examination of the sources of error in the figures suggests that the indirect estimates are likely to be more accurate than the direct estimates.[58] Second, as we shall see below, the price data rather unambiguously indicate that the gold-purchase program was the more important. As it happens, the estimates in line 6 are also the ones comparable to those we have used in our several charts showing the relation between relative prices and capital movements (Charts 9, 17, and 36).

From the estimates for the three years 1934–36, mostly before French and Swiss devaluation, and the three years thereafter, 1937–39, the dominance of the gold-purchase program appears to be clearly greater in the second period than in the first. By providing gold, as it were, from their monetary balances to exporters of capital, the gold-standard countries facilitated the direct offsetting of the capital and the gold movements described earlier. Indeed, the figures for both lines 5 and 6 indicate that, during the earlier years, the capital movement had more impact on the balance of trade than did the gold flow.

The price data in the third section of Table 20 indicate that the gold program was more important than the capital flow, despite the divergent movement of prices in different countries, mostly reflecting the impact of different dates of devaluation. Though many other forces may in principle affect relative prices, these other forces have in practice been quite minor. In the whole period from 1879 to 1914, for example, when both Britain and the United States were continually on gold, the price ratio like that in Table 20 (given annually in Table A-4, column 1, for 1871–1960) varied only between 90 and 106, and some of that variation, as we have seen, can be accounted for by capital movements. Hence, these

---

[58] See *Balance of Payments, 1949–1951*, Office of Business Economics, 1952, pp. 115–117. What is in question is whether errors and omissions are to be interpreted as primarily unrecorded capital items or unrecorded trade and service items. If the former, the estimates in line 1 should be more accurate; if the latter, the estimates in line 2 should be more accurate. It should be noted that our inclination to accept the latter interpretation is contrary to the most widely held view.

price ratios are sensitive and accurate indicators of the effects of monetary changes and of such major factors as the gold program and the capital flow.

To judge from implicit prices in the United States and cost-of-living indexes for Britain, France, and Switzerland, U.S. prices, adjusted for changes in exchange rates, were lower relative to prices in other countries after 1933 than in either the twenties or 1930–33. This is the result to be expected if the gold price-support program had a greater effect than the capital inflow had.

The difference between British prices, on the one hand, and French and Swiss prices, on the other, before the French and Swiss devaluation in 1936 reflects the disproportionate initial impact of the gold-purchase program on France and Switzerland referred to above: their gold losses implied a large balance of payments deficit reflecting high prices internally relative to U.S. prices. Once they devalued, the differential effect was eliminated. Had the gold-purchase program alone been operating, one might have expected a decline in the ratio in the table for Britain balancing a rise in the ratios for France and Switzerland—just the reverse of the movements after the British devaluation in 1931. In fact, what happened was that the British ratio stayed roughly the same, while the French and Swiss rose sharply to meet it. The reason is that the capital outflow from those countries affected all alike and tended to raise all those ratios above the level that would have been produced by the gold price-support program alone.

To digress for a moment: in some ways the most striking feature of Table 20 is the greater similarity between the balance-of-payments figures for 1923–29 and those for 1930–33 than between either and those for 1934–39. The first two sets of figures show remarkably little trace of the economic holocaust that was sweeping the world. The United States was supposedly ceasing to lend to the world, yet it exported almost as much capital in absolute amount per year from 1930 to 1933 as from 1923 to 1929 and more as a percentage of national income. The reason is, figuratively, that, given no basic change in conditions of production, the incentives to invest in various countries, or monetary arrangements, the preservation of the general pattern of the figures in Table 20 was precisely the vehicle for the international transmission and coordination of the economic collapse, whatever its initial source. The attempt to change these figures—for example, the attempt by the United States to cease foreign lending—produced repercussions abroad that largely frustrated the attempt and forced this country, as it were, to continue lending.

Of course, had the capital flight occurred in the absence of the gold price-support program, the U.S. balance of trade in commodities and services other than gold after 1934 would have been less than it actually

TABLE 20

United States Balance of International Payments and Ratio of Purchasing-Power Parity to Exchange Rates, 1923-39

	1923-29	1930-31	1932-33	1930-33	1934-36	1937-39	1934-39
	ANNUAL AVERAGE AMOUNT (billions of dollars)						
Balance of trade in commodities and services other than gold (exports minus imports) lines 1, 2							
1. Estimated directly	1.07	0.74	0.34	0.54	0.16	0.78	0.47
2. Estimated from capital movements	0.86	0.95	0.41	0.68	0.47	1.27	0.87
3. Capital inflow minus unilateral transfers to foreign countries	-0.84	-0.90	-0.49	-0.69	0.86	0.74	0.80
4. Gold outflow	-0.02	-0.05	0.08	0.02	-1.33	-2.01	-1.67
	AVERAGE PER CENT OF NATIONAL INCOME						
Balance of trade in commodities and services other than gold (exports minus imports) lines 5, 6							
5. Estimated directly	1.32	1.03	0.78	0.91	0.33	1.09	0.71
6. Estimated from capital movements	1.07	1.32	0.94	1.13	0.89	1.76	1.32
7. Capital inflow minus unilateral transfers to foreign countries	-1.03	-1.28	-1.13	-1.21	1.42	1.01	1.21
8. Gold outflow	-0.04	-0.04	0.19	0.08	-2.31	-2.76	-2.54

(continued)

TABLE 20 (concluded)

	1923–29	Jan. 1930 to Aug. 1931 Before Britain Abandoned Gold	Sept. 1931 to Dec. 1933 After	1930–33	Jan. 1934 to Sept. 1936 Before France and Switzerland Devalued	Oct. 1936 to Aug. 1939 After	Jan. 1934 to Aug. 1939
				MONTHLY AVERAGES (per cent)			
9. Ratio (1929 = 100) of purchasing-power parity to exchange rates, U.S. implicit price index relative to:							
a. British cost of living divided by cents per pound	98.8	97.4	108.2	103.7	87.7	85.5	86.6
b. French cost of living divided by cents per franc	112.2	86.9	71.6	78.0	52.0	80.2	66.5
c. Swiss cost of living divided by cents per franc	100.7	94.2	79.4	85.6	58.1	80.3	69.5

NOTE: Because of rounding, there may be discrepancies in the last decimal place.

SOURCE, BY LINE

1. Balance of trade in commodities and services as reported includes excess of gold production over nonmonetary gold consumption (see Balance of Payments, 1949–1951, Office of Business Economics, Dept. of Commerce, 1952, pp. 23, 113). Excess obtained by subtracting gold sales (Balance of Payments, 1958, pp. 11–12, line 8) from gold outflow (line 4 of the present table) was subtracted from the reported balance (ibid., pp. 11–12, line 23).

2. Sum, with sign changed, of lines 3 and 4 of the present table. (Line 2 minus line 1 is the OBE'S "errors and omissions.")

3. Ibid., pp. 11–12, sum of lines 24, plus 30, plus 41.

4. 1923–33: Banking and Monetary Statistics, Board of Governors of the Federal Reserve System, 1943, p. 538. 1934–39: Federal Reserve Bulletin, 1947–49 issues.

5–8. Same as lines 1–4, except that each item for each year was first divided by national income from same source as for Chart 62.

9. U.S. implicit price index: Same source as for Chart 62. British and Swiss cost of living: Statistical Yearbook of the League of Nations, 1931/32–1939/40 issues. French cost of living: 1923–June 1931, Oct. 1931–Dec. 1938, ibid. (data are quarterly for Paris only); July–Sept. 1931, data from ibid. were interpolated to months by average monthly price of 34 household commodities in Annuaire Statistique, 1946, France, Institut National de la Statistique, p. 199; Jan.–Aug. 1939, League of Nations data were extrapolated by a quarterly cost-of-living index in ibid., 1940–45, p. 211.
Exchange rates: Banking and Monetary Statistics, pp. 670, 680–681.

was, and U.S. prices relative to foreign prices would have fallen less than they actually did or perhaps would have risen. This is so because the appreciation of the U.S. dollar relative to other currencies produced by the capital flow would have discouraged exports and encouraged imports. How much less would the balance of trade have been? Since the capital flight itself would have meant an import of gold, the balance of trade would certainly not have been less by more than $1.67 billion (Table 20, line 4, last column)—but this is so outside a limit that it is of little practical value. Similarly, in the absence of the capital flight, the balance of trade would have been higher, but again no useful estimate of how much higher can readily be made.

If we use the period 1923–29 as a basis of comparison, speak in terms of nominal dollar sums, and neglect other factors, we may summarize the combined impact of the gold price-support program and the capital flight as follows. For the six years 1934 through 1939, the statistics show that the U.S. government was buying some $1.7 billion per year more in gold than it and its citizens were wont to; and, at the same time, the U.S. economy was reducing the excess of its sales abroad over its purchases abroad of other commodities and services by some $0.6 billion per year— i.e., selling net that much less or buying net that much more—or holding that excess constant, depending on the treatment of the $0.6 billion consisting of errors and omissions in the recorded accounts (compare the difference between lines 1 and 2 of Table 20 for 1923–29 and the same difference for 1934–39). The foreign currency to finance that recorded $2.3 or $1.7 billion net increase in purchases was provided by a shift from net lending or acquisition of assets by U.S. citizens abroad of $0.8 billion a year to net borrowings or sale of assets of some $0.8 billion a year, or by an even larger shift in the same direction if the errors are assigned to the capital items. The shift from the net export to the net import of capital, in its turn, reflected mainly the desire on the part of many foreigners to hold assets in the form of U.S. dollars or U.S. securities rather than in the form of currencies and securities of European nations.

The same evidence is given year-by-year and over a longer period in Chart 36 which shows the relation between relative prices in the United States and other countries, adjusted for exchange rate changes, and capital movements into and gold movements out of the United States (expressed as a fraction of net national product) from 1920 to 1960.

Before 1932, the lines showing capital imports and unilateral transfers alone and this sum plus the gold outflow (or its equivalent, with the opposite sign, the balance of trade in commodities and services other than gold) differ little from one another either in level or year-to-year movements. The capital movements are so much larger in magnitude that they dominate the gold movements. Before 1929 the year-to-year movements of

CHART 36

**U.S. Net International Capital Movement as a Ratio to National
Income, and Purchasing-Power Parity, 1920–60**

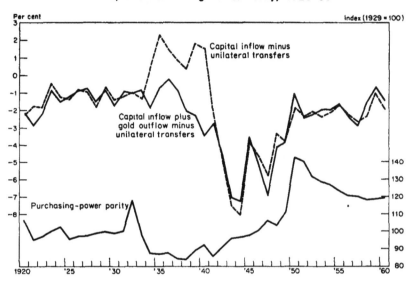

NOTE: Capital inflow, minus unilateral transfers, is plotted as plus. Gold outflow is plotted
as plus.
SOURCE: Table A-4.

both capital and the payments balance show the kind of loose relation to
movements in relative prices in the U.S. and Britain that we found for
earlier periods (see Charts 9 and 17 above).

From 1929 to 1933, a wide divergence developed between the U.S.–
British price ratio and capital movement. The price ratio rose in 1932
to a peak higher than any other value attained since 1871, the year the
series starts. The payments balance shows only a mild reflection of the
sharp rise in the price ratio and the capital movement alone a still milder
one. The reason is that Britain's departure from gold in 1931 and the
emergence of a sterling bloc and a gold bloc introduced wide diversity
into the world pattern of prices. It is not possible during that period to
regard movements in British prices as a reliable index of movements in
world prices. This is shown in Chart 51 (p. 586) by the series expressing
U.S. prices relative to Swiss prices, which is linked to the U.S.–British
series in 1929. There was a sharp divergence between the two from 1929
to at least 1937, when they came fairly close together, only to diverge
again after World War II began in 1939. In 1933, U.S. devaluation

produced the same kind of decline in U.S. prices relative to Swiss prices that British devaluation had earlier produced in British prices relative to both U.S. and Swiss prices. For the period from 1931 on, some curve intermediate' between the British and the Swiss would seem the appropriate continuation of the earlier U.S.–British price ratio.

After 1932 and particularly after 1933 up to 1941, there was a dramatic divergence between capital movement figures and the figures for the balance of trade in commodities and services other than gold, a divergence of a very much larger order of magnitude than occurred before or since. That divergence represents the unprecedentedly large gold movements produced by the gold-purchase program and the flight of capital from Europe. In relation to the capital movement figures alone, U.S. prices were much lower relative to British, and even more, relative to Swiss prices than during the twenties or later during the forties and fifties. As we have seen, the difference reflects largely the effect of the gold-purchase program. The balance of trade figures alone, on the other hand, show much more nearly the same relation to the relative prices as earlier, if we use a curve intermediate between the British and Swiss.

THE SILVER-PURCHASE PROGRAM[59]

The Thomas amendment, passed on May 12, 1933, and containing a provision authorizing the President to reduce the gold content of the dollar, also gave the President sweeping powers with respect to silver. They were hardly used until December 21, 1933, when, disappointed by the effects of the gold-purchase program and under pressure from Senators from silver states as well as other proponents of currency expansion, President Roosevelt used the authority granted by the Thomas amendment to direct U.S. mints to receive all newly produced domestic silver offered to them up to December 31, 1937, at $64\frac{64}{99}$ cents an ounce (i.e., \$0.6464 . . . an ounce).

The market price of silver was at that time about 44 cents an ounce, or some 75 per cent above the level at the end of 1932 and in early 1933. The rise, only slightly greater than the simultaneous depreciation of the dollar, reflected mostly the effect on all commodities with a worldwide market of the changed foreign exchange value of the dollar. But no doubt it was in part also a speculative rise promoted by expectations, raised by the Thomas amendment as well as by an agreement on silver with other countries reached at the ill-fated London Economic Conference, that the U.S. government would "do something for silver."

The nominal monetary value of silver was, and still is, $\$1\frac{29}{99}$, or \$1.2929 . . . an ounce. This value dates from 1792, when the silver dollar

[59] We have drawn heavily on Paris, *Monetary Policies,* in connection with this and with the preceding section.

was defined as containing 371.25 grains of pure silver.[60] But it had not been an effective market price since the gold content of the dollar had been reduced in 1834. From 1834 to 1873, the Mint ratio then established overvalued gold, hence the market value of silver was higher than $1.29+, and none was coined; the United States, though nominally bimetallic, was effectively on gold (excluding the greenback period). After 1873, when free coinage was not permitted, silver fell in value relative to gold (Chapter 3, footnote 52), a trend that though irregular was interrupted significantly only in 1889–90, thanks to the earlier silver purchase programs of 1878–90 and 1890–93, and again during World War I. Except for World War I, the market price since the turn of the century had generally been less than half the nominal mint value. Since that date, the U.S. government had made no substantial silver purchases, except after World War I to replace silver that had been shipped to India during the war (see above, Chapter 5, footnote 31). Silver had remained in a monetary limbo with respect to new acquisitions: it was used for subsidiary coin, a small volume of standard silver dollars circulated mostly in silver states, and a roughly fixed stock of silver certificates remained as a relic of the earlier silver agitation.[61] The amount of silver in use as coin or as backing for currency both inside and outside the Treasury totaled about 650 million ounces in December 1933 and had a nominal monetary value of $840 million, of which $300 million was in the form of subsidiary coin. The total market value of the stock of silver at the time the purchase program began was of course very much smaller, approximately $285 million, and that figure was some 70 per cent higher than at the end of 1932. The rather bizarre purchasing price of $64\frac{64}{99}$ cents an ounce was arrived at by adopting the fiction that silver was being accepted at its monetary value with a seigniorage charge of 50 per cent.

The President's directive to purchase newly mined silver did not stop agitation for further measures on the part either of those interested primarily in silver or of those who saw silver as a useful device for expanding the money stock. Numerous bills were introduced providing for additional action with respect to silver, many coupling that action with the use of the "seigniorage profits" for specific purposes, such as soldiers' bonus, purchase of farm products, and the like. The result was the Silver Purchase Act of June 19, 1934, which closely followed recommendations

[60] An ounce troy equals 480 grains. An ounce of silver is therefore worth 480 divided by 371.25 or $1.2929 . . . .

[61] The stock of silver dollars and certificates in and outside the Treasury increased from about $270 million in 1920, when the Treasury began to purchase silver to replace bullion shipped to India during World War I, to $540 million in 1928, at which amount it remained until the start of the silver-purchase program in Dec. 1933. Silver certificates in circulation fluctuated with changes in the public's demand for currency. The stock of subsidiary silver, as well as amounts in circulation, grew until the 1929–33 contraction.

made by the President in a message of May 22, 1934, and which directed the Secretary of the Treasury to purchase silver at home and abroad until the market price reached $1.29+ an ounce, or until the monetary value of the silver stock held by the Treasury reached one-third of the monetary value of the gold stock. The Secretary was given wide discretion in carrying out that mandate.

A purchase program under the authority of this and subsequent acts was still legally in effect in 1962, repeated efforts to repeal silver-purchase legislation having been blocked.[62] Under the authority of these acts and the initial and subsequent Presidential proclamations, the Treasury acquired some 3,200 million ounces of silver, approximately half in the four years ending December 31, 1937, and half from then to June 30, 1961.

Of the total, some 110 million ounces was silver that was "nationalized" on August 9, 1934, when the President required all holders of silver, with exceptions for silver being used in the arts and for silver coins, to turn their holdings in to the U.S. Mint at a price equivalent to 50.01 cents per fine ounce, a measure similar to the nationalization of gold and adopted for the same reason: to capture for the government profits expected to result from raising the price of silver.[63]

Another 880 million ounces was newly mined domestic silver. Since the Treasury price for newly mined domestic silver until 1955 was higher than the market price, nearly all domestic silver went to the Treasury and the demand of American silver users was met by foreign silver. From then until November 1961, when the Treasury discontinued sales, the market price approximated the support price, and silver users not only absorbed current output but also purchased from Treasury stocks. The price paid by the Treasury for the newly mined domestic silver varied between 64.64 . . . cents and 90.5050 . . . cents an ounce (corresponding to 30 per cent seigniorage). In April 1935, when the market price rose above 64.64 . . . , reaching a peak of over 81 cents at the end of April, the Treasury twice raised its price, first to a trifle over 71 cents an ounce (corresponding to 45 per cent seigniorage) then to 77.57 . . . cents (corresponding to 40 per cent seigniorage). The market price then fell, par-

[62] On Jan. 22, 1962, President Kennedy requested Congress to repeal silver-purchase legislation under which the government is required to buy all newly mined silver offered to it at the currently fixed price of 90½ cents per ounce. He also called for repeal of the silver transfer tax, under which the government takes 50 per cent of the profit from silver transactions. Legislation embodying the President's request was passed on June 4, 1963, when this book was in press.

[63] The one important difference was the recall of gold but not silver from circulation as coins. The reason for the difference, of course, is that the silver content of coins even when nominally full-bodied, as the silver dollar is, was worth less in the market than the face value, and that of subsidiary silver coins decidedly less. (The weight of silver in a silver dollar equals the face value if silver is valued at $1.2929 . . . an ounce; for smaller silver coins the weight so valued is less than their face value.)

ticularly sharply at the end of 1935, and reached a level of 45 cents in early 1936, but the Treasury price remained 77.57 . . . cents until December 1937, when it was lowered to the earlier level of 64.64. . . . After the Presidential proclamation authorizing purchases at that level expired in June 1939, an act was passed on July 6, 1939, directing the purchase of all domestic silver offered at a seigniorage charge of 45 per cent. The Treasury's silver purchases dwindled to nearly nothing soon after we entered the war. By the end of 1945 the market price had risen above 71 cents, so on July 31, 1946, an act was passed reducing seigniorage to 30 per cent—effectively establishing a buying price of 90½ cents per ounce for newly mined domestic silver—and authorizing the Secretary of the Treasury to sell nonmonetized (seigniorage or free) silver to domestic industry at not less than 90½ cents per ounce.[64] As noted above, the market price rose by 1955 to the neighborhood of the Treasury support price. From that year until November 1961, sales from Treasury stock pegged the market price at the Treasury support price. The Treasury then announced it would end sales on November 28. Once the Treasury suspended sales, the market price rose above the support price.[65]

The remaining amount purchased by the Treasury, totaling 2,210 million ounces, was silver purchased abroad at prevailing market prices. All in all, total expenditures for silver from December 31, 1933, to mid-1961 amounted to roughly $2 billion.

In spite of silver purchases of $2 billion and the accompanying sextupling of the physical quantity of silver in use as coin and currency

[64] During World War II, because of increased industrial demand for silver, some 170 million ounces were sold by the Treasury from nonmonetized silver in the General Fund, under the Green Act of July 12, 1943, for industrial uses and for Philippine coinage. The act expired on Dec. 31, 1945. In addition, over 900 million ounces were loaned temporarily to war industries for nonconsumptive electrical use. Some 410 million ounces were lend-leased to India and other countries to be returned within five years after the signing of the Japanese Peace Treaty in April 1952. All but 15 million ounces had been returned by the end of 1961.

Under the act of 1946, 138 million ounces were sold to industry, mostly after 1958. The reduction of the stock of nonmonetized silver held by the Treasury from nearly 200 million ounces at the end of 1958 to 22 million ounces when sales were suspended in 1961 reflected, in addition to sales to industry, withdrawals for subsidiary silver coinage.

[65] Within a few weeks after the order suspending sales was issued, the market price rose to $1.04¾. After declining somewhat in early 1962, the price rose to $1.09 during Aug. 1962, the highest price since Aug. 1920, when the Treasury was in the market to buy silver to retire Pittman Act certificates (see Chap. 6, footnote 60), and by June 1963, when this book was in press, to within 1½ cents of the monetary price of $1.2929. . . . When and if the market price of silver reaches the monetary price, under existing law it will be pegged close to that price by Treasury redemption of silver certificates, so long as the Treasury's silver stock holds out, and by melting down of coined silver dollars.

or held by the Treasury, the U.S. silver program never came close to achieving either of the objectives specified in the 1934 Silver Purchase Act: a market price equal to the monetary value of $1.2929 . . . , or a ratio of the monetary stocks of silver and gold of 1 to 3. The market price of silver in 1960 was about 91.4 cents an ounce and had never been much higher between 1934 and 1960.[66] The rise from 25 cents an ounce at the end of 1932 was larger than the concurrent rise in wholesale prices in general, but not by much. In 1960, the price of silver was 3.7 times the end-of-1932 level; wholesale prices, 2.9 times. The ratio of monetary silver to monetary gold stocks, both at their nominal monetary values, was just over 1 to 5 immediately before the rise in the official price of gold in January 1934; the change in the gold price reduced the ratio to 1 to 9; the heavy silver purchases restored the ratio of 1 to 5 by early 1936; until the war, continued silver purchases on the average just balanced increases in gold stock, so that the ratio fluctuated about that level. Since then the ratio has been dominated by changes in the gold stock. At the postwar peak in the gold stock in 1949, the ratio stood at 1 to 7. By the end of 1960, gold outflow had raised the ratio to 1 to 4.

In terms of its domestic effects, the silver-purchase program, like the gold-purchase program, is best regarded as a price-support program for a particular commodity, or perhaps a combination of a price-support program and a stockpiling program. In contrast with gold and as for wheat, only the price of domestic output has been effectively supported On the other hand, like gold and in contrast with wheat, purchases have been made of both domestic output and silver drawn from foreign output and stocks. Indeed, two and a half times as much has been purchased from abroad as from domestic output. Again, as with both gold and wheat, the silver program offers dramatic evidence of the high elasticity of supply of stockpiled products and the resulting difficulty of substantially altering their relative prices by a governmental purchase program, even one of very large size relative to initial output. Domestic silver output more than tripled—from under 2 million ounces a month to nearly 6 million—in the four years from the Presidential proclamation of December 21, 1933, to December 31, 1937, the period covered by that proclamation.

As with gold, the one important domestic monetary element in the silver program has been the automatic link between silver purchases and authorization to issue currency. The large so-called seigniorage charge for

---

[66] From 1957 to 1961 world monetary and nonmonetary consumption of silver rose at an annual rate of 4 per cent, world production at an annual rate of about 1.5 per cent. Prices and output of silver would undoubtedly have been higher in the absence of sales by the U.S. at the support price. World output may be expected to rise at a faster rate in response to the rise in the market price since the Treasury suspended sales.

newly mined silver, and the difference between the monetary value and the market price for foreign silver, have meant that silver purchases increased the authorization to issue currency by a considerably larger sum than the amount paid for the silver. In practice, the Treasury has apparently issued silver certificates equal to the amount actually paid for the silver, and has treated the excess monetary value as a miscellaneous budget receipt.

It is not easy to judge the purely domestic monetary effects of the silver-purchase program. It has involved the printing of additional silver certificates totaling over $2 billion and so in the first instance has added this much to the stock of money. However, the Federal Reserve System has always been in a position to offset this direct effect, and, as we shall see, the silver purchases to some extent reduced the gold inflow. The additional silver certificates may therefore have been simply a substitute for additional Federal Reserve notes which would otherwise have been printed. In view of the generally passive behavior of the Federal Reserve System, particularly in the period up to the end of 1937 when silver purchases were greatest, it is likely that the truth is somewhere between, and that the silver purchases led to a somewhat more rapid increase in the stock of money than would otherwise have occurred. In any event, the sums involved were small compared to either the total increase in the stock of money or the concurrent inflow of gold.

The effects on the United States other than these monetary effects were twofold. In the first place, the program involved public expenditures to stockpile a commodity and therefore increased federal government outlays—not in terms of budget accounts but in terms of economic effects. The expenditures were not large relative to the government budget. At their highest, from the end of 1933 through 1937, they averaged $220 million a year (for foreign and domestic silver combined) in comparison with federal government expenditures of the order of $7 billion a year. However, they were extremely large in comparison with the outlay of the industry they were at least partly intended to help. Total domestic silver output, even valued at the price paid by the Treasury, averaged only about $40 million a year, 1934–37,[67] and, of course, the excess of that value over the returns which the resources employed could have earned in other ways was much smaller still. Hence, viewed as a measure to "help" silver producers—including in that term not only enterprises producing silver but also persons supplying labor and other resources for production of silver—even the immediate returns from the silver-purchase program involved gross Treasury expenditures of well over $5, perhaps as much as $25 or more, for each dollar of return to silver

[67] *Historical Statistics of the United States, Colonial Times to 1957*, Bureau of the Census, 1960, p. 351, Series M-36.

producers, though, for a reason given in the next paragraph, this over-states the net cost of the program substantially.[68] And the long-run effects of the silver-purchase program have surely offset much of this immediate gain, if they have not converted it into a loss, by reducing the monetary use of silver in the rest of the world—a point to which we shall return.

The second effect on the United States, besides the direct effect on the money stock, was on the balance of international payments. Like the gold purchases, the silver purchases involved in effect the offer of dollars for foreign currencies (in order to buy foreign silver), and thereby helped finance the capital inflow into the United States. In the absence of the silver purchases, the potential U.S. payments surplus would have been larger, and hence gold inflows would have been larger as well. Given our gold policy, therefore, silver purchases were to some extent a substitute for gold purchases. This offset reduced both the net cost of the silver program and the amount by which it can be supposed to have increased the stock of money.

The most important effects of the silver program were not these domes-tic effects—which, though major in relation to the silver industry, were relatively minor in relation to the economy as a whole—but the effects on other countries. The silver program is a dramatic illustration of how a course of action, undertaken by one country for domestic reasons and relatively unimportant to that country, can yet have far-reaching consequences for other countries if it affects a monetary medium of those countries.

China was most affected. At the time, China was on a silver standard, though for minor transactions it also used local currencies of copper and nickel, whose value in silver varied from time to time.[69] Because the ex-change value of silver varied relative to gold, China was spared the initial effects of the worldwide depression. Its currency depreciated relative to other currencies, so its internal prices could remain relatively stable despite the fall in world prices. After Britain's devaluation at the end of 1931, and still more after the United States' departure from gold in 1933, the situation changed drastically. China's currency appreciated, the country was subject to the pressure of internal deflation, and it experienced widen-ing economic difficulties. The initial pressure was, of course, felt as a decline in exports relative to imports. The potential deficit in the balance of payments was met by export of silver, which in its turn tended to con-

[68] "Well over $5" is obtained by dividing $220 million, peak average annual Treasury expenditures for silver, by $40 million, annual value of domestic silver output. "Perhaps as much as $25 or more" is a conjecture that not more than one-fifth of the $40 million is the excess over the amount that resources employed in silver output could have earned in alternative uses.
[69] See Arthur Salter, *China and Silver*, New York, Economic Forum, 1934, pp. 46–47, 56–57.

tract the internal money supply. The pressure was somewhat eased by the availability of minor copper and nickel coinage which could change in value relative to silver, but it is doubtful that the offset was of major significance.

The U.S. silver-purchase program greatly intensified the pressure on China. As we have seen, from early 1933 to the end of the year the market price of silver rose nearly 75 per cent, and by mid-1935, under the impact of the silver-purchase program, its initial price had nearly trebled. The effect on China's international trade position can perhaps be appreciated best by expressing these figures in terms more familiar to the reader. It was as if, when Britain and the United States were both on the gold standard in the 1920's, Britain had been confronted over the course of two years with a rise in the dollar price of the pound sterling from $4.86 to nearly $15.00, resulting from changes in the U.S. gold price, without any change in the pound price at which Britain was obligated to sell gold, and without any substantial change in external or internal circumstances affecting the supply of or demand for products it purchased or sold. The result of the silver-purchase program, of course, was to drain China of silver. Its government imposed the equivalent of an export embargo on silver in an attempt to offset the appreciation of its currency. Not surprisingly, the legal obstacles to export were of no avail. Smuggling drained silver from China as rapidly as legal export had earlier.[70] Finally, in November 1935, China nationalized silver in circulation, officially abandoned the silver standard, and replaced it with a managed fiduciary standard. The new standard specified that a fractional silver reserve be held by the bank of issue, but it gave the public no right to redeem notes or deposits in silver.[71]

The owners of silver benefited, of course, from the high foreign exchange value of silver. Had silver been simply a commodity, the U.S. purchase program would have been a largely unalloyed boon, enabling the holders of silver to sell their stocks at an unexpectedly high price. Because silver served as the monetary base of China, however, students of the period are unanimous that the boon was more than offset by the economic effects of the drastic deflationary pressure imposed on China and the resulting economic disturbances. The deflationary pressure and disturbances, aside from their economic effects, certainly did not contribute to the political stability of China. Much of the limited stock of political capacity had to be devoted first to unsuccessful attempts to prevent the export of silver, then to the sweeping monetary "reform" of 1935. Furthermore, by converting China from a commodity standard effectively to a

---

[70] See Paris, *Monetary Policies*, p. 66.
[71] See Frank M. Tamagna, *Banking and Finance in China*, New York, Institute of Pacific Relations, 1942, pp. 142–150.

paper standard, the so-called reform rendered it both easier and more tempting to finance later war expenditures by inflationary currency issues. Under pressure of the needs of war and then revolution, China probably would in any event have departed from silver, resorted to paper money issues, and have succumbed to hyperinflation. But there can be little doubt that the effects of U.S. silver policy on China's monetary structure increased the likelihood of those events and speeded up their occurrence.

Though the Chinese experience is the most dramatic, China was by no means the only country affected by the silver-purchase program. Mexico, a major silver producer and user, was led to proclaim a bank holiday in April 1935 because the bullion value of the peso had risen above its monetary value. All coins were ordered to be exchanged for paper currency, and the export of silver money was prohibited. A year and a half later, after the world price of silver had fallen, silver coinage was restored.[72] Similar events occurred in numerous other countries throughout the world. A U.S. Treasury order in May 1935 prohibiting the import of foreign silver coins was of course ineffective. It simply meant that the coins were melted down outside the United States and the bullion shipped in instead of the melting being done, as earlier, in New York.

A policy undertaken as part of a broader program to promote adoption of "a permanent measure of value, including both gold and silver, [as] . . . a world standard," to quote from President Roosevelt's silver message of May 22, 1934,[73] had the effect of a major diminution in the worldwide monetary role of silver.

COMPOSITION OF THE CURRENCY

The effect of changes discussed in the preceding sections is in part recorded in the figures on the composition of U.S. currency, 1932–60, in Table 21. From one-sixth of the total currency in circulation, gold has declined to a negligible sum representing gold certificates lost in the course of time, held in numismatic collections, or held illegally. The figures record no coin as in circulation. However, there surely has been some in these same categories, although since 1955, there have been no limits on the possession of gold coin, all such coins having been designated rare coin (see above, footnote 45). Silver, which rose from one-eighth to one-fourth of total currency during the height of the silver-purchase program, has continued to rise in absolute amount but so much less rapidly than the total that it is back to roughly its initial proportion. National bank notes, accounting for over one-eighth of the currency in 1932, have been in the process of retirement since 1935 and are now a

[72] Paris, *Monetary Policies*, p. 71.
[73] As reproduced by Paris, pp. 187–188.

TABLE 21

COMPOSITION OF UNITED STATES CURRENCY IN CIRCULATION, OUTSIDE THE
TREASURY AND FEDERAL RESERVE BANKS, SELECTED DATES, 1932–60

End of June	Total	Gold Coin	Gold Certifi-cates	Silver[a]	National Bank Notes[b]	Other Treasury Currency[c]	Federal Reserve Notes
			MILLIONS OF DOLLARS				
1932	5,408	166	716	640	701	406	2,780
1933	5,434	34	265	647	920	508	3,061
1938	6,461	0	78	1,612	217	438	4,114
1945	26,746	0	52	2,565	120	1,142	22,867
1960	32,065	0	30	3,917	56	968	27,094
			PERCENTAGE DISTRIBUTION				
1932	100.0	3.1	13.2	11.8	13.0	7.5	51.4
1933	100 0	0.6	4 9	11 9	16.9	9.3	56.3
1938	100.0	0	1.2	24 9	3 4	6.8	63.7
1945	100 0	0	0 2	9.6	0.4	4.3	85.5
1960	100.0	0	0.1	12.2	0.2	3.0	84.5

[a] Includes standard silver dollars, silver certificates, Treasury notes of 1890, and subsidiary silver.

[b] After Aug. 1935, national bank notes became liabilities of the Treasury on a par with "other Treasury currency."

[c] Includes minor coin, U.S. notes, and Federal Reserve Bank notes. Before Mar. 1935, Federal Reserve Bank notes were liabilities of the issuing Reserve Banks.

SOURCE: *Circulation Statement of United States Money:* 1932–38, *Banking and Monetary Statistics,* p. 409; 1945, *Federal Reserve Bulletin,* Aug. 1946, p. 889; 1960, *FRB,* Aug. 1960, p. 883.

negligible fraction of the total. The variety of items under "other Treasury currency," including minor coin, U.S. notes, and Federal Reserve Bank notes, has, like silver, risen in absolute amount but fallen as a fraction of the total from over 7 per cent to 3 per cent. Evidencing the continued centralization of monetary authority, and the shift from a quasi-commodity standard to a dominantly fiduciary standard, Federal Reserve notes have taken up the slack, rising from 51 per cent of currency in circulation in 1932 to 84 per cent in 1960.[74]

[74] The Nov. 1961 order suspending silver sales from the Treasury's nonmonetized stock also directed the Treasury to use the silver cover for silver certificates for future subsidiary coinage and to replace silver certificates consequently retired by Federal Reserve notes. Only $5 and $10 denominations were affected by the order. In Jan. 1962, the President asked Congress to authorize the Federal Reserve System to issue $1 and $2 Federal Reserve notes to make possible the gradual retirement of silver certificates of those denominations. The authorization was included in the act of June 4, 1963, repealing the silver purchase acts.

CHAPTER 2

Cyclical Changes, 1933–41

As we have seen, severe contractions tend to be succeeded by vigorous rebounds. The 1929–33 contraction was no exception. Net national product rose no less than 76 per cent in current prices and 59 per cent in constant prices from 1933 to the next cyclical peak in 1937, or at average rates of growth of 14 and 12 per cent per year, respectively (see Chart 37). These are extraordinary rates of growth. Two other four-year periods show larger rises in income in current prices, but both are wartime periods, one, terminating just after World War I, the other, during World War II. No other four-year period from the time recorded annual figures start in 1869 to 1960 shows so large a rate of rise in income in constant prices.

1. Changes in Money, Income, Prices, and Velocity

It is a measure of the severity of the preceding contraction that, despite such sharp rises, money income was 17 per cent lower in 1937 than at the preceding peak eight years earlier and real income was only 3 per cent higher. Since population had grown nearly 6 per cent in the interim, per capita output was actually lower at the cyclical peak in 1937 than at the preceding cyclical peak. There are only two earlier examples in the recorded annual figures, 1895 and 1910, when per capita output was less than it was at the preceding cyclical peaks in 1892 and 1907, respectively. Furthermore, the contraction that followed the 1937 peak, though not especially long, was unusually deep and proceeded at an extremely rapid rate, the only occasion in our record when one deep depression followed immediately on the heels of another.

In consequence, the most notable feature of the revival after 1933 was not its rapidity but its incompleteness. Throughout the revival, unemployment remained large. Even at the cyclical peak in 1937, seasonally adjusted unemployment was 5.9 million; by the trough thirteen months later, it had risen to 10.6 million out of a labor force of nearly 54 million.

The revival was initially erratic and uneven. Reopening of the banks was followed by a rapid spurt in personal income and industrial production (see Chart 37). The spurt was intensified by production in anticipation of the codes to be established under the National Industrial Recovery Act (passed June 16, 1933), which were expected to raise wage rates and

CHART 37
Money Stock, Income, Prices, and Velocity, Personal Income
and Industrial Production, in Reference Cycle Expansions
and Contractions, March 1933–December 1941

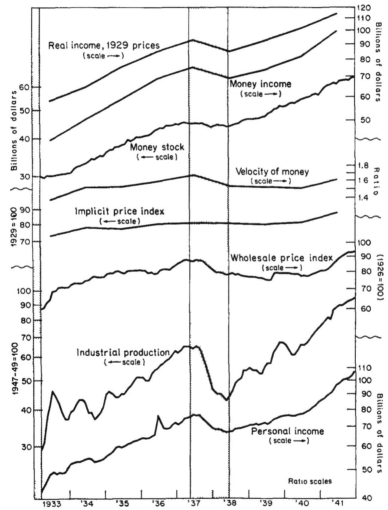

NOTE: Shaded areas represent business contractions; unshaded areas, business expansions.
SOURCE: Industrial production, same as for Chart 16. Personal income, same as for Chart 28.
Other data, same as for Chart 62.

prices, and did. A relapse in the second half of 1933 was followed by another spurt in early 1934 and then a further relapse. A sustained and reasonably continuous rise in income and production did not get under way until late 1934; and then it was disproportionately concentrated in the production of nondurable goods and services and of goods for government purchase as compared with previous and subsequent experience. At the cyclical peak in 1937, the nondurables component of the index of industrial production was more than 21 per cent above its value at the 1929 peak, whereas the durables component was some 6 per cent below its value at the 1929 peak. The difference reflected largely an unusually low level of private capital formation. Net private investment remained negative until 1936. When it became positive in 1936 and early 1937, an unusually large part consisted of additions to inventories.[1] At its highest in early 1937, private construction was only one-third of the highest level reached in the mid-twenties.

In his detailed analysis of the revival, Kenneth Roose quite plausibly attributes the unusually low level of private investment at that time mainly to the effects of governmental policies. Those policies tended to make profits relatively low. Wage rises were promoted first through the NIRA codes and then, when the codes were declared unconstitutional in 1935, through the National Labor Relations Act and the enactment of minimum wage laws. Other labor costs were raised by laws imposing a variety of new taxes, notably social security taxes, enacted in 1935 and effective in 1936–37, along with federal provision for unemployment compensation and old age security payments. The undistributed profits tax law, both enacted and effective in 1936, reduced profits net of tax. In addition, and perhaps even more important, business confidence in possibilities for future returns, already shaky because of the 1929–33 experience, was weakened still further by these and other measures: some regulating business (such as the Securities Act of 1933 and the Securities Exchange Act of 1934, the divorce of investment banking from commercial banking under the Banking Act of 1933, restrictions on public utility holding companies enacted in 1935); others expanding government activities into areas up to then reserved mostly for private enterprise (such as the creation of the Tennessee Valley Authority in 1933, the Resettlement Administration and the Rural Electrification Administration in 1935, the Social Security Board in 1935, the Home Owners Loan Corporation in 1933, and the Federal Farm Mortgage Corporation in 1934); still others seeming to threaten the sanctity of private contracts and property (such as the cancellation of gold clauses and the "nationalization" of gold and

[1] See K. D. Roose, *The Economics of Recession and Revival,* Yale University Press, 1954, pp. 45–47. Roose describes the inventory accumulation as unplanned (p. 186).

silver). The effects of these measures were exacerbated by the deliberate maintenance of an unbalanced budget, by attacks on "economic royalists" and "monopoly" by the President and other administration spokesmen, and by the President's proposal to reorganize the Supreme Court. Social tension was heightened by establishment of the Congress of Industrial Organizations, use of the sit-down strike, widespread labor troubles and— from the other side—establishment of the Liberty League and similar organizations by opponents of the New Deal. The result was "a highly emotional controversy as to desirable methods and goals for the political, social, and economic life," and "a bitter division of opinion over the New Deal, its measures and philosophy," hardly calculated to establish an atmosphere conducive to vigorous enterprise and confident risk taking.[2]

The unusually small demand for funds to engage in capital formation contributed to a fall in the level of long-term interest rates, and the low level of rates is in its turn an additional bit of evidence that there was, in fact, an unusually small demand. During the 1920's, high-grade corporate bonds yielded around $4\frac{1}{2}$ to 5 per cent; in the later 1930's, such bonds yielded 3 to $3\frac{1}{2}$ per cent. Lower-grade bonds also fell in yield, though the spread between lower- and higher-grade bonds widened—evidence of the unwillingness of the saver, like the entrepreneur, to undertake risk. The same phenomenon may help account for the widening spread between long- and short-term rates, which brought short-term rates to unprecedentedly low levels. The commercial paper rate fell to $\frac{3}{4}$ of 1 per cent in the second half of 1934 and remained at that level until early 1937; the Treasury bill rate fluctuated around a level of $\frac{1}{8}$ of 1 per cent from April 1934 to the end of 1936 and at even lower levels after a temporary rise in 1937. As we have seen, the desire for liquidity on the part of banks played an especially important role in bringing down the short-term rates (see Chart 35).

Interest rates were not only low; in addition, they declined during the cyclical expansion of 1933–37. The reversal of the usual cyclical pattern was probably the result of the large inflow of capital from abroad, discussed in the preceding chapter, which added sharply to the supply of loanable funds, reinforcing the effect of an unusually small demand on the level of rates and more than offsetting the cyclical expansion in demand that doubtless did occur.

Like production, wholesale prices first spurted in early 1933, partly for the same reason—in anticipation of the NIRA codes—partly under the stimulus of depreciation in the foreign exchange value of the dollar. Wholesale prices then stabilized to rise again at a more moderate pace throughout most of the period to mid-1937, interrupted only by a mild decline in 1936. All told, from the 1933 trough to the 1937 peak, wholesale

[2] Quotations from Roose, *Economics of Recession*, p. 61.

prices rose nearly 50 per cent. Cost of living rose decidedly less, by 13 per cent. The comprehensive index implicit in Kuznets' deflation of the net national product, available only on an annual basis, was only 11 per cent higher for 1937 than for 1933. While the wholesale price index generally shows a wider amplitude than the cost-of-living index or the implicit index, the differences were much wider than usual. They reflect in part the differential impact of devaluation on goods entering international trade; those goods are more important in the wholesale price index than they are in the other indexes. But it may also be that the differences reflect in part an understatement of the price rise by the cost-of-living and implicit indexes; the recorded prices of many items included in those indexes, but not in the wholesale price index, are much more stable than the actual prices of those items.

As in the other episodes we have considered, the broad movements in the stock of money correspond with those in income. From its trough in April 1933, the recorded stock of money rose 53 per cent to its subsequent peak in March 1937, or at an average annual rate of nearly 11 per cent per year. So large a rise has occurred in a four-year period only immediately after resumption (1879–83), in reaction to the deep depression of the early 90's (1897–1901), and during the two world wars. Yet the stock of money in 1933–37, like money income, did not regain its average 1929 level. The difference was, however, much smaller for money than for income. Velocity, though it rose some 20 per cent in the four years, was still some 15 per cent below its 1929 level, so a difference between 1929 and 1937 of 2 per cent in the stock of money was converted into a 17 per cent difference in money income. The 1937 peak was followed by an unusually severe contraction in money as in income. We have seen that the stock of money generally rises during contractions in general business, though at a slower pace than during the preceding expansions. It falls in absolute level primarily during unusually severe contractions. In 1937 it fell absolutely. The fall was only 3 per cent, from specific cycle peak to specific cycle trough, yet it was the first time since the 1890's that the stock of money had fallen absolutely in two successive contractions in general business.

An extremely interesting feature of the 1933 to 1937 expansion is the relation between the rise in the stock of money and the rise in prices. We may obtain a standard of comparison from two earlier cyclical expansions, which involved a reaction to deep depressions comparable in duration to the 1929–33 contraction (1879–82 in reaction to the 1873–79 contraction, and 1896– or 1897–99 in reaction to the generally depressed years 1891–96 or –97). If we rely on annual figures for all three expansions —monthly figures are available only for the third—the stock of money rose 53 per cent from 1879 to 1882, 41 per cent from 1896 to 1899, and

46 per cent from 1933 to 1937. The rise in implicit prices was also of roughly the same order of magnitude in the three expansions: 10 per cent, 6 per cent, and 11 per cent, respectively. But the rise in wholesale prices was much larger in the third expansion: in annual averages, 20 per cent in 1879–82, 12 per cent in 1896–99, and 31 per cent in 1933–37; in terms of the change from the three months centered on the specific cycle trough to the three months centered on the specific cycle peak, 28 per cent from 1879 to 1882, 26 per cent from 1897 to 1900, and 45 per cent from 1933 to 1937.[3]

What accounts for the greater rise in wholesale prices in 1933–37, despite a probably higher fraction of the labor force unemployed and of physical capacity unutilized than in the two earlier expansions? One factor, already mentioned, was devaluation with its differential effect on wholesale prices. Another was almost surely the explicit measures to raise prices and wages undertaken with government encouragement and assistance, notably, NIRA, the Guffey Coal Act, the agricultural price-support program, and National Labor Relations Act. The first two were declared unconstitutional and lapsed, but they had some effect while in operation; the third was partly negated by Court decisions and then revised, but was effective throughout the expansion; the fourth, along with the general climate of opinion it reflected, became most important toward the end of the expansion.

There has been much discussion in recent years of a wage-price spiral or price-wage spiral as an explanation of post-World War II price movements. We have grave doubts that autonomous changes in wages and prices played an important role in that period. There seems to us a much stronger case for a wage-price or price-wage spiral interpretation of 1933–37—indeed this is the only period in the near-century we cover for which such an explanation seems clearly justified. During those years there were autonomous forces raising wages and prices.[4] The wage and

[3] The specific cycle dates are:

Trough	Peak
June 1879	Aug. 1882
June 1897	Mar. 1900
Feb. 1933	Apr. 1937

[4] The wage-price spiral or price-wage spiral is often stated as if the existence of strong unions or strong producer monopolies were sufficient to set in motion autonomous forces raising wages and prices. This is wrong and involves the confusion between "high" and "rising" that is so common a fallacy in reasoning about economic matters. Strong unions and strong producer monopolies simply imply high wages for the unionized labor and high prices for the commodities monopolized relative to the wages of other labor and the prices of other commodities; they do not imply a continuous tendency for those wages and prices to be forced still higher. Such autonomous upward pressure is to be expected only from *increasingly* strong unions, and *increasingly* strong monopoly groups in the process

price rises occurred in an environment of rapid growth in the money stock, and so they could take place without meeting a monetary barrier or producing an absolute increase in unemployment. In what is perhaps the most common version of the wage-price spiral analysis, the monetary barrier which would block a wage-price spiral is looked upon as being removed by monetary authorities committed to a full employment policy and hence willing to increase the stock of money to prevent unemployment resulting from rises in wages and prices. That was not the sequence from 1933 to 1937; the rise in the money stock was produced not by the monetary authorities but by the gold inflow. Though accidental gold inflow served the same economic function as compliant monetary authorities would have, it occurred despite rather than because of the actions of unions, business organizations, and government in pushing up prices.

If this analysis is right, it suggests that, in the absence of the wage and price push, the period 1933–37 would have been characterized by a smaller rise in prices and a larger rise in output than actually occurred. Moreover, that tendency would have been reinforced by its indirect effects on the stock of money. A smaller rise in domestic prices would have meant a still larger favorable balance of trade and hence a still larger gold inflow. The changed political and economic climate might well have evoked a greater demand for investment, a smaller decline in interest rates or perhaps even a rise instead of a decline, and a less rapid fall in the ratio of deposits to reserves desired by commercial banks. The rise in the stock of money would therefore probably have been greater on two scores: high-powered money would have risen more, and the ratio of the money stock to high-powered money would have declined less. The rise in output would also therefore probably have been greater on two scores: the fraction of the increase in money income accounted for by an increase in output would have been larger; and the increase in money income itself would have been larger.

2. *Factors Accounting for Changes in the Money Stock*

Chart 38 facilitates a more detailed examination of changes in the money stock and of the factors accounting for them. High-powered money was the major factor accounting arithmetically for the change in the money

---

of raising their wages and prices to levels consistent with their newly acquired monopoly power.

In 1933–37, this condition was clearly satisfied for unions. They experienced a major growth in numbers and strength. Union membership increased two and a half times, and just about doubled as a percentage of nonagricultural employment from 1933 to 1937 (*Historical Statistics of the United States, Colonial Times to 1957*, Bureau of the Census, 1960, Series D-743 and D-745, p. 98). For producer groups, the legislation referred to had the same effect, increasing their effective power to make prices approximate more closely the level that would be optimum for a monopoly.

CHART 38
The Stock of Money and Its Proximate Determinants,
March 1933–December 1941

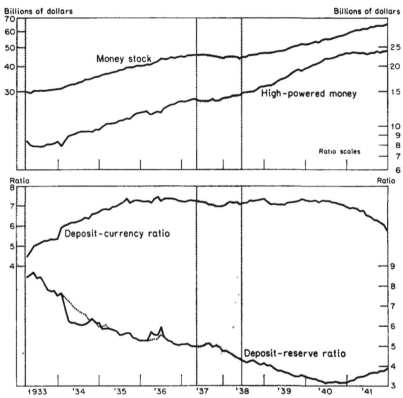

NOTE: Shaded areas represent business contractions; unshaded areas, business expansions.
SOURCE: Tables A-1 (col. 8) and B-3. Dotted section of deposit-reserve ratio smoothes deposits and reserves (see Chart 44 and the accompanying text).

stock over the period as a whole as well as for smaller fluctuations in sub-periods of 1933 to 1941. The stock of money grew by 51 per cent from March 1933 to the reference peak in May 1937, and high-powered money, by 60 per cent. The concurrent rise in the ratio of deposits to currency, which alone would have made for a more rapid rise in the money stock than in high-powered money, was more than offset by the decline in the ratio of deposits to bank reserves. The deposit-currency ratio behaved very smoothly, rising sharply from 1933 to 1935 and making its largest contribution to the growth of the money stock in those years, then tapering off to remain roughly constant until 1940. The deposit-reserve ratio was more irregular, particularly in 1934 and in 1936. In both years, those irregularities offset corresponding irregularities in high-powered money and so left an impress on the stock of money only in much muted form.

From 1937 to mid-1940, money and high-powered money, though they have the same pattern of movement, converged sharply. The convergence resulted from the continued decline, at an accelerated pace, of the deposit-reserve ratio, this time neither offset nor intensified by movements in the deposit-currency ratio. From mid-1940 to 1945 (see Chart 46), the movements of the two deposit ratios were reversed, the deposit-currency ratio falling and the deposit-reserve ratio rising, so that they again offset one another, and the stock of money moved roughly proportionately to high-powered money.

The composition of additions to high-powered money from 1933 to 1940 differed according to whether it is viewed in terms of the liabilities of the monetary authorities—which is to say, the assets of the public and the banks holding the high-powered money—or in terms of the assets carried on the books of the monetary authorities as the counterpart of those liabilities. From the point of view of the public and the banks, the increase was primarily in Federal Reserve money (Chart 39A), most of the increase being in Federal Reserve deposits. Treasury currency rose a trifle (mostly because additions to silver currency exceeded the volume of national bank notes that were retired). Recorded gold fell to zero after it became illegal to hold, though some gold was probably held illegally. On the other hand, on the consolidated books of the monetary authorities, the increase in high-powered money was matched almost entirely by an increase in gold. Federal Reserve claims on the public and the banks fell to nearly zero, as discounting went out of fashion, and the System's holdings of acceptances became negligible. The remaining category of assets—which we designate other physical assets and fiat—fluctuated within a narrow range. The major fluctuations reflected the Treasury gold sterilization and desterilization operations in 1937 and 1938, which we consider in more detail below. Sterilization corresponded to the replacement of fiat by gold (on the liability side, of noninterest-bearing obligations by interest-bearing ones if financed by borrowing, or net reduction in obligations if financed by a budget surplus), and desterilization corresponded to the opposite.

The 1933–40 relationships were in interesting contrast with those that prevailed during both the twenties and the 1929–33 contraction. In the first place, the ratio of deposits to currency receded from an active and strategic role to a largely passive and secondary role. During the twenties, the steady rise in the deposit-currency ratio was the major factor account-

CHART 39
High-Powered Money, by Assets and Liabilities of the Treasury and Federal Reserve Banks, 1933–41

A. Liabilities

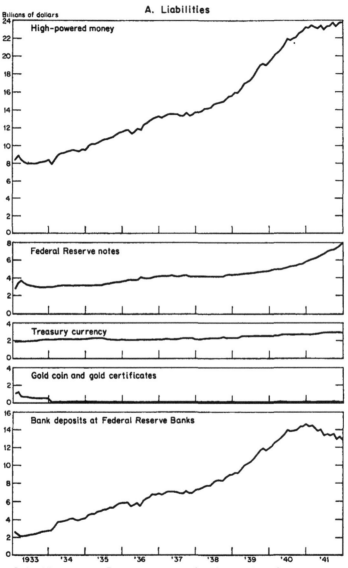

NOTE: Federal Reserve notes, Treasury currency, and gold coin and certificates are outside the Treasury and Federal Reserve Banks.

SOURCE: Same as for Chart 19, but the cumulated devaluation profit was deducted from the seasonally adjusted official gold stock. Devaluation profit as of Jan. 31, 1934, from *Banking and Monetary Statistics*, p. 538. For subsequent months, annual devaluation profit, from the *Annual Report* of the Secretary of the Treasury, 1940, pp. 634–635, and 1941, p. 428, was cumulated to the Jan. 31, 1934, figure.

CHART 39 (Concluded)

B. Assets

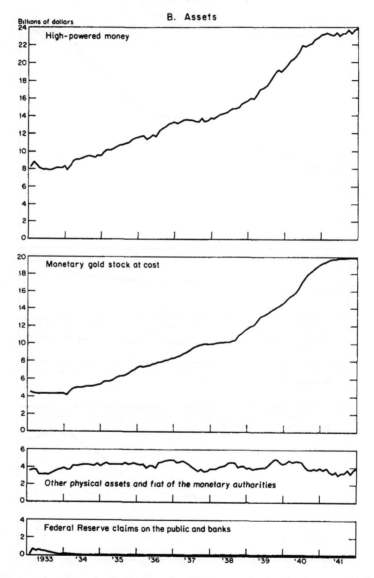

ing for the concurrent rise in the stock of money; from 1930 to 1933, recurrent declines in the ratio signaled renewed liquidity crises. After 1933, the initial sharp rise in the ratio is partly spurious, reflecting the defects in our money estimates analyzed in Chapter 8 (section 1) and arising from the reclassification of deposits in unlicensed banks. The re-classification had the effect of raising the ratio of deposits to currency.[5] If this effect is allowed for, there remains a gradual rise in the ratio of deposits to currency from the low point reached in 1933 to mid-1935. Thereafter, the ratio was highly stable until 1940, when it began to de-cline. The rise from 1933 to 1935 was clearly a reaction to the prior decline. It was a sign of renewed confidence in banks, of renewed willing-ness to hold deposits instead of currency, just as the 1930–33 decline had been a result of a loss of confidence in bank deposits. However, the level around which the ratio fluctuated between 1935 and 1940, about 7.20, was much lower than the peak of 11.57 attained in 1929. It was about the same as the level reached in 1921, which in turn was somewhat below the level in the years immediately before World War I. Cagan's detailed analysis of the deposit-currency ratio implies that the low level between 1935 and 1940 was primarily attributable to the cost of holding deposits, which was higher than at earlier dates—interest on demand deposits was outlawed and instead service charges were imposed.[6] The decline after 1940 we consider in connection with wartime developments (Chapter 10).

A second and more interesting contrast is found in the tools employed by the Reserve System and in the relative roles of the Reserve System and the Treasury. During the 1920's and to a lesser extent the early 1930's, there was little connection between movements in high-powered money and in the gold stock because of a clear inverse relation between movements in the gold stock and in Federal Reserve credit outstanding (see Chart 25). The Federal Reserve System used its powers, particularly during the twenties, to sterilize gold movements and to prevent erratic short-term changes in high-powered money. After 1933, on the other hand, Federal Reserve credit outstanding was almost constant and the

[5] Our estimates include currency in the vaults of unlicensed banks as part of currency held by the public. The opening of a previously unlicensed bank or its merger with a licensed bank, therefore, increased the numerator of the deposit-currency ratio and reduced the denominator. The reclassification also had a lesser effect on the deposit-reserve ratio. Our estimates treat deposits of unlicensed member banks at Federal Reserve Banks as part of total member bank reserves and therefore include them in the denominator of the deposit-reserve ratio. The open-ing of a previously unlicensed bank or its merger with a licensed bank increased the numerator of the deposit-reserve ratio by the full amount of the released de-posits, but increased the denominator only by vault cash.

[6] Phillip Cagan, *The Demand for Currency Relative to the Total Money Supply*, New York, NBER, Occasional Paper 62, 1958, pp. 20–22.

discount rate was not altered from early 1934 to mid-1937 (see Chart 41, below). As we have seen, the changes in high-powered money reflected mainly movements in the gold stock. Such deviations as there were between the changes in high-powered money and the gold stock reflected offsetting measures by the Treasury, which altered its cash holdings and deposits at the Federal Reserve. This contrast applies not only to year-to-year movements but equally to seasonal movements. In the 1920's and early 1930's, Federal Reserve credit outstanding had a distinct seasonal movement, corresponding to the seasonal movement in currency outside the Treasury and Reserve Banks (Chart 26). After 1933, currency had the same seasonal movement as earlier, but Federal Reserve credit outstanding had essentially no seasonal movement. The System discarded almost entirely the role it had assumed in the 1920's and along with it the tools it had developed at that time. For such actions as it engaged in it used new tools acquired in 1933–35—control over margin requirements on securities and over reserve requirements of member banks.

A third and closely related contrast appears in the connection between movements in high-powered money and in the ratio of deposits to bank reserves. In the 1920's, both rose, though the rise in high-powered money had nearly stopped by 1925, while the rise in the deposit-reserve ratio continued steadily throughout the decade; and both were highly stable in their shorter-term movements. After 1930, the two began to move inversely, high-powered money rising and the ratio of deposits to bank reserves declining, as banks sought to strengthen their liquidity position. The general inverse movement continued after 1933, with addition of a much more regular tendency for the short-term irregularities in the deposit-reserve ratio to offset corresponding irregularities in high-powered money. The distinction between the general inverse movement over a period of years, and the shorter-term, month-to-month offsetting movements deserves more attention and we shall return to it. The short-term tendency is related to the preceding contrast. The Federal Reserve was no longer smoothing minor irregularities in high-powered money, hence the banks adjusted to them. The short-term irregularities in the deposit-reserve ratio can therefore correctly be interpreted as a fairly passive response on the part of banks to the short-term irregularities in high-powered money. This has fostered the view that the longer-term decline— a manifestation of the accumulation of excess reserves, discussed above— was also a passive reaction to the growth of high-powered money, a view discussed above and rejected (Chapter 8, section 1).

The first of these contrasts requires no further discussion. In connection with the other two, we shall consider factors accounting for changes in high-powered money (section 3); policy actions of the Federal Reserve (section 4); changes in the deposit-reserve ratio (section 5); and, finally, by way of a summary of the rest, the role of monetary measures in the 1937–38 contraction and the subsequent recovery (section 6).

3. Changes in High-Powered Money

The breakdown of high-powered money by assets of the monetary authorities, presented in Chart 39B, consolidates the accounts of the Treasury and the Federal Reserve System. Though appropriate for analyzing the joint effect of the monetary authorities on the money stock, the consolidation conceals the relative roles of the two separate agencies and hence cannot be used to document our conclusion that the Treasury had become the active monetary authority. For this purpose, we need to separate out the items over which the Treasury had direct control: its cash and its deposits at Federal Reserve Banks. Since those deposits are a liability of the Banks, they cancel out when Treasury and Reserve accounts are consolidated.

When the Treasury bought gold, it paid with a check on its account at one of the Federal Reserve Banks. At the same time, however, it could print gold certificates of a corresponding amount and either add them to its cash balances or deposit them at the Reserve Banks. Such a transaction therefore meant a rise in high-powered money equal to the value of the gold purchase and no change in Treasury cash and deposits at Reserve Banks. As we have seen, transactions of this kind accounted for the major movements in high-powered money from 1933 to 1941. This point is demonstrated again in Chart 40 with a series on the monetary gold stock slightly different from that given at cost in Chart 39B. This one is expressed in official values, which changed abruptly at the end of January 1934 when the official price of gold was raised. We use official values in this chart in order to make the gold series comparable with the series on Treasury cash plus deposits at the Reserve Banks, also plotted on the chart.

The gold series is smoother than the high-powered money series. The main reason is that movements in Treasury cash and in deposits at Federal Reserve Banks altered the impact of the gold stock, and accounted almost entirely for the discrepancies between movements in high-powered money and the gold stock. Though changes in Treasury cash and deposits at Reserve Banks need not affect high-powered money, during that period they did. The Treasury can change its cash and deposits at Reserve Banks by various bookkeeping operations such as printing Treasury currency authorized but not issued, or destroying Treasury currency it holds, or selling securities to or buying them from the Reserve Banks. None of these operations will affect high-powered money. However, with one exception, no such transaction of any size was undertaken from 1933 to 1941. Other operations changing Treasury cash and deposits at Reserve Banks all

CHART 40

Major Factors Accounting for Changes in High-Powered Money,
1933–41

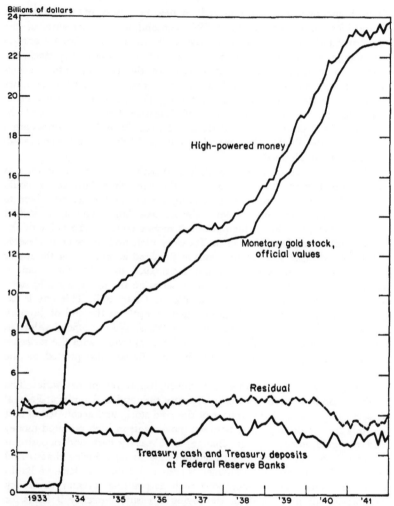

SOURCE: High-powered money, Table B-3. Monetary gold stock, same as for Chart 19. Treasury cash and deposits, Table A-3. Residual, see text.

change high-powered money by the same amount but in the opposite direction, since they consist of a transfer of cash or deposits at Reserve Banks from the public and banks to the Treasury, or conversely.[7]

We did not find it necessary in the preceding chapter to take explicit account of Treasury cash and deposits at Federal Reserve Banks, for two reasons. In the first place, Treasury cash and deposits at the Banks fluctuated much less in the twenties than they did later. In the second place, in the twenties and early thirties, the Reserve System deliberately undertook to offset seasonal changes in Treasury holdings as well as in other short-term factors tending to introduce irregularities into the total volume of high-powered money. After 1933, the System apparently gave up any attempt to smooth short-term movements. In consequence, high-powered money became more erratic in its month-to-month movements after 1933 than before (compare Chart 38 with Charts 23 and 31).

The extent to which the gold stock and changes in Treasury cash and deposits at the Reserve Banks jointly fail to account for movements in high-powered money is shown by the line in Chart 40 labeled "residual." It plots the excess of high-powered money over the sum of the gold stock and Treasury cash and deposits at Reserve Banks. It therefore reflects all other factors. The movements in the residual are small and even some of these are Treasury induced, reflecting bookkeeping transactions that make our series on Treasury cash and deposits at Reserve Banks an inexact index of the effects of Treasury operations on high-powered money. Only the movements in the residual in 1933 and early 1937 and the sharp decline in 1940 can be plausibly attributed to Federal Reserve rather than Treasury action. The first reflects Reserve System operations in the wake of the bank holiday; the second, operations accompanying the reserve requirement changes; and the third, reduction of Federal Reserve credit outstanding through open market sales (see Chapter 10).

Though the initial sharp jump in the gold stock from January to February 1934 is accounted for primarily by the revaluation of gold, part of it was produced by the substantial amount of gold imported, as foreigners took advantage of the higher buying price. The new gold price became official on January 31, 1934. Gold was almost immediately shipped

---

[7] Such operations, when they increase Treasury cash or deposits at Reserve Banks, involve the Treasury's taking in from the public and the banks, in the form of cash or checks on Reserve Banks, more from sales of securities or taxes or other receipts than it pays out in the same form to redeem securities or to meet current expenses. But this means that the public and the banks transfer part of their high-powered money to the Treasury. Since our series on high-powered money refers solely to money held outside the Treasury and the Reserve System, it follows that such a transfer reduces high-powered money by the same amount that it adds to Treasury cash and deposits at the Reserve Banks; and conversely, when the transfer is from the Treasury to the public and the banks. In practice, the initial transfer from the public is typically to Treasury accounts at commercial banks. The Treasury then transfers its deposits at commercial banks to Reserve Banks.

to the United States. In the six weeks from February 1 to March 14, more than $0.5 billion of gold (valued at the new price) was imported. At the same time, Treasury cash and deposits at Federal Reserve Banks, excluding the profit from revaluation of gold, declined. The two factors together account for the sharp rise in high-powered money from the end of January to the end of March—a rise of $1 billion or one-eighth of the initial level, much the largest percentage change in so short an interval during the whole period—1907 to 1960—for which monthly data on high-powered money are available.

Once the initial rush of gold imports was over, the gold stock continued to rise at a fairly steady rate to the end of 1937. Until France left gold in late 1936, roughly half of U.S. gold imports came from France. For the next year, France was a net importer of gold from the U.S. rather than a net exporter. During the last quarter of 1937, a large-scale withdrawal of foreign short-term balances followed rumors that further devaluation of the dollar was being considered as a possible counter-cyclical measure.[8] On net, the United States lost gold from October 1937 to February 1938. Withdrawal of European short-term funds from the United States ceased in July 1938. These counter movements roughly offset the forces making for a continued flow of gold to this country, so the total gold stock remained fairly steady from autumn 1937 to autumn 1938. Munich then led to a further flight of capital from Europe and a sudden increase in the rate of gold inflow. The outbreak of war simply maintained the rate of the gold inflow. The intensification of Britain's war effort after the fall of France in early 1940 and her attempt to tap American supplies of war material, as she had in World War I, produced a further increase. Finally, the enactment of lend-lease in early 1941, which relieved Britain and her allies of the necessity of acquiring dollars to finance war purchases, brought an end to the rapid growth of the gold stock.

Many of the minor fluctuations (Chart 40) in Treasury cash holdings

[8] The Gold Reserve Act of Jan. 30, 1934, empowered the President to establish the gold content of the dollar anywhere between 50 to 60 per cent of its former weight. The devaluation he proclaimed the following day established the gold content at about 59 per cent of the former weight. Hence he still had authority to change the purchase price of gold or the weight of the dollar. The power to devalue was allowed to expire in 1943 but *de facto* devaluation can still legally be effected by the Secretary of the Treasury under the power he acquired in the Gold Reserve Act to buy and sell gold, with the approval of the President, "at such rates and upon such conditions as he may deem advantageous to the public interest."

However, M. A. Kriz has pointed out that the Secretary of the Treasury's authority to change the market price of gold has been limited by the obligations assumed by the U.S. as a member of the International Monetary Fund and by the provision in the Bretton Woods Agreements Act of July 31, 1945, requiring legislative action by Congress before any change is made in the par value of the U.S. dollar ("Gold in World Monetary Affairs Today," *Political Science Quarterly*, Dec. 1960, p. 504 n.).

and deposits at Federal Reserve Banks, which are mirrored in corresponding fluctuations in high-powered money, probably reflect largely seasonal discrepancies between receipts and expenditures. Although the series plotted have been seasonally adjusted, both expenditures and receipts of the federal government changed so radically that the statistical adjustments probably have not succeeded in eliminating all seasonal effects.

There remain for comment a number of discrepancies of more moment.

(1) The marked irregularity in the first half of 1936 in high-powered money reflects an abnormal accumulation of Treasury deposits at Federal Reserve Banks from both March income- and gift-tax collections and, more important, from a large flotation of bonds and Treasury notes.

(2) The failure of high-powered money to reflect the growth of the gold stock in the first nine months of 1937 is a result of the gold-sterilization program adopted by the Treasury in December 1936. During that period, the Treasury paid for the gold it bought by borrowing rather than by using the cash balances it could create on the basis of the gold; the purchase of gold was therefore accompanied by a rise in its cash plus deposits at the Reserve Banks (see Chart 40).

The operation was economically identical with the sterilization actions of the Federal Reserve in the 1920's, when the System sold bonds on the open market to offset the increase in high-powered money that would otherwise have arisen from a gold inflow. The difference was that the Treasury rather than the System sold the bonds and took the initiative in sterilizing gold. As we shall see, the program became effective at about the same time as the second of two rises in reserve requirements imposed by the Federal Reserve. The sterilization program sharply reinforced the effect of the rise in reserve requirements in producing monetary tightness: the rise in reserve requirements increased the demand for high-powered money; simultaneously, the Treasury's action virtually brought to a halt an increase in the stock of high-powered money which had been proceeding with only minor interruptions since 1933.

(3) The more rapid increase in high-powered money than in the gold stock in the first half of 1938 reflected the reverse process: desterilization of gold by the Treasury, which is to say, its printing of gold certificates corresponding to some of the "inactive" gold in the Treasury; deposit of the certificates at the Reserve Banks, and drawing on those balances to pay government expenses or to redeem debt. Again, the operation was essentially an open market purchase of securities but one undertaken by the Treasury at its initiative.

A start toward desterilization was made in September 1937, when the Board of Governors of the Federal Reserve System requested the Treasury to release $300 million from the inactive gold account.[9] There was, of

---

[9] Board of Governors of the Federal Reserve System, *Annual Report*, 1937, p. 9.

course, no technical reason the Board itself could not have taken the economic equivalent of that step by buying $300 million of government securities. The Treasury released the amount requested by the Federal Reserve in a bookkeeping sense. However, it continued to sterilize all further gold purchases, which amounted to $174 million in that month, so that inactive gold held by the Treasury fell only $126 million in September 1937. The net effect of those actions as well as of other transactions affecting Treasury accounts was a decline of $136 million in Treasury cash and deposits at the Federal Reserve. This is the amount by which high-powered money grew in September, as a result of Treasury operations, over and above the increase in the gold stock in that month.

As of January 1, 1938, the Treasury limited the addition to the inactive gold account in any one quarter to the amount by which total gold purchases exceeded $100 million, and on April 19, 1938, discontinued the inactive gold account, which then amounted to about $1.2 billion. Once again, that was largely a bookkeeping step, the economic effect of which can be judged only by taking into account the simultaneous changes in other Treasury accounts. Initially, the inactive gold was simply moved from Treasury cash to Treasury deposits at Federal Reserve Banks, and so had no immediate monetary effect. Effective desterilization did not occur until more than a year after formal desterilization. Over that period the sum of Treasury cash holdings and deposits at Reserve Banks fell about $0.75 billion, then rose about $1 billion, and only after February 1939 began to decline toward the level that had prevailed before the sterilization program (Chart 40).

(4) The marked month-to-month irregularity in high-powered money in 1941 reflects a correspondingly increased irregularity in Treasury balances in that year, arising partly from sharper fluctuations in income-tax receipts as a result of the increased taxes imposed under the Revenue Acts of June 25 and October 8, 1940, partly from a series of bond issues which about coincided in time with the seasonal peaks in tax receipts. Again, this is an example of precisely the kind of irregularity that, by the late 1920's, the Federal Reserve System had learned to smooth with great effectiveness.

•

4. Federal Reserve Policy

In the period under consideration, the Federal Reserve System made essentially no attempt to alter the quantity of high-powered money by using either of the two instruments which had been its major reliance up to 1933: open market operations, which, as we saw in Chapter 6, had developed in the twenties from a means to acquire earnings into the major technique of monetary control; and rediscounting, which had initially been regarded as the primary instrument of Federal Reserve policy but had become one blade of the scissors of which open market operations was the other. Open market purchases and sales were made continually but, with only a few exceptions, in order to maintain the total portfolio intact or to alter its composition and thereby affect the structure of rates of return, not to alter the total amount of Federal Reserve credit outstanding. As President Harrison described it in 1939, the System had, in the course of those years, shifted its attention from "credit control" to "market control."[10]

After a decline and later rise in 1933, Federal Reserve credit outstanding was almost perfectly constant from 1934 to mid-1940. (There was then a sharp decline to a new level in 1941, discussed in Chapter 10.) The only change that shows up at all noticeably on a scale the size of Chart 41 is an increase and then a decrease on the occasion of the outbreak of World War II. Comparison of Chart 41 with Charts 25 and 33 shows how sharp the contrast with earlier experience was. In the five years 1934 through 1938, taken as a whole, Federal Reserve credit outstanding varied within a range of $177 million. In each of the seven years from 1924 through 1930, taken separately, the range is wider and in six of the seven years, more than twice as wide.

As Chart 41 shows, after a series of declines in 1933 and early 1934 following the rise in March 1933, the rediscount rate at New York remained at 1½ per cent for nearly three and one-half years and was lowered to 1 per cent in August 1937, some three months after the cyclical peak in May. It remained at that level for over five years. The longest preceding period of constancy was nineteen months—in 1915–16 and again in 1918–19.

Even this evidence understates the contrast between the use of these instruments by the Federal Reserve System in the period under consideration and in the earlier period. Whatever fluctuation occurred in Federal Reserve credit outstanding arose largely from variation in "float" (the difference between the amounts credited and debited to member bank accounts for items in the process of collection) and in bills bought and bills discounted. From January 1934 through March 1937, government securities held at month's end fluctuated within a range of $17 million; on successive Wednesdays, within a $4 million range; and was exactly equal to $2,430 million in 133 out of 170 weeks. In early 1937, the System purchased $96 million of bonds in connection with money-market tightness and a sharp flurry in short-term rates accompanying the final rise in reserve requirements. It then kept the level fixed for half a year, bought $38 million more in November 1937 and kept the new level fixed until

---

[10] George Leslie Harrison Papers on the Federal Reserve System, Columbia University Library, Harrison, Notes, Vol. VII, Dec. 7, 1939. For a full description of the Papers, see Chap. 5, footnote 41 and the accompanying text.

CHART 41
Use of Tools by Federal Reserve System, March 1933–December 1941

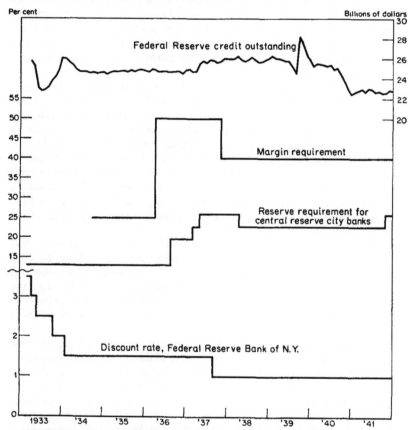

SOURCE: Federal Reserve credit outstanding, end-of-month data, from *Banking and Monetary Statistics*, pp. 376–377, seasonally adjusted by Shiskin-Eisenpress method (see source for Chart 21). Other series, *Banking and Monetary Statistics*, pp. 400, 441–442, 504.

mid-1939. Use of open market operations to influence the volume of Federal Reserve credit outstanding from day to day, week to week, and month to month ceased to be a continuous activity of the System.

Discounting, too, fell into even greater disuse than the constancy of the rate alone suggests. In the earlier period, the discount rate was seldom above short-term open market rates. For example, the New York discount rate was never above the average open market rate on 4- to 6-month commercial paper in any week from 1919 through 1931. From 1934 on, the discount rate was seldom below short-term open market rates. The New York discount rate was never below the average 4- to 6-month commercial paper rate in any week in the eight years from 1934 through 1941. The result, of course, was negligible use of rediscounting facilities. From 1918 to August 1933, the average amount of bills discounted in any month never fell below the $155 million of August 1931 and was generally several times that sum; from September 1933 through August 1941, it never rose above $138 million, after June 1934, never above $24 million, and was mostly below $10 million.

The Federal Reserve System repeatedly referred to its policy as one of "monetary ease" and was inclined to take credit—and, even more, was given it—for the concurrent decline in interest rates, both long and short. It is hard to accept this view in terms of the traditional instruments of the System and, as we shall see, the new instruments it used—control over reserve requirements and over margin requirements on securities— were employed entirely as restrictive devices. As to open market operations, failure to reduce the System's portfolio was, it is true, an act of self-restraint which permitted gold inflows to have full effect on high-powered money. But there is no reason gold inflows should provide the appropriate growth in high-powered money month after month. Moreover, Federal Reserve officials expressed recurrent concern in meetings of the Federal Open Market Committee about the inflationary effect of the gold movements but were inclined to leave any offsetting open market operations to the Treasury. They used instead their new tool of changes in reserve requirements.

With respect to discount policy, the Federal Reserve was misled by the tendency, present recurrently throughout its history before and since, to put major emphasis on the absolute level of the discount rate rather than on its relation to market rates. The rate in the thirties was low in comparison with rates in earlier periods but, as we have seen, it was much higher compared with market rates than it had ever been. By relevant standards, the discount policy was abnormally tight, not easy. The System regarded the lack of discounting as a reflection of the large accumulation of excess reserves and hence as a lack of need for accommodation. That view no doubt had some validity, but the causal chain ran the other way as well. With discount rates so high relative to market rates, discounting was an expensive way to meet even temporary needs for liquidity. Banks, therefore, had an incentive to rely on other sources of liquidity, including the accumulation of larger than usual reserves.[11]

---

[11] As we have seen above, the System's belief that it was being "easy" in 1930 and 1931 reflected the same fallacy in the interpretation of discount rates, and, as we shall see in Chap. 11, so did the emphasis on "free reserves" in the policy

Given the large inflow of gold, a relatively tight discount policy was probably the correct policy for most of the period. The stock of money rose steadily throughout the period except for 1937, when the rise was interrupted by Treasury sterilization of gold and the doubling of reserve requirements. And, as we have seen, the rate of rise was large. It is by no means clear that a still larger rate of rise was desirable. And even if it were, given the attitudes of the commercial banks, it probably would have been preferable to provide them with more reserves through open market purchases than through encouragement of discounting. Our point therefore is not at all that the discount policy followed was a mistake, but only that it cannot be regarded as having contributed to monetary "ease."

Up to 1941 at least, whatever may have been the reasons for the low and declining levels of interest rates, Federal Reserve policy was clearly not one of them. The System's high discount rate relative to market rates and, as we shall see, increases in reserve requirements probably induced banks to resort to short-term paper rather than to discounting as a source of secondary reserves, and thereby helped to produce the abnormally low level of short-term rates relative to long-term rates that prevailed in the thirties. But the low level of long-term rates and its declining tendency must clearly be attributed to other factors. We have already expressed the view that the most important were probably the combination of a low demand for funds for private capital formation and an increase in the supply of funds arising out of the flight of capital from Europe to the United States. In addition, a gradual downward revision of expectations about the level of future short-term rates doubtless served to narrow the spread between short- and long-term interest rates after the mid-1930's.

One other piece of evidence of the radical change in Federal Reserve policy is the absence of any substantial pattern in the seasonal movement in Reserve credit outstanding (see Chart 42). As we saw, the seasonal movement in Reserve credit in the twenties—roughly similar in amplitude and pattern to that in currency outside the Treasury and Federal Reserve Banks—largely protected member bank deposits at the Reserve Banks from seasonal changes in the demand for currency (Chart 26). In the thirties, currency had about the same seasonal movement as before, and Treasury deposits at Reserve Banks, now at least ten times their former volume, had a very large seasonal movement. But the seasonal movement in Reserve credit in the thirties was negligible in amplitude and did little to offset those forces. Accordingly, member bank deposits at Reserve Banks were subject to wide seasonal variation.

The Securities Exchange Act of 1934 and the Banking Act of 1935

---

discussions of the 1950's. The fallacy is also identical with that embodied in the pegging of government security prices, which the System took so long to perceive at all fully.

•

CHART 42
Seasonal Patterns Affected by Federal Reserve Policy, 1933–41

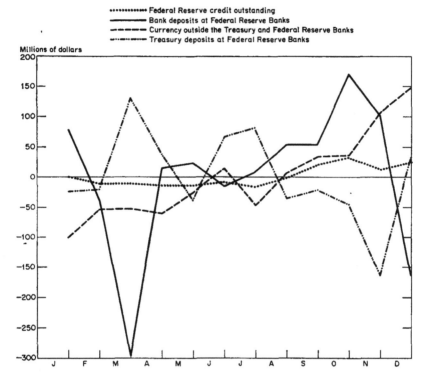

NOTE: Treasury cash is not shown because no seasonal movement was discernible after 1933.
SOURCE: Federal Reserve credit outstanding, bank deposits at Federal Reserve Banks, same as for Chart 26. Currency, same, using seasonal index computed from 1934–41 data. Treasury deposits at Federal Reserve Banks, same, using original data and 1931–43 seasonal index underlying seasonally adjusted data in Table A-3.

gave the System two permanent powers: control over margin requirements on securities, and authority to raise or lower reserve requirements of member banks between the legal level before 1933 and twice that level.[12] Both powers were lodged in the Board alone. Chart 41 shows the use that was made of them. Margin requirements were imposed as soon as the power was granted, then raised sharply at the beginning of 1936 when the Board was increasingly concerned with potential inflation,

[12] In Aug. 1948, Congress granted the Board a temporary power, terminating June 30, 1949, to raise the maximum percentages permitted under the Banking Act of 1935 by 4 points on demand deposits and by 1½ points on time deposits.

then lowered part way in late 1937 when the recession was in process. Both the granting of that power and its use were a result of the experience during the late 1920's when the Board, among many others, was concerned with the bull market in stocks and felt constrained to check "speculation." In our view, the imposition of those requirements and their variation had negligible monetary consequences and can be ignored for our purposes. The power to alter reserve requirements is a different matter. It is an extremely potent control and was used in what seems retrospectively a drastic fashion, the requirements being doubled to the maximum level permitted in three steps within a nine-month period. The System thus abandoned its old tools—open market operations and rediscounting—and applied with vigor its new tool for the earlier purpose. Yet even so drastic a use of that new power does not contradict the view that the Federal Reserve System was following a largely passive policy. The rise in reserve requirements was not imposed primarily to affect current conditions but to enable the System to control future developments it feared might be set in train by the large excess reserves.

The Reserve System's neglect of seasonal and other short-term movements, the maintenance of a constant portfolio of government securities, the absence of change in discount rates, and the doubling of reserve requirements all had common roots in the sharp rise in member bank excess reserves and in the System's interpretation of the significance of excess reserves.

Retrospectively, the initial accumulation of excess reserves, after the banking panic of 1933 and before the devaluation of the dollar, to a level of about $800 million was welcomed in explicit recognition that the experience of prior years had altered commercial bank attitudes: a volume of reserves which would have been expansionary before 1929 might be contractionary in 1934.[13] However, as excess reserves accumulated in

---

[13] The retrospective view was stated in a memorandum on excess reserves, dated Dec. 13, 1935, for a Federal Open Market Committee (FOMC) meeting, and on Jan. 23, 1936, by Harrison in a meeting with his directors (Harrison, Open Market, Vol. II; Notes, Vol. VI). The open market purchase program which created the initial accumulation of excess reserves was not, however, voted primarily for that purpose. An Apr. 1933 Governors Conference, according to Harrison, "was not in favor of embarking on another excess reserve program," but the governors favored purchases of government securities if necessary to meet Treasury requirements; the New York Bank approved the Conference resolution to that effect (Notes, Vol. III, Apr. 24, 1933). A similar view had been expressed at the Apr. 22, 1933, meeting of the Open Market Policy Conference, which authorized the executive committee to purchase up to $1 billion of government securities "to meet Treasury requirements." Deputy Governor McKay of Chicago voted against the resolution. The Board thought the authorization too narrow, and approved the recommendation without the limitation "to meet Treasury requirements" (Open Market, Vol. II, minutes of meeting; telegram, dated May 12, 1933, Board—signed Chester Morrill—to Harrison). Purchases were not made until after May 23, when Governor Black—appointed the week before to replace

amounts which dwarfed any earlier levels, attitudes changed. As an internal memorandum, dated December 13, 1935, and prepared at the New York Bank, put it: "It seems very probable that with excess reserves of such extraordinary dimensions there comes a point when further increases have no constructive effects."[14] The view, always held by many, that excess reserves were idle funds serving little economic function and reflecting simply absence of demand for loans or lack of supply of investments came to be accepted and taken for granted by almost all—albeit, of course, with minor qualifications expressed from time to time.

Given this interpretation, it seemed pointless to try to offset seasonal and other short-term movements. The excess reserves could and, as we shall see, did cushion their effects to a large extent. Similarly, variation in discount rates could not be expected to affect credit conditions. If the commercial banks were passive, ready and willing to make loans or purchase securities, and were being kept from doing so only by lack of demand, there was little to be gained by making it cheaper or more expensive for them to acquire still more reserves.

This interpretation also explains the reason the System engaged in no extensive purchases of government securities after November 1933. Why add to excess reserves, which were being so rapidly expanded by gold inflows and which served no current economic function? It does not explain why the System kept its security holdings constant. Certainly, after mid-1935, gold inflows were viewed as expanding excess reserves at too rapid a rate and as raising dangers of future inflation. The obvious reaction would be to sell government securities and thereby offset the gold inflow. At first, that measure was not taken because the System was unwilling to do anything that could be interpreted as contractionary at a

---

Eugene Meyer as governor of the Board—met with the executive committee of the Open Market Policy Conference. The New York view was that an increase in excess reserves was desirable at the time but not beyond an accumulation of $500 million (Open Market, Vol. II, minutes of executive committee meeting; Notes, Vol. III, May 15, July 6, 1933).

Early in Aug., when excess reserves had reached $550 million, the executive committee of the Conference proposed to discontinue purchases, and again in Sept. and Oct., when the excess was even larger. Purchases were nevertheless continued until Nov. 15, 1933—totaling $600 million—because of administration pressure. The committee had been warned, that cessation of purchases "might . . . precipitate immediate and definite inflation through the issue of greenbacks," on the insistence of Senator Thomas and others in Congress (Conversations, Vol. II, Sept. 16, 1933, conversation with Governor Black). Owen D. Young, however, saw no merit in increasing excess reserves beyond existing levels through open market purchases in preference to the issue of greenbacks—authorized to be issued up to $3 billion by the Thomas amendment to the Agricultural Adjustment Act of May 12, 1933 (Notes, Vol. III, Sept. 7, 1933).

[14] The memorandum, a revision of an earlier version, dated Sept. 19, 1935 (Notes, Vol. VI) and Oct. 22, 1935 (Open Market, Vol. III), was circulated to the members of the FOMC before its meeting on Dec. 17–18, 1935 (ibid.).

time when economic conditions were extremely depressed, when there were repeated threats of legislative measures that many officials within the System regarded as "greenbackism," when the System felt itself in a delicate position vis-à-vis both the administration and Congress, and when the Treasury with its Stabilization Fund was in a position to off-set any action the System might take. Later, those considerations were greatly reinforced by concern about earnings. As excess reserves mounted, sales of securities large enough to reduce reserves to levels regarded as appropriate would also have reduced the income of the Reserve Banks to negligible amounts. Governor Harrison was reported to have told his directors in September 1935 "he realized that central banks cannot give primary consideration to the question of earnings, but . . . he also realized that they must have some funds with which to stay in business."[15]

The result was that the System drifted into a policy of holding a rigid portfolio of government securities. It did not want to buy and felt it could not sell. Time and again, at meetings of the New York Bank's directors and of the Federal Open Market Committee, the desirability of achieving flexibility in the System's portfolio by selling some securities or letting some run off was stressed and agreed to by almost everyone present. The System felt itself in a straitjacket from which it urgently wished to be freed. Yet the considerations mentioned in the preceding paragraph re-peatedly inhibited such action. And, of course, the longer the portfolio was held constant, the stronger the inhibitions against selling, because the constant portfolio became a public symbol in which a change might be interpreted as signaling a major change in policy. It should be empha-sized that keeping the volume of securities constant from week to week, as securities matured and had to be replaced, was no easy task. We have described the System's policy as passive—and so it was if judged by the total volume of securities held—but it took unremitting and skilled ac-tivity to keep the total constant.

While the total was kept constant, the distribution among maturities altered from time to time. Much attention was devoted to the appro-

[15] Harrison, Notes, Vol. VI, Sept. 26, 1935. Listing of reasons for initial failure to sell government securities is based on: Office, Vol. IV, Oct. 16, 1935; Notes, Vol. V, memorandum, dated Mar. 15, 1934, another dated Mar. 16, 1935, on excess reserves; *ibid.*, minutes of directors' meetings, Jan. 24, Feb. 21, Mar. 7, 21, Sept. 26, Oct. 6, 1935; Open Market, Vol. III, minutes of meetings, Oct. 22–24, and memorandum, dated Dec. 13, 1935. Other reasons noted were the risk of starting a liquidation of government security holdings by banks and the public and the likelihood of Board disapproval of sales. Burgess apparently had some qualms because of the disastrous sequel to sales in Jan. 1933. He said, ". . . we had tried the idea of flexibility . . . in January 1933, and had made a mess of it" (Notes, Vol. IV, Mar. 8, 1934; also the same view in Notes, Vol. V, Jan. 24, 1935).

priate composition of the portfolio, and there was a persistent attempt to use changes in the composition of the portfolio to foster an "orderly market" in government securities. That objective increasingly came to the fore in the System's considerations in view of the growing importance of government securities, the large federal deficits requiring financing, and hence the growing concern of the Treasury with the bond market. Beginning in early 1935, much deliberate attention was directed toward the problem. The System uniformly agreed that it should not "rig" the market by pegging the prices of government securities; and nearly as uniformly that it should maintain an orderly market. But how to distinguish the one from the other and how to keep the one from degenerating into the other raised problems. Transactions to maintain an orderly market were of course conducted predominantly in New York, so it was the New York Bank that considered the distinction and its explicit formulation most fully. Harrison described the Bank's operating principle as "our . . . practice of putting bids in under the market just so that there would be no air pockets and no disorder," and as quite different from "putting a floor under it" or pegging.[16] As we shall see in Chapter 10, once the United States entered the war, there was a rapid transition from maintaining an orderly market to pegging the prices of government securities.

The 1936–37 increases in reserve requirements apparently had their origin in proposals made by the New York Bank. Beginning in early 1934, the Bank's staff prepared a series of internal memoranda, some circulated also to the Federal Open Market Committee, in which it examined the problem of excess reserves, emphasized potential dangers they raised, and considered alternative ways to control them. In the key memorandum (dated December 13, 1935, from which we have already quoted) it was concluded that open market operations would be an inefficient technique because of the size of the excess reserves, and that the discount rate would be inefficient because of the absence of borrowing. Hence, the appropriate tool was a change in reserve requirements, a discontinuous policy instrument poorly suited for continuous short-term adjustments but an appropriate means of immobilizing excess reserves and thereby establishing a situation in which the flexible instrument of open market operations could be used. Moreover, it was argued that accumulation of excess reserves was itself a consequence of a discontinuous

[16] Harrison, Conversations, Vol. III, Apr. 2, 1937; Office, Vol. V, memorandum, dated Mar. 16, 1938, Harrison to Burgess.

In addition to executing orders for the System account, the New York Bank continued to serve as the Treasury's agent in the government securities market. Harrison commented, ". . . the Treasury acts somewhat as a long-range investor, more or less always having funds to put into Government securities for various accounts, whereas the Open Market Committee acts as a market stabilizer" (Notes, Vol. VI, Feb. 4, 1937).

measure—the devaluation of the dollar. "Must we not," to quote the memorandum, "recognize that the devaluation of the dollar carried with it, as one of the necessary conditions of its successful operation, the need for a fundamental readjustment of reserve requirements?" Or, as Harrison put it to his directors, "the larger part of the existing excess reserves is the result of government actions, and correction by government action will be necessary before control will be back in central bank hands."[17]

In the December 1935 memorandum, the author recognized possible dangers in raising reserve requirements, and in taking that step too soon. It should not be taken "until production has returned to normal, or at least until the present trend toward a return to normal provides unmistakable evidence of continuing." The operating officials were usually less cautious. At an October 31, 1935, meeting with his directors, Harrison said that if he were a dictator, he would raise reserve requirements immediately by 25 per cent; a week later, he said he would raise them by 50 per cent in two steps.[18] The Federal Open Market Committee at a meeting on October 22 to 24, 1935, passed a resolution urging the desirability of reducing the volume of excess reserves preferably by raising reserve requirements. The resolution continued: "There are also risks incident to . . . raising reserve requirements. This method of control is new and untried and may possibly prove at this time to be an undue and restraining influence on the desirable further extension of bank credit." It included a recommendation that the Board of Governors make studies of the distribution of excess reserves and of the effects of a rise in requirements.[19]

Two months later, at the December 17–18, 1935, meeting of the Federal Open Market Committee, with the technical memorandum serving as one of the background documents, the matter again received extensive attention. A clear majority of the governors (the Federal Open Market Committee had not yet been reorganized in accordance with the Banking Act of 1935 and hence still consisted of the operating heads of all the Banks, who until March 1, 1936, retained the title governor) were in favor of action by the System to immobilize excess reserves but did not agree on the appropriate means. Some wanted to sell securities, others to

[17] The memorandum is in Harrison, Open Market, Vol. III; Harrison's remarks, in Notes, Vol. VI, Sept. 26, 1935; see also his remarks at the Sept. 19, 1935, meeting of directors. The dates of earlier memoranda on excess reserves are Mar. 15, 1934, and Mar. 6, 1935 (Harrison, Notes, Vol. V); Mar. 21, 1935 (Open Market, Vol. III); Sept. 19, 1935 (Notes, Vol. VI); Oct. 22, 1935 (Open Market, Vol. III); Nov. 7, 1935 (Notes, Vol. VI, and Special, no. 7).

[18] Harrison, Notes, Vol. VI. Interestingly enough, Owen D. Young, then chairman of the board of directors of the New York Bank, was opposed to an immediate rise in reserve requirements for what seems to us the correct reason: there was no point in taking such a step simply as a precautionary matter, with the danger that it might have adverse consequences; there would be ample time to take it when the need was clear (ibid., Nov. 7, 1935).

[19] Harrison, Open Market, Vol. III.

urge the Board to raise reserve requirements. The result was that an initial resolution urging the Board to raise reserve requirements was voted down, 7 to 5. Harrison then drafted a revised resolution making clear that some who voted for the resolution favored open market sales rather than a rise in reserve requirements but favored the latter rather than no action. The resolution was passed by a vote of 8 to 4.

William McChesney Martin, governor of the St. Louis Bank, summarized in a statement to the FOMC the views of those opposed to action at that time. "It is true," he said, "that the System having an excess reserve of $3,000,000,000 affords the possibility of a run-away condition, but we should not be fooled by considering a possibility as a probability . . . . [C]onditions at present do not offer signs of an immediate probability. In any action taken at the present time there is too great danger of discouraging efforts toward recovery . . . ."[20]

The detailed record makes clear that two factors other than those cited in the technical memorandum led Harrison and other governors to favor reserve requirement changes rather than open market operations. One, already mentioned, was the problem of earnings. The other, more subtle and less clearcut, was a consequence of the continuing conflict between the Banks and the Board. The Board alone had the power to change reserve requirements. Harrison envisaged the change as a once-for-all change which would not be reversed. Let reserve requirements rise to their legal limit, and the chief monetary power the Board alone could exercise would be immobilized along with the excess reserves. Open market operations—in which the Banks shared power with the Board— and discount rates—which the Banks established subject to Board review—would then resume their place as the continuing instruments of monetary policy.[21]

Technique aside, why seek to immobilize reserves at that time? Why not, in Martin's words, wait until the possibility became a probability? Granted that the proponents of the move did not expect the rise in reserve requirements to have any significant effect and hence viewed it as immediately harmless. Why not wait until the need was clearer? One reason was strictly political and accounts for any probable difference about timing between the author of the technical memorandum and Harrison. The Board was in process of reorganizing the System in accordance with

[20] Harrison, Open Market, Vol. III, statement, read by Governor Martin at Dec. 17, 1935, meeting.

[21] Harrison told a special meeting of his directors (Dec. 16, 1935) called to discuss excess reserves and Federal Reserve policy: "If we increase reserve requirements, we shall put the Reserve Banks in the position where they will have a chance to control the situation by open market operations and changes in discount rates. If we sell government securities first, we shall put whatever control is left in the hands of the Board of Governors which alone has power to increase or decrease reserve requirements" (Harrison, Notes, Vol. VI, Dec. 16, 1935).

the Banking Act of 1935. Harrison felt that if action was not taken at the end of 1935, it probably would not be taken for a full year—in his view, too long to wait.

The technical reasons for taking action were spelled out in the December 1935 memorandum. "At such a point [when further increases in excess reserves have no further constructive effects] excess reserves may contain possibilities of positive harm . . . [1] may give rise to disproportionate bank investment in government securities . . . [2] banks may acquire government and other bonds at prices which later may not be sustained . . . [3] with money so freely available, states, municipalities, and the national government, and other borrowers as well, may be tempted to over-borrow . . . [4] general fear which many people entertain that excess reserves of the present magnitude must sooner or later set in motion inflationary forces which, if not dealt with before they get strongly under way, may prove impossible to control . . . [5] the very fact of such inordinately large excess reserves may, by causing foreign expectation of favorable conditions for speculative investment, accentuate the gold inflow which is the real source of our problem."

In this list, the technical reasons we have numbered 1, 2, and 3 are inconsistent with the literal interpretation of excess reserves as idle funds accumulating because of the absence of desirable loans and investments; they clearly involve an effect of excess reserves on bank assets and hence on the rate of expansion of total bank credit. They are not, however, inconsistent with the actual somewhat mixed Reserve System interpretation which also included recognition, either implicitly as above or explicitly, that it was an oversimplification to regard excess reserves as idle funds having literally no effect. The listed reasons correctly reflect the almost exclusive preoccupation of the System with the "credit" effects of monetary policy as opposed to its effects on the stock of money. In all the discussion between 1930 and 1940 at the New York directors' meetings, as recorded in the Harrison Papers, we have noted only one explicit discussion of the quantity of money and its velocity as relevant to monetary policy—by Marriner Eccles, appointed governor of the Federal Reserve Board, November 1934, Black having resigned in August.[22] Otherwise, changes in the volume of demand deposits were sometimes referred to because of their relation to required reserves and as a reflection of changes in commercial bank credit; changes in currency in circulation were considered because of their effect on bank reserves and as a source of demand for Federal Reserve credit. There was no consideration—systematic or unsystematic—

[22] The discussion occurred in the course of a long meeting with the New York directors on the proposed Banking Act of 1935 (Harrison, Notes, Vol. V, Feb. 18, 1935). See also Chap. 7, footnote 93, above, and Chap. 11, sect. 3.

of the total stock of money as a magnitude that either was or should be controlled by the System, nor of changes in the stock as measuring the impact of the System. The System's role was seen exclusively in terms of conditions in the money market, i.e., the market for loans and investments.

Technical reason 5 is a most curious one, since it is precisely the reverse of the view repeatedly expressed during the climactic period from 1931 to 1933. Then the view had been that fear of inflation in the United States would lead foreigners to withdraw gold; now, that it would produce an inflow. A reconciliation is possible: whereas earlier foreign balances were mostly governmental and had to be held primarily in fixed dollar form, now the capital inflow was primarily private and either was channeled into equities or could be so channeled—though we have no evidence that that explanation was either true or believed to be true. More likely, the inconsistency simply reflects the fact that different people composed the System. The natural tendency to regard the System as one individual, holding consistent or at least connected views through time, is in the main correct. There does develop a System position which impresses itself on the members of the organization and which they come to accept and, of course, also to shape—almost without knowing it. But the explanation is not correct in every detail. The System's personnel had changed since 1933, and System philosophy was not all-pervasive.

Technical reason 4 is the only one publicly stated at the time in justifying the rise in reserve requirements in August 1936 and in March and May 1937. In the words of the 1937 *Annual Report,* "the Board's action was in the nature of a precautionary measure to prevent an uncontrollable expansion of credit in the future."[23] The Board contended at the time that the action was not a reversal of the System's easy-money policy. It made extensive studies before it took that action to assure itself that excess reserves were widely distributed geographically and among banks, so that most banks could satisfy the higher reserve requirements without mechanical difficulties. It denied then—and has continued to ever since—that the measure had any significant current influence.[24]

When the rise in reserve requirements was recommended by the FOMC at the end of 1935, and even when the first rise was imposed in August 1936, there was apparently no intention to exert a contractionary influence. By January 1937, when the two later rises were scheduled, the situation was somewhat different. In his briefing of the FOMC on January 26, 1937, Goldenweiser (who had been appointed its

[23] Board of Governors of the Federal Reserve System, *Annual Report,* 1937, p. 2.
[24] See Board of Governors of the Federal Reserve System, *Annual Report,* 1936, pp. 2, 14–15; 1937, p. 2; M. S. Eccles, *Beckoning Frontiers,* New York, Knopf, 1951, pp. 289–293; and E. A. Goldenweiser, *American Monetary Policy,* New York, McGraw-Hill, 1951, pp. 176–179.

economist while continuing to serve as the Board's director of research)
said: "the most effective time for action to prevent the development of
unsound and speculative conditions is in the early stages of such a
movement when the situation is still susceptible of ʾcontrol, and that, as
present indications were that such a time had arrived, as the technical
market situation is favorable for action at the present time, and as short-
term rates had been abnormally low in relation to long-term rates and
some stiffening of the former would be desirable, action to absorb excess
reserves should be taken at this time." John H. Williams (economic adviser to the New York Bank, 1933–52, and a vice-president, 1936–47,
and in 1937 associate economist of the FOMC) said of the business and
economic situation, "in certain respects it was going beyond a normal
state," and joined Goldenweiser in advocating a further rise in reserve
requirements.[25] In discussions at meetings of the New York Bank directors
in January 1937, Harrison made clear his awareness that a rise in reserve
requirements would have a tightening effect and his approval of such
an effect; most of the directors agreed.[26]

The desire to tighten in early 1937 is entirely understandable. Economic expansion had been proceeding irregularly for four years and
steadily for two; wholesale prices had risen nearly 50 per cent since March
1933; stock market prices had roughly doubled between 1935 and the end
of 1936. Harrison and others in the System felt strongly that, in the past,
the System had always been late in reacting; by their criterion of the
absolute level of interest rates, the money market was abnormally easy.

[25] Harrison, Open Market, Vol. IV, minutes of meeting, Jan. 26, 1937.
[26] Harrison, Notes, Vol. VI, Jan. 7,.14, 21, 28, 1937.
Clark Warburton has noted that the extensive studies of the Board regarding
the ability of banks to satisfy the higher reserve requirements (see footnote 24,
above) missed an important element in the impact, namely, the loss of reserves
by central reserve city banks as other banks drew on their correspondent balances
("Monetary Difficulties and the Structure of the Monetary System," *Journal of
Finance*, Dec. 1952, pp. 543–544). That element was discussed at a Jan. 1937
meeting of the New York Bank directors, but did not change Harrison's views.
G. W. Davison, a banker, who recommended using only half the remaining power
to raise reserve requirements, pointed out that "some of the central reserve and
reserve city banks would feel the shock of an increase in reserve requirements
'both ways'; in addition to having their own reserve requirements increased, they
would be subject to withdrawals of funds by out-of-town banks" (Harrison, Notes,
Vol. VI, Jan. 21, 1937). The Board had apparently been urged to make the increase in reserve requirements applicable only to central reserve and reserve city
banks. Country banks, it was suggested, would give up Federal Reserve membership if reserve requirements of state banking systems were substantially lower.
Goldenweiser argued, however, that reserve requirements were not an important
factor in a bank's decision regarding membership and, furthermore, country banks
"as a group had a large aggregate amount of excess reserves and excess balances
with correspondents and could easily meet the increased requirements" (Open
Market, Vol. IV, minutes of meeting, Jan. 26, 1937). He did not mention the
impact of the withdrawal of those balances on the central reserve city banks.

What rendered the action unfortunate in retrospect was, as we shall see, that the System failed to weigh the delayed effects of the rise in reserve requirements in August 1936, and employed too blunt an instrument too vigorously; this was followed by a failure to recognize promptly that the action had misfired and that a reversal of policy was called for. All those blunders were in considerable measure a consequence of the mistaken interpretation of excess reserves and their significance.

While the desire to take restrictive action in early 1937 is understandable, it is difficult to have much sympathy with the argument in the technical memorandum, and the explicit justification of its action by the Board: it was desirable to reduce excess reserves solely as "a precautionary measure to prevent an uncontrollable expansion of credit in the future." Even if the Board had been right in its opinion that the action taken would have no immediate effects, why, if no current effects were desired, take a step that could just as readily be taken when undesirable expansion of credit started to occur? What would make such future expansion "uncontrollable"? The Board's only argument was that excess reserves were larger than the System's total government security holdings, and that the increase in reserve requirements reduced excess reserves to a level below that total. Even if the comparison were relevant, a later increase in reserve requirements would have had the same effect. Harrison's earlier argument (see above) that the reorganization of the Board would force a delay was clearly a tenable reason for advance action. But by the time the Board acted, the reorganization was completed and that reason no longer had any substance.

Our conclusion, expressed above, is that the increase in reserve requirements did have important current effects. Comparison of the timing of the increases in requirements with the timing of the behavior of the money stock documents this conclusion in detail. The decision to impose the first rise in reserve requirements was announced in July 1936, and the rise was effective in August. In the next five months, from the end of July to the end of December 1936, the ratio of deposits to bank reserves declined sharply as banks sought to restore their excess reserve position. In consequence, although high-powered money grew by decidedly more in those five months than in the prior seven months, the stock of money grew by less than half as much.[27] The month-to-month figures are even more impressive. They show high rates of growth of the money stock in April, May, and June 1936, and a sharp drop in the rate of growth thereafter. The second rise in reserve requirements was announced on

[27] And even this understates the contrast, since most of the increase in high-powered money in the prior seven months came at the very end, and hence might have been expected to have delayed effects. The increase from June 1936 to July 1936 was six-sevenths of the increase from the end of Dec. 1935 to the end of July 1936.

January 30, 1937, and became effective in two steps, on March 1 and May 1. High-powered money was at the same time held roughly constant by Treasury sterilization of gold. The money stock reached an absolute peak in March and fell with only minor interruptions to the end of the year. The cyclical expansion reached its peak in May 1937.[28] The March and May rises in reserve requirements were also accompanied by a general rise in market yields. Treasury bills, longer-term governments, and many private bonds fell sharply in price and, as noted, the Federal Reserve was induced to engage in minor offsetting open market purchases.

Those minor open market operations were taken only after an extensive series of discussions, which revealed wide disagreement within the System, and partly in response to pressure from the Treasury. A meeting was called by the Board, after the March rise in reserve requirements and accompanying market disturbances, to consider whether to rescind the May rise or whether to offset the rises by purchases in the open market. Harrison and most of the other Bank presidents were opposed to any action. The System policy was to reduce excess reserves, they argued, and the flurry in the bond market was insufficient reason to alter the policy. The most that should be done, in their view, was to promote an orderly market but without pegging and without preventing a decline in the price of government securities which was on the whole desirable. Governor Eccles, almost alone among the members of the FOMC, took the opposite view. He favored large-scale purchases or rescinding of the final rise in reserve requirements. His position, as summarized in a memorandum by Williams, was that "there was no inconsistency in decreasing excess reserves by a large amount, through the relatively clumsy instrument of increasing reserve requirements, and then effecting a partial increase by the elastic and adjustable instrument of open market operations, in order to facilitate an orderly process of transition." And, of course, this is the technique the Reserve System has since come to adopt. The final compromise at the time, involving purchases of a moderate amount of securities, satisfied no one. It was acceded to by the majority, not only in deference to Eccles, but also partly because of the strong views expressed

[28] In a first draft of a memorandum, dated Jan. 27, 1938, dealing with the question, "Did the Raising of the Reserve Requirements Cause the Depression?", Williams analyzed the change in assets and liabilities of banks and reached a negative conclusion. Looking only at the absolute changes in demand deposits—which increased substantially from June 30, 1936, to Dec. 31, 1936, and declined only $300 million from Dec. 31, 1936, to June 30, 1937—and without reference to earlier changes, Williams arrived at his answer to the question. Apparently, he did not recognize that the significance of a given change might depend upon whether it represents a continuation or a radical departure from earlier trends. His emphasis throughout was on effects in the credit market. He mentioned changes in demand deposits only as evidence on the total earning assets of commercial banks (Harrison, Special, no. 22. The memorandum was prepared at the request of the FOMC).

by Secretary of the Treasury Morgenthau, who blamed the whole setback in the bond market on the increase in reserve requirements.[29]

Although the peak of the expansion is dated May 1937, and although the following contraction was one of the sharpest on record, it was apparently not until August or September that the technical staff of the System became seriously concerned about the state of business or began to suggest the desirability of expansionary action. At a September 11, 1937, FOMC meeting, Goldenweiser reported only that "there was a possibility that the uncertain situation . . . might lead to a decline in business and to a recession of indeterminable magnitude." Williams reported he was changing his mind: "there might be some recession." On the basis of these reports, the Committee decided to ask the Treasury to desterilize $200 or $300 million of gold and to direct the executive committee to purchase securities to meet seasonal needs.[30] As we have seen, the System purchased $38 million in November 1937, and then made no further changes in the total volume of securities until mid-1939.

Reserve requirements were not reduced until April 1938, some two months before the cyclical trough in June 1938, to a level that eliminated only one-quarter of the combined effect of the earlier rises. The action was taken by the Board despite opposition to it by Harrison. Reserve requirements remained unchanged at the new level until November 1, 1941.[31]

Despite the close connection in time between the reserve requirement changes, the money market disturbances, and the subsequent business contraction, Harrison and the other chief proponents of the increase in reserve requirements insisted there was no connection. They regarded assertions to the contrary by economic analysts outside the System as simply ill-informed and persistently opposed expansionary monetary policies to counter the contraction. At the September 11, 1937, FOMC meeting, Harrison "expressed himself as feeling that non-monetary measures were probably the ones to be used at this time since the adverse developments in business were of a non-monetary nature." To his directors, he pointed out in December that "most of the executives of the Reserve System do not believe that monetary action would afford relief in the present business situation, regardless of whether the causes of the recession are monetary or non-monetary but rather that it was felt that improvement

[29] Harrison, Conversations, Vol. III, memorandum, dated Apr. 14, 1937, Williams to Harrison; see also *ibid.*, Harrison's reports of conversations with Morgenthau, Eccles, and other Board members, Mar. 31, Apr. 2, 9, 14, 15, 16; another memorandum, dated Apr. 14, 1937, by Williams, and one, dated Apr. 23, 1937, by Allan Sproul; and Open Market, Vol. IV, minutes of executive committee meetings, Mar. 13, 22, and 23, and of FOMC, Apr. 3 and 4, 1937.

[30] Open Market, Vol. IV, minutes of meetings, Sept. 11 and 12, 1937.

[31] Open Market, Vol. IV, minutes of meeting, Apr. 29, 1938.

in the business situation would be more influenced by actions of the Administration."[32]

The irony is that Harrison's arguments against open market purchases at this juncture very nearly duplicated those he encountered when he urged open market purchases in 1930. He now upheld views that he then so vigorously opposed. The difference, of course, was that he was then on the offensive and was not burdened with a prior position inconsistent with purchases, whereas now he was on the defensive. For him to favor an expansion of excess reserves, when they were very large by standards he had earlier adopted, would have meant reversing a position he had espoused for years. His situation was in many respects precisely that of his opponents in 1930. His experience is a striking illustration of how difficult it is for anyone—whether in practical affairs, politics, industry, science, the arts—however able and disinterested, as Harrison was in unusual measure, to reverse a strongly held intellectual position.

In economic aspects, the years 1937–38 are strikingly reminiscent of 1920–21. On both occasions, in the course of a rapid rise in the money stock, the System took vigorous action with untried tools that produced a sharp retardation in the rate of growth of the stock, followed shortly by an absolute decline. On both occasions, the action was also accompanied by a pause in a rising tide of economic activity, followed by an exceptionally sharp but fairly brief decline. On both occasions, the System was slow to recognize the onset of contraction and, even after it did, refrained from reversing its policies for some time. On both occasions, it undertook significant expansionary action just two months before the cyclical trough, each time using the same tool it had used in its initial contractionary actions—in 1921, reducing discount rates, in 1938, reducing reserve requirements. On both occasions, it was strongly criticized for having produced or fostered a contraction, and on both it staunchly contended that the timing relation between the monetary actions and the contraction was purely coincidental and that nonmonetary factors were at fault.

The parallelism of the two periods is shown in Chart 43, which plots for both contractions the money stock, month-to-month changes in the stock, and the index of industrial production. The month of vigorous Federal Reserve restraining action in 1920 was clearly January, when discount rates were raised sharply. The counterpart in 1937 is less obvious. We have taken it to be January 1937, when the forthcoming rises in reserve requirements were announced, rather than either March or May, when they became effective. January 1937 was chosen on the grounds that the announcement gave banks an incentive to prepare for the forthcoming rises, even if not required to at once, just as the rise in discount rates in January 1920 gave banks an incentive to reduce their discounts,

[32] Notes, Vol. VII, Sept. 16, Dec. 9, 1937.

CHART 43
Money Stock, Change in Money Stock, and Industrial Production,
During Two Similar Episodes in Federal Reserve History:
1919–22 and 1936–39, Superimposed

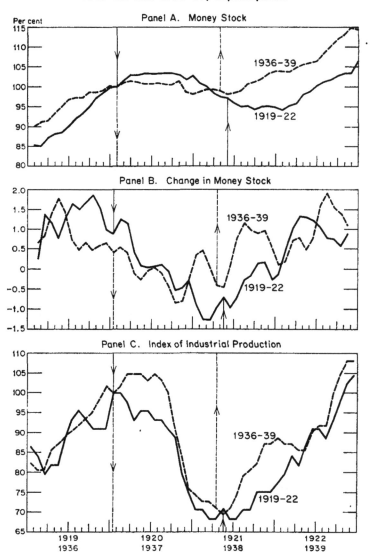

even if not required to at once. Accordingly, we have expressed the stock of money and industrial production as 100 in January 1920 for the earlier contraction and in January 1937 for the later, and have superimposed the two months in plotting the series. The month-to-month rates of change are expressed as percentages of the money stock in the base month of January 1920 or January 1937 and are smoothed by a three-term moving average (with weights of 1,2,1). The initial downward pointing arrows mark the months of vigorous restraining action, the later upward pointing arrows; the months of reversal of monetary action.

There is certainly an extraordinary resemblance between the curves in each pair. The major difference is that the money stock was rising at a faster rate in 1919 than it was in 1936, was carried further above 100 by its momentum, and subsequently fell further and for a longer time. That difference is not reflected in the index of industrial production but is reflected in wholesale prices, which rose more rapidly in 1919 than in 1936 and fell more after 1920 than after 1937—by about 45 per cent compared with 15 per cent. In the later contraction, the initial drop in the rate of change in the money stock reflects the August 1936 rise in reserve requirements.

The 1936–37 episode is also an instructive example of how technical defects in a monetary tool may greatly enhance mistakes in policy arising from erroneous analysis and thus play an independent role.[38] Had the power to vary reserve requirements not been available, the System could have sought to reduce excess reserves by the same amount through open market operations instead. It might at first be supposed that, given its analysis of excess reserves, it would have done that and would also thereby have produced the same deflationary effects, i.e., that the key defect was in the analysis, not in the particular instrument used to implement the analysis. However, even a rough calculation of the orders of magnitude involved shows this supposition to be wrong, even if we put entirely to one side the System's nearly complete abandonment of open market operations as a major instrument of monetary policy. The initial reserve requirement increase, effective in August 1936, reduced

[38] For a discussion of the defects of variable reserve requirements as a tool of monetary policy, see Milton Friedman, *A Program for Monetary Stability*, New York, Fordham University Press, 1960, pp. 45–50.

Notes to Chart 43.

NOTE: In Panels A and C, monthly data are expressed as percentages of the base month, Jan. 1920 or Jan. 1937—the months marking the onset of Federal Reserve pressure.

In Panel B, month-to-month changes in the money stock are expressed as percentages of the money stock in Jan. 1920 or Jan. 1937, and the percentages averaged by a weighted 3-term moving average (weights = 1,2,1).

The solid and dashed vertical lines pointing downward mark the month in each period of the onset of F.R. pressure; pointing upward, the month in each period of the start of F.R. easing measures.

SOURCE: Money stock, Table A-1, col 8. Index of industrial production, same as for Chart 16.

excess reserves by about $1.5 billion, and the second and third increases, effective in March and May 1937, reduced them by another $1.5 billion. On the System's analysis that the reserves were excess in the economic as well as legal sense, to achieve the same result through open market operations would have required sales of those amounts on the corresponding dates. The amounts were exceedingly large relative to other magnitudes of the time. The $3 billion involved in the three steps together ‘exceeded by one-fifth total holdings of government securities by the Federal Reserve System and amounted to nearly one-quarter of total high-powered money. Even if the System had had enough government securities in its portfolio, it is hardly conceivable that it would have sought to sell $1.5 billion of securities in the course of a few weeks and then only seven months later a further $1.5 billion in the course of two months. And even if it had begun, it would not have been committed to see the whole operation through as it virtually was, once a reserve requirement change was announced, and hence could have readily reversed course when the results became manifest. The tool used was, therefore, not simply the means whereby a defective policy was put into effect but also materially affected the outcome.

We have explained both the extreme passivity of the Federal Reserve System during the thirties and the one notable exception as resulting from its interpretation of excess reserves. But, to a large extent, this is a superficial explanation. Why was the System so ready to adopt that interpretation or, if it did, to let the interpretation condemn it to inactivity? Why, for example, did it ask the Treasury on several occasions to take actions that the System could equally well have taken?

First, the passivity reflected partly the natural tendency of individuals and, especially, official bodies to avoid responsibility for unfavorable occurrences by pleading limited power. The shattering of earlier high hopes made the tendency especially strong in the present instance. The belief that traditional instruments of monetary policy had been impotent in the decline of 1929–33—largely a rationalization of failure—strongly fostered their neglect in the later thirties.

Second, a passive policy was fostered also by the changing locus of power in the System and the changing personalities in positions of power that played such an important part in the System's performance during the contraction (see Chapter 7). In 1930, New York's commanding role in the System was reduced when the other Banks and the Board succeeded in limiting its freedom of action. The New Deal sealed the shift of power away from New York and concentrated it in Washington rather than in the other Banks. The dominant role of the Board was formalized by the Banking Act of 1935, and there were no subsequent developments to counteract the shift.

The transfer of power from a financial institution in the active financial center of the country to a political institution in the active political center fostered a shift in policy from the kind of continuous day-to-day concern with market activity, and continuous involvement in it, that is the mark of the active trader and participant in economic matters, to the discontinuous occasional pronouncement and enactment of legislation or rules, that is the mark of political activity. The difference was clearly foreshadowed in 1929 in the divergent opinions on how to deal with speculation. New York favored the quantitative impersonal technique of monetary restriction affecting directly the interests of operators in the market; Washington favored exhortation and administrative action on examination of each case by the lenders, which affected only at one remove the operators in the market. The difference, after the Board took over, is reflected more subtly in the virtual absence of continuous and day-to-day open market operations affecting the total volume of holdings, and in increased reliance on discontinuous instruments such as changes in reserve requirements and, above all, on public pronouncements.

Third, the preceding factors were reinforced by a change in the climate of intellectual and political opinion about economic matters. There developed a far readier acceptance of government intervention in the details of economic activity that fostered emphasis on such policy measures as margin requirements, bank examination and regulation, and control of security issues. More important from our point of view, emphasis shifted from monetary to fiscal measures. It was widely accepted that monetary measures had been found wanting in the twenties and the early thirties. The view that "money does not matter" became even more widely held, and intellectual study and analysis of monetary institutions and arrangements probably reached an all-time low in the study of economics as a whole. Emphasis shifted to fiscal measures, to influencing economic activity by government expenditure and taxation. Deficit spending, pump priming, and public works—not central bank policies—were widely regarded as the means to recovery. No wonder the Treasury became the active center of monetary policy as well.[34]

The Keynesian revolution in economic theory was a manifestation of that trend and helped to foster it. But certainly until 1937 and probably for some time thereafter, it played little role in the monetary developments we have described. Use of Keynesian ideas subsequently to promote "cheap-money" policies has led to the view that the Federal Reserve

[34] Harrison was critical of the Board's 1938 *Annual Report*, which stated, "Under existing conditions the Treasury's powers to influence member bank reserves outweigh those possessed by the Federal Reserve System" (p. 5). He said "he felt that the powers of the Board of Governors for credit control were belittled in the report which at the same time tended to over-emphasize the credit control powers of the Treasury" (Harrison, Notes, Vol. VII, Feb. 2, 1939).

System actively followed a cheap-money policy before 1937. We have seen that it did not. The Keynesian approach involved a shift of emphasis away from the "monetary" effects of monetary policy—that is, the effects on the stock of money—to the "credit" effects—that is, the effects on interest rates. The Federal Reserve System, as we have seen, had always emphasized interest rates and the use of credit, rather than the monetary effects. It did, however, make a different shift after 1937, from seeking to affect credit conditions indirectly through member bank reserves to seeking to affect them directly by operations in the government securities market involving changes in the composition of its portfolio.[35]

Marriner Eccles, who served as chairman of the Board of Governors (before 1936, governor of the Federal Reserve Board), November 1934 to April 1948, and as a member of the Board until July 1951, vividly documents some of these points in his memoirs. He stresses: (1) the Banking Act of 1935 and its importance in centering formal power in the Board—he regarded his shepherding of the act through the Congress as perhaps his major accomplishment and as comparable in importance to the establishment of the Federal Reserve System; (2) achievement of coordination in bank examination among the different regulatory agencies and adoption of an examination policy that would exert countercyclical influence; and (3) the importance of deficit spending for achieving recovery. He emphasizes that his support of deficit spending predated his acquaintance with Keynes' work, and that his policy position owed little to Keynes. He attributes the contraction of 1937–38 almost entirely to a change in the difference between government expenditures and receipts and ascribes little or no importance to the changes in reserve requirements and the stock of money.[36]

5. Changes in the Deposit-Reserve Ratio

Our view that the shorter-term movements in the deposit-reserve ratio require a different interpretation than the longer-term movements do

[35] For example, "This change [in open market policy] reflected a shift in emphasis in the use of open-market operations from their influence on member bank reserves to their direct influence on conditions in the capital market" (Board of Governors of the Federal Reserve System, *Annual Report*, 1939, p. 2).

[36] Eccles, *Beckoning Frontiers*, pp. 166–174; 202; 221–228; 266–268; 272–278; 130–132; 293–295; 309–320. Eccles claims (pp. 272–273) that it was upon his initiative that representatives of the Federal Deposit Insurance Corporation, the Comptroller of the Currency, and the Federal Reserve System were brought together to reach an agreement on a joint bank examination policy and ignores the impetus provided by the FDIC. He views the other agencies, as well as the Treasury Department and the state bank examiners, as obstructionist because they opposed Federal Reserve policies on examination procedures. The changes adopted in examination procedures did not in fact yield an examination policy that was countercyclical in influence, since the other supervisory agencies did not share the Federal Reserve view that the examination process should be subordinate to monetary policy (see Chap. 8, footnote 16).

was recorded above. The shorter-term movements are mostly temporary adaptations to short-term irregularities in high-powered money and deposits, reflecting, as it were, departures from the desired ratio which the banks tolerate, either because the irregularities are expected shortly to be reversed or because it takes time to adjust to unexpected changes. The inverse correlation between these irregularities in the deposit-reserve ratio and in high-powered money is an essential characteristic of the adjustment process. The long-term movements, on the other hand, represent mostly deliberate adaptation of the deposit-reserve ratio to a level desired by the banks in accordance with the interest rates at which they can lend and borrow and with the value they place on liquidity. That value, in its turn, depends on their confidence in their ability to raise cash at need from either the System or other banks. Such a deliberate adaptation by the banks does not occur instantaneously when there is a change in the desired level of the deposit-reserve ratio. Rather, it proceeds at a desired pace, just as an individual whose conception of the desirable pattern of his assets suddenly changes may take considerable time to readjust his portfolio. The observed inverse correlation between these longer-term movements in the deposit-reserve ratio and in high-powered money during the period under consideration is a coincidence, not an essential characteristic of the adjustment process, as the positive correlation in the twenties and again in the forties attests.

Two short-term irregularities require comment: (1) the sharp drop in the deposit-reserve ratio from January to March 1934, its mild rate of decline from March to July, and its rise from July to October; (2) the irregularities in early 1936.

The initial sharp drop in 1934, like the contemporaneous rise in high-powered money, is unprecedented in our series. There is no other two-month period since 1907, when our monthly data begin, that shows anything like so sharp a fall. The initial sharp drop seems quite clearly to reflect the large gold imports in February and March; the subsequent movements, the gradual adjustment of the banking system to that shock and the return to a desired position. Gold imports have two direct effects on the deposit-reserve ratio. First, gold raises bank deposits when it is deposited to the credit of the importer; second, it raises bank reserves when the recipient bank deposits at its Federal Reserve Bank the Treasury check it receives in payment for the gold, which it is legally required to turn over to the Treasury. The arithmetic effect of gold imports is, therefore, to raise the numerator and denominator of the deposit-reserve ratio by the same absolute amount. Since the ratio is greater than one, the numerator is raised by relatively less than the denominator and hence the ratio tends to decline. The increase in reserves encourages banks to expand. But that takes time, and the amount of time must surely depend on the size and unexpectedness of the change, and its temporal and geographic concentration.

In the 1934 instance, as we have noted, the change was unprecedentedly large and both temporally and geographically concentrated, the bulk of it occurring within the course of six weeks from January 31 to March 14 in New York City. Over the six-week period, high-powered money, affected as we have seen chiefly by changes in the gold stock and in Treasury cash holdings and deposits at Federal Reserve Banks, increased by $855 million and member bank deposits at Reserve Banks by $800 million or by 30 per cent.[37] We have weekly figures on deposits owned by the public and on their breakdown between banks in New York City and outside it only for weekly reporting member banks. In the same six-week period, deposits of all weekly reporting member banks at Reserve Banks increased $720 million and their net demand deposits $650 million. New York banks account for roughly 60 per cent of the increase both in deposits at Reserve Banks and in net demand deposits of all weekly reporting member banks, although they held initially only 46 per cent of net demand deposits and less than 40 per cent of deposits at Reserve Banks. Deposits of New York weekly reporting banks at Reserve Banks rose by 56 per cent in the course of the six-week period, and at a time of year when both deposits and reserves tend to fall seasonally. Little wonder that the first impact was on the deposit-reserve ratio, and that it took time for the banking system to adjust to the increase in reserves.

On this interpretation, the slow decline in the deposit-reserve ratio from March to July 1934 and the subsequent rise to October reflect primarily the adjustment by banks to the accession to their reserves; secondarily, the continued increase in high-powered money to July and then its rough constancy to October. This would imply an adjustment period of something like seven months, which seems not unreasonable. The level of the deposit-reserve ratio reached at the end of October was decidedly lower than the January level. However, if our interpretation is correct, the difference was not a passive reaction to the gold inflow, like the drop from January to March, but a continuation of the declining trend of 1933, representing a process of adjusting the deposit-reserve ratio to the level desired by banks.

A rough indication of the effect on the deposit-reserve ratio of the erratic movements in high-powered money can be obtained by a hypothetical calculation distributing the increment to the gold stock more evenly. The dotted line in Chart 44 is the result of such a calculation: the growth in high-powered money from January 1934 to March 1935 was assumed to have occurred by equal absolute amounts each month;

[37] Weekly figures for high-powered money were derived following the same procedures described in Table B-3 for the monthly figures.

CHART 44

**Deposit-Reserve Ratio, March 1933–December 1941, and
Hypothetical Ratio, Assuming Even Growth of High-Powered Money,
January 1934–March 1935 and February–June 1936**

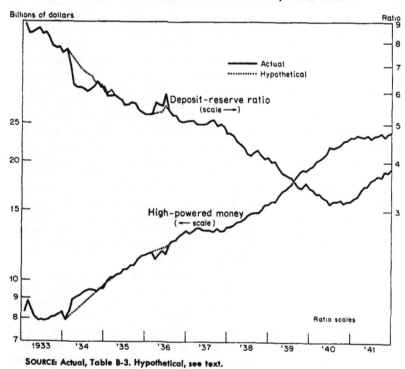

SOURCE: Actual, Table B-3. Hypothetical, see text.

the difference between actual high-powered money and this hypothetical stock was subtracted from both deposits and bank reserves. The dotted line is the ratio of the two resulting hypothetical figures. It will be seen that it produces a continuation of the 1933 trend in the deposit-reserve ratio and is fairly close to the actual ratio from October 1934 on. This dotted line is, on our interpretation, an estimate of the longer-run deposit-reserve ratio that banks were seeking to achieve.

The second short-term irregularity in the deposit-reserve ratio of sufficient size to merit attention occurred in the first half of 1936. We have already noted that the fluctuation in high-powered money of which that was a reflection arose largely from an unusual accumulation of and variation in Treasury deposits at Federal Reserve Banks. If we smooth that fluctuation by the procedure followed for 1934—substituting for actual high-powered money the values interpolated along a straight line between the actual February and July values—the result is that depicted by the dotted line in Chart 44. This computation eliminates the sharp rise in March, but not a noticeable peak in June. The latter reflects an unusual outflow of currency into circulation, as does the concurrent dip in the deposit-currency ratio (Chart 38), associated with the redemption during the latter half of June of adjusted service bonds in the amount of $800 million.[38]

The longer-term movements in the deposit-reserve ratio in Chart 44 readily lend themselves to interpretation in terms of our earlier analysis (Chapter 8, section 1). In May 1933, after the immediate readjustment to the banking panic, the deposit-reserve ratio began to move downward. If the dotted lines of Chart 44 are substituted for the actual to allow for the short-term perturbations just discussed, and if attention is concentrated on the period through June 1936, the decline appears to be proceeding at a steadily decreasing rate and the ratio to have reached a fairly steady level in early 1936. In July the first increase in reserve requirements was officially announced and, coincidentally, the deposit-reserve ratio resumed its downward course but at a very mild pace. Later reserve increases left no immediate impact on the ratio, which was fairly constant to August 1937, when it started declining at a pace roughly comparable to that after mid-1933, until it leveled off again in 1940.

In our view, that behavior is to be interpreted as the result of two successive shifts in the preferences of banks for reserve funds, and the adaptation of portfolio positions to the changed preferences. The first shift occurred as a result of the experience during 1929-33, and the adaptation took about three years, from 1933 to 1936. The second occurred as a result of the successive rises in reserve requirements, reinforced by the occurrence of a severe contraction that was a stern reminder of earlier experience. The adaptation to it took about the same length of time, from 1937 to 1940.[39] In both cases, the adaptations occurred in an environment of generally declining interest rates which, even with stable preferences, would have induced banks to hold larger reserves. The 1933-

[38] Under the terms of the Adjusted Compensation Act of Jan. 27, 1936, passed over Presidential veto, more than $1.5 billion in bonus nine-year interest-bearing bonds, convertible into cash at any time, was distributed on June 15 to World War I veterans.

[39] Phillip Cagan has analyzed the reserve ratio adjusted for requirement changes —in his terminology, the usable reserve ratio. By 1938, the usable ratio had returned to its 1936 level. He is doubtful that the banks desired to hold larger usable reserves than in 1936, but offers no alternative explanation for the rise in usable reserves from 1938 to 1940 (see his forthcoming monograph on the determinants and effects of changes in the U.S. money stock, a National Bureau study).

36 shift in preferences was one factor contributing to the sharp fall in the ratio of short-term to long-term rates; the reserve increases in their turn produced a temporary rise in short-term rates, as banks sought cash instead of secondary reserves in the form of short-term securities; and the 1937–40 shift in preferences contributed to a decline, even sharper after mid-1937 than from 1933 to 1936, in the ratio of rates on short-term U.S. securities to long-term rates. Throughout, the high level of the discount rate relative to market rates reinforced the banks' reluctance (bred of their 1929–33 experience) to rely on borrowing from the Federal Reserve Banks for liquidity and led them instead to rely on cash reserves in excess of legal requirements and on short-term securities.[40]

This interpretation dates the second shift in preferences as occurring at the end of 1936 or early in 1937. In terms of the numerical behavior of the deposit-reserve ratio itself, as recorded in Chart 44, the second shift in preferences could as readily be dated as occurring at the end of 1937 or in mid-1938. If it were, it would have to be interpreted as a reaction to the 1937–38 contraction and as unrelated to the reserve re-

[40] The rise in reserve requirements in 1936 and 1937 was accompanied by a reduction in total holdings of government securities by member banks. The reduction was concentrated in bills and notes, which the banks largely replaced by deposits at the Reserve Banks. As a result, member bank holdings of government bonds rose from 45 per cent of their total holdings of government securities in 1936 to 74 per cent in 1941. The yield on 9-month Treasury bills rose from about 0.1 per cent per annum in Nov. 1936 to over 0.7 per cent on May 1, 1937, when the final rise in reserve requirements became effective, as a result of the pressure to convert from bills to cash. After the pressure subsided, banks presumably sought again to acquire bills. But the supply outside the Federal Reserve was so small that their attempt served only to reduce yields on bills to a level so close to zero—much of the time less than 0.01 per cent per annum—as to induce banks to hold cash or notes instead. Indeed, yields on Treasury bills were occasionally negative in 1940, when their price was bid up by purchasers seeking to convert cash into other assets for short periods to reduce tax liability under personal property tax laws.

At a directors' meeting of the New York Bank on Aug. 26, 1937, when the discount rate was reduced from 1½ to 1 per cent, effective the next day, Harrison reported a discussion he had had with commercial bankers, the upshot of which was agreement "that it would be better to borrow at the Federal Reserve Bank than to sell securities" if additional reserves were needed. He was interrupted by G. W. Davison, a banker, who said he "was shocked by Mr. Harrison's resumé of the views of the New York bankers because it differed so materially from his own impressions gained from contacts with certain of the bankers." Davison said bankers preferred to dispose of their holdings of bankers' acceptances and Treasury bills rather than borrow at the Reserve Bank. He had argued with the bankers that the Reserve System would not change reserve requirements every day, that they "certainly don't want the Federal Reserve to buy more Governments, and don't want the Treasury to abandon sterilization of gold, and that, consequently, borrowing at the Federal Reserve Bank was the logical way to supply needed reserves for seasonal requirements." Harrison's reply was that "if the banks want to see a return to normal banking relationships he couldn't understand why they were reluctant to conduct their affairs in such a way that borrowing at the Federal Reserve would ensue" (Harrison, Notes, Vol. VII, Aug. 26, 1937).

quirement increase. The rough constancy from late 1936 to August 1937 would have to be interpreted as the final stage of adjustment to the earlier shift in preferences. The main reason we reject this alternative interpretation is that it does not allow for the effects of the gold-sterilization program of the Treasury, which kept high-powered money roughly constant from December 1936 to late 1937. Just as the unusually rapid increase in high-powered money in early 1934 temporarily lowered the deposit-reserve ratio, with adaptation to the decline taking some seven months, the sterilization program must have had the opposite effect in 1937.

Suppose bank preferences had not been affected by the reserve changes. The abrupt cessation—as a result of gold sterilization—of a rise in high-powered money that had been proceeding for over three years would have produced a temporary bulge in the deposit-reserve ratio and a later return to the desired level. Given about the same seven-month adjustment time required in 1934, the temporary bulge would not have disappeared until about June or July of 1938, some seven months after high-powered money resumed its rise. The deposit-reserve ratio shows no such absolute bulge but it does show a flattening in 1937, such as would have been produced by the superposition of a temporary bulge lasting until mid-1938 on a declining longer-run desired level. The peak discrepancy between the bulge and the hypothetical desired level came in August 1937, when the amount of "inactive gold" in the Treasury balance reached its maximum.

Although we explain the behavior of the deposit-reserve ratio from 1937 to 1940 as an adaptation by banks to changed preferences resulting primarily from the increase in reserve requirements, and as reflecting the impact of gold sterilization, we do not exclude an effect due to the 1937–38 contraction. It must have been an additional factor inducing banks to prefer a lower deposit-reserve ratio.

If, as we argue, banks were primarily concerned about reserves in excess of legal requirements, the reduction in reserve requirements in April 1938 should have satisfied some of their desire for liquidity. But that change leaves no clear impress on the recorded deposit-reserve ratio. It is tempting to extrapolate the trend of the deposit-reserve ratio before July 1938 forward, and after September 1938 backward, and interpret the difference as a delayed reaction to the reduction in reserve requirements. But this is reading more into the data than can be justified without a much more detailed study than we have made.

The deposit-reserve ratio reached a trough in 1940 and thereafter began to rise, a rise that continued through 1946, though at a much milder pace from mid-1943 on than from 1940 to 1943. The rise from early 1942, when the Federal Reserve System officially began supporting the yield on bills and, in effect, on other government securities as well (see below, Chapter 10), raises no problem of interpretation. With fixed prices guaranteed by the Reserve System, government securities were the equivalent of cash and yielded some return, leaving no reason to hold reserves in excess of requirements for liquidity purposes. Hence "excess reserves" quickly fell to a low level which remained relatively stable.

The more interesting question is why the ratio rose from 1940 to 1942. If the 1940 level represented the attainment of a desired liquidity position, what produced the rise after 1940? One factor was doubtless the sharp change in the behavior of high-powered money. From rapid growth, it rather suddenly shifted in early 1941 to rough constancy, as a result of a sharp decline in gold imports. This constituted another short-term irregularity which banks might be expected initially to absorb and then react to only after a considerable lag. However, we are inclined to doubt that the adaptation by banks to that irregularity can account for the whole rise in the deposit-reserve ratio, since this explanation would mean that there had been essentially no adjustment at all for the whole year 1941, whereas the earlier evidence suggests a lag of about seven months.[41]

A second contributing factor might have been a rise in yields on alternative investments, which would make it more expensive to hold cash and thus induce banks to hold relatively less, even with given preferences for liquidity. However, the behavior of interest rates contradicts this view. Rates on private obligations, including commercial loans by banks, remained roughly stable from 1940 to early 1942; the yield on long-term governments fell slightly; the only rates that rose were on Treasury bills, so there was a narrowing of the spread between long-term and short-term government securities (see Table 22). But the narrowing of the spread suggests that the rise in short-term rates was a consequence of a decreased preference for liquidity rather than of a movement along an unchanged liquidity preference schedule. Just as the earlier shift in preferences of banks toward a desire for greater liquidity produced a widening in the spread, a shift in the opposite direction might be expected to produce a narrowing of the spread.

Hence, we are inclined to believe that the rise in the deposit-reserve ratio from 1940 to early 1942 reflected in part a shift in the preferences of banks in the opposite direction from the shifts in 1933 and 1937. We have already suggested why such a shift seems reasonable. The accumulation of experience under FDIC and a seven-year period without serious banking difficulties might well promote a reversal of the drive for liquidity that arose from the 1929–33 experience. A similar though less drastic sequence had followed earlier and less severe banking panics.

[41] The same percentage growth in high-powered money from Dec. 1940 to Dec. 1941 as from Dec. 1939 to Dec. 1940 would have added $4.5 billion to high-powered money. If this sum is added to both deposits and bank reserves in Dec. 1941, it yields a hypothetical deposit-reserve ratio almost identical with the actual ratio in Dec. 1940.

TABLE 22

AVERAGE RATES OR YIELDS ON SELECTED ASSETS, JUNE 1940–MARCH 1942

	Prime Commercial Paper, 4- to 6-Month		90-Day Bankers' Acceptances	Business Loans of Commercial Banks, 79 Cities		Basic Yield of 40- to 50-Year Corporate Bonds	U.S. Bonds Not Due or Callable for 12 Years or More	3-Month Treasury Bills	(7) − (8)
	NBER	FRB		Shifting Weights	Constant Weights				
	(1)	(2)	(3)	(4)	(5)	(6)	(7)	(8)	(9)
June 1940	0.81	0.56	0.44	2.59	1.9	2.68	2.39	0.071	2.319
June 1941	0.69	0.56	0.44	2.55	2.1	2.65	1.91	0.089	1.821
Mar. 1942	0.69	0.63	0.44	2.48	2.0	2.65	2.00	0.212	1.788

SOURCE, BY COLUMN

(1) Same source as for Chart 35.

(2–4, 7–8) Banking and Monetary Statistics, pp. 451, 460, 464; Federal Reserve Bulletin, Aug. 1942, p. 825. In col. 4 the rates charged are weighted according to the dollar volume of new loans made at each rate.

(5) FRB, Mar. 1949, p. 231. The rates charged in 4 size groups of loans are weighted according to the loans outstanding in each group on Nov. 20, 1946.

(6) Straight-line interpolation between annual (Feb.) figures in Historical Statistics, 1949, p. 279.

This analysis of the behavior of the deposit-reserve ratio yields, as a by-product, estimates of the reaction time of the banking system, of interest in their own right, especially for analysis of lags in the response to monetary policy measures taken by the Reserve System. We have suggested that it takes some seven months for banks to adjust to an unanticipated discrepancy between their actual and desired reserve positions produced by a change in their actual position, and some three years for banks to carry through a thoroughgoing revision of their actual reserve position as a result of a change in the desired position.

6. *Role of Monetary Factors in the 1937 Contraction and Subsequent Recovery*

The preceding sections have analyzed the factors accounting for the behavior of the money stock in the period 1933–41. Before we leave that period, a few explicit comments on the effect of the changes in the money stock on economic activity are in order. Extensive controversy has arisen about this issue, particularly about the 1937 contraction. Because the final increases in reserve requirements preceded the cyclical peak in May by such a short interval, many commentators have regarded them as partly or wholly responsible for the subsequent contraction. On the other hand, the Federal Reserve System has argued that those changes could not have had such an effect since they only absorbed excess reserves. Further, the much greater importance attributed by economic analysts, during the 1930's and ever since, to government fiscal operations than to monetary changes has led students to attach more importance to the contemporaneous shift in the government's budget from a deficit toward a surplus than to monetary policy measures. In his recent exhaustive study of that episode, Kenneth Roose concludes:

> In broad outline, the causation may be reduced to a relatively few important elements . . . . [N]et government contribution to income was drastically reduced in January 1937 . . . .
> [A]t the same time . . . the Federal Reserve action on excess reserves caused short-term governments to weaken and set up thereby a chain of reactions which resulted in increased costs of capital and the weakening of the securities markets to which business expectations are very sensitive, especially in the United States. The operation of the undistributed profits tax, in addition to its effects on business expectations, also reduced the cash position of even the large companies. The imperfect supply of capital funds and their increased cost made it more difficult for borrowers to obtain capital. Most important of all, however, was the reduced profitability of investment, beginning in the first quarter of 1937. This resulted from the increased costs, in which labor costs played a prominent part . . . . [T]he immediate decline in profit ratio, accompanied by the prospect of sharp declines in future profits, is adequate reason for the occurrence and timing of the recession.[42]

[42] Roose, *Economics of Recession*, pp. 238–239.

It is symptomatic of the change in intellectual outlook of which we have spoken that this judicious, eclectic statement should stress solely the "credit" aspects of monetary action and omit entirely the "monetary" aspects. Precisely the same is true of a draft of a memorandum prepared at the New York Federal Reserve Bank by John H. Williams in answer to the question whether the reserve requirement changes caused the 1937–38 depression. Williams emphasized essentially the same factors as Roose, except that he gave even less weight to Federal Reserve action on the grounds, first, that up to June 1937, "there was no contraction of bank deposits or bank assets," and, second, "if the action on reserve requirements was in any degree responsible for the business recession, it was because of its effect on interest rates," yet "at the end of the fiscal year 1937 money rates were but little changed from the rates existing at the beginning, and were throughout the year . . . at abnormally low levels."[43]

Consideration of the effects of monetary policy on the stock of money certainly strengthens the case for attributing an important role to monetary changes as a factor that significantly intensified the severity of the decline and also probably caused it to occur earlier than otherwise. As we have seen, the money stock grew at a rapid rate in the three successive years from June 1933 to June 1936—at continuous annual rates of 9.5 per cent, 14.0 per cent, and 13.0 per cent. The rapid rise was a consequence of the gold inflow produced by the revaluation of gold plus the flight of capital to the United States. It was in no way a consequence of the contemporaneous business expansion: the only way the expansion could significantly have increased the money stock would have been by inducing banks to hold smaller reserves, yet they were in fact doing the opposite. And the rapid rate of rise in the money stock certainly promoted and facilitated the concurrent economic expansion.

The combined impact of the rise in reserve requirements and—no less important—the Treasury gold-sterilization program first sharply reduced the rate of increase in the money stock and then converted it into a decline. From June 1936 to June 1937, the money stock grew at the continuous annual rate of 4.2 per cent per year and then in the following year fell at the rate of 2.4 per cent. The absolute peak in the money stock came in March 1937; the trough in May 1938, though December 1937 was almost as low.[44] The cyclical peak is dated in May 1937; the cyclical trough, in June 1938. As we have seen, neither the retardation in the rate of rise in the money stock nor the subsequent decline in the money stock

---

[43] Harrison, Special, no. 22, draft of memorandum, dated Jan. 27, 1938.

[44] If we measure the changes from June 1936 to the peak in the money stock in Mar. 1937 and then to the subsequent trough in May 1938, the resultant continuous annual rates of change are +6.3 and −2.9 per cent.

—any more than the preceding rapid rise—can be attributed to the contemporaneous course of business; they were produced by deliberate policy measures that offset the expansionary influence of the continuing gold inflow. The sharp retardation in the rate of growth of the money stock must surely have been a factor curbing expansion, and the absolute decline, a factor intensifying contraction. Though the decline may not seem large in absolute amount, it was the third largest cyclical decline recorded in our figures, exceeded only by the 1920–21 and 1929–33 declines.

Recovery came after the money stock had started to rise. It rose at continuous annual rates of 7.8, 13.1, and 12.1 per cent in the three years from June 1938 to June 1941, once again mostly as a result of the continued inflow of gold, and despite a continued decline in the deposit-reserve ratio to 1940 as an aftermath of the increases in reserve requirements. Munich and the outbreak of war in Europe were the main factors determining the U.S. money stock in those years, as Hitler and the gold miners had been in 1934 to 1936. Doubtless, other factors helped to account for the onset of recovery and for its pace, but the rapid increase in the money stock certainly at the very least facilitated their operation.

The rates of growth of the money stock during the periods of expansion from 1933 to 1936 and from 1938 to 1941 were unusually high and make more credible than otherwise widespread concern with dangers of inflation in the midst of large-scale unemployment. Yet, they were so high chiefly because of the unprecedented magnitude of the preceding decline. Averaged over the dozen years from 1929 to 1941, the rate of growth of the money stock was less than 2½ per cent per year and of real output less than 2 per cent per year—both well below the long-time average U.S. experience. In 1941, Kuznets' implicit price index was 13 per cent below its 1929 level, and even wholesale prices were some 8 per cent below their 1929 level, despite a rise of over 10 per cent from 1940 to 1941 alone under the impact of the first stage of the wartime boom. How different the history of that fateful dozen years might have been if the money stock had grown steadily at its average rate of 2½ per cent per year, let alone at the higher long-term historical rate, instead of first falling by one-third from 1929 to 1933 and then doubling from 1933 to 1941.

CHAPTER 3

World War II Inflation, September 1939–August 1948

THE OUTBREAK of war in Europe in September 1939 ushered in a period of inflation comparable to the inflations which accompanied the Civil War and World War I, though more protracted than either. By the postwar price peak nine years later (August 1948), wholesale prices had more than doubled, the implicit price deflator had somewhat less than doubled, the stock of money had nearly tripled, and money income had multiplied more than two-and-a-half-fold (see Chart 45). As this comparison indicates, velocity on net fell over the period. After an initial rise to 1942, it fell sharply to 1946 and then rose mildly to 1948. According to annual data, wholesale prices rose at the average rate of 8.2 per cent per year; the implicit price deflator, 6.5 per cent per year; the stock of money, 12.3 per cent per year; money income, 10.7 per cent per year; real income, 4.2 per cent per year; and velocity fell at the average rate of 1.7 per cent per year.[1] Substantial though these rates of change are, the rate of rise in the money stock was slightly lower than in World War I and about half the rate in the Civil War; the rate of rise in prices was less than three-fifths the rate in World War I and only one-third that in the Civil War.[2]

As in World War I, wholesale prices jumped on the outbreak of war, then stayed roughly constant for about a year before resuming their

[1] Paralleling World War I figures, our income figures for 1942–45 are modifications of Kuznets' estimates on the basis of Kendrick's "national security version" of net national product (see Chap. 5, footnote 16).

[2] For prices and money stock, the comparison between the three wars is as follows:

	World War II	World War I	Civil War
Start of war	Sept. 1939–[a]	July 1914–[b]	April 1861–
Price peak	Aug. 1948	May 1920	Jan. 1865
	RATE OF RISE, PER CENT PER YEAR		
Money stock	12.1	12.9	24.0[c]
Wholesale prices	8.7	15.3	24.5

[a] Measured from Aug. 1939, see Table 23.

[b] Measured from June 1914, see Table 16.

[c] From June 1861 through fiscal year ending June 1865. Data for those years are from Milton Friedman, "Price, Income, and Monetary Changes in Three Wartime Periods," *American Economic Review*, May 1952, p. 624.

These figures for World War II differ from those given in the text, because they are derived from monthly rather than annual data.

CHART 45
Money Stock, Income, Prices, and Velocity, and Industrial Production, in Reference Cycle Expansions and Contractions, 1939–48

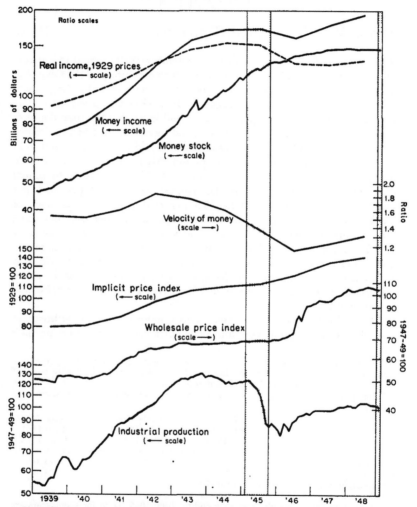

NOTE: Shaded areas represent business contractions; unshaded areas, business expansions.
SOURCE: Industrial production, same as for Chart 16. Other data, same as for Chart 62.

upward movement. As in World War I also, prices rose more rapidly before and after involvement than during the United States' active participation in the war, at least as judged from the available indexes. Again as in World War I, the sources of the rise in the stock of money were quite different in the three periods just distinguished: the period of U.S. neutrality, the period of our active participation in the war, and the postwar period. Table 23 records the changes in prices and the stock of money during those periods and the factors accounting for the changes in the stock of money.

1. U.S. Neutrality, September 1939–November 1941

Politically, the period of U.S. neutrality was clearly demarcated. Economically, it was not. During its early months—the so-called "phony war" period—the war had little impact on the U.S. economy. After a brief speculative movement in the final quarter of 1939, production, employment, and personal income in general declined until May 1940. The Nazi attack on the Low Countries and the subsequent fall of France brought a dramatic reversal. Britain and her remaining allies started placing large-scale orders for war material in the United States. As we saw earlier, there was a sharp increase in mid-1940 in the rate of flow of gold to the United States, as gold was shipped to pay for war material. The United States simultaneously embarked on a greatly expanded defense program. Those developments spurred a rapid expansion in industrial production, employment, and personal income. Because of the large absolute amount of unemployment and unused industrial capacity, wholesale prices at first remained stable, starting to rise only in the fall of 1940. Economically, therefore, the beginning of the war for the United States as a neutral might better be dated in the month when its effects first began to be felt—say, May 1940.

To mark the close of that phase and the active involvement of the United States in the war, the month when lend-lease began, March 1941, is probably a better date than early December when war was declared against Germany and Japan. Before lend-lease, Britain paid for war purchases by transferring over $2 billion in gold, drawing down British dollar balances by $235 million, and selling $335 million in U.S. securities —the last two requisitioned in large part by the British government from British subjects.[3] Thereafter, the U.S. government paid for much of the war material, nominally in return for services rendered in exchange to the United States. Lend-lease, under which some $50 billion was spent by the end of the war, was the counterpart in World War II of U.S.

[3] See *International Transactions of the United States During the War, 1940–1945*, Economic Series No. 65, Office of Business Economics, Dept. of Commerce, 1948, pp. 112–115. The figures cited cover the period Sept. 1939–Dec. 1940.

TABLE 23

CHANGES IN PRICES AND IN STOCK OF MONEY, AND SOURCE OF CHANGES IN STOCK OF MONEY, DURING THREE SEGMENTS OF THE PERIOD AUGUST 1939–AUGUST 1948

	U.S. Neutrality Aug. 1939 Through Nov. 1941	War or Wartime Deficits		To Postwar Price Peak		Period as a Whole Aug. 1939 Through Aug. 1948
		Nov. 1941 Through Aug. 1945	Nov. 1941 Through Jan. 1946	Aug. 1945 Through Aug. 1948	Jan. 1946 Through Aug. 1948	
Number of months	27	45	50	36	31	108
Percentage change in:						
1. Wholesale prices	23	14	16	55	53	118
2. Stock of money	29	102	107	14	11	197
3. High-powered money	29	80	83	7	5	149
Per cent change per year in:						
4. Wholesale prices	9	4	4	15	16	9
5. Stock of money	11	19	18	4	4	12
6. High-powered money	11	16	15	2	2	10
Fraction of change in stock of money (total change = 1.00) attributable to change in:						
7. High-powered money	0.99	0.84	0.83	0.53	0.49	0.84
8. Ratio of commercial bank deposits to vault cash plus deposits at Federal Reserve Banks	0.16	0.39	0.38	0.01	−0.02	0.31
9. Ratio of commercial bank deposits to currency held by the public	−0.15	−0.15	−0.14	0.46	0.52	−0.09
10. Interaction of ratios	−0.01	−0.07	−0.07	0	0	−0.05

SEGMENT

Fraction of change in high-powered money (total change = 1.00) consisting of change in:

11. Monetary gold stock	1.15	−0.14	−0.14	1.15	1.58	0.26
12. F.R. claims on the public and banks	0.02	0.04	0.03	0	0.03	0.03
13. Other physical assets and fiat of monetary authorities	−0.17	1.10	1.11	−0.15	−0.61	0.71

NOTE: Because of rounding, components may not always add to 1.00.

SOURCE, BY LINE

1, 4. Continuation of Historical Statistics, pp. 47, 78.

2–3, 5–13. Same as for corresponding lines of Table 10, except that original data for lines 11–12 from 1942 on are from Federal Reserve Bulletin. Result in lines 11–13 is the same whether or not the gold stock is adjusted approximately to cost by subtracting the cumulated devaluation profit.

loans to its allies in World War I. Within a month after the enactment of lend-lease, the rapid rise in the gold stock that began in 1938 and accelerated after the fall of France came to an end.

Whichever pair of dates is used—whether August 1939, just before the outbreak of war in Europe, through November 1941, just before Pearl Harbor (the dates used in Table 23) or those just suggested of May 1940 through March 1941—the growth of the money stock during the period of U.S. neutrality was attributable entirely to the concomitant growth of the gold stock (see Table 23, lines 7 and 11, for the first pair of dates). The gold stock played the same role between those dates as it did during the period of neutrality in World War I, when about 80 per cent of the increase in the stock of money was attributable to the increase in the gold stock. During the neutrality period in World War II, the stock of money grew by 29 per cent, high-powered money by the same percentage, and the increase in high-powered money was less than in the gold stock, the difference being absorbed by a decline in the sum of Federal Reserve Bank private claims and the fiat of the monetary authorities.

A rise in the ratio of commercial bank deposits to reserves, as banks reduced their excess reserves, tended to increase the money stock but was about offset by a concomitant decline in the ratio of deposits to currency (Chart 46 and Table 23). These deposit ratios were to continue to move in opposite directions throughout the war, just as they had during most of World War I.

In the World War I neutrality period, the Federal Reserve System had been powerless to offset the effects of the gold inflow, since it possessed no earning assets to sell. In the World War II period, the Federal Reserve was in a much stronger technical position. It had a portfolio of over $2 billion of government securities which it could have sold at will. True, even the sale of its whole portfolio would have offset less than half the gold inflow from August 1939 to November 1941. However, the Treasury could have offset the rest—or indeed the whole or more than the whole—of the gold inflow by sterilization operations like those it had conducted in late 1936 and early 1937, when it sold securities and used the proceeds to pay for gold rather than printing gold certificates to do so. Between them, therefore, the Treasury and the Federal Reserve were technically in a position to control the changes in high-powered money (see Chart 47 for the breakdown of high-powered money, by assets and liabilities of the monetary authorities).

The behavior of prices gave reason to be concerned with the growth of the money stock. From August 1939 to November 1941, wholesale prices rose 23 per cent, or at the rate of 9 per cent per year and, as we have seen, nearly the whole of the increase occurred in the final fifteen months of

CHART 46
The Stock of Money and Its Proximate Determinants, Monthly,
August 1939–August 1948

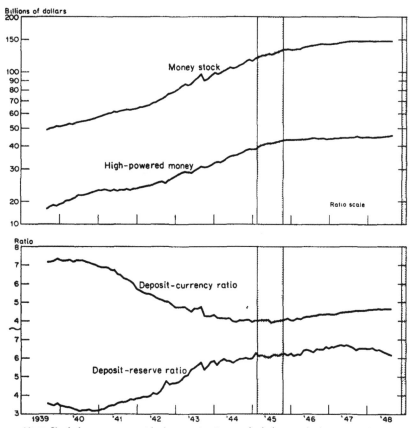

NOTE: Shaded areas represent business contractions; unshaded areas, business expansions.
SOURCE: Tables A-1 (col. 8) and B-3.

the period, when wholesale prices rose nearly 20 per cent and the stock of money over 16 per cent. Yet, as is clear from Chart 49, below, the Federal Reserve engaged in no extensive open market operations. In the three weeks after the outbreak of war in September 1939, it purchased some $400 million of government securities to offset a sharp drop in the prices of U.S. government bonds.[4] These were sold off in the next few

[4] These operations were regarded by the Board as a departure from past practice,

months so that, by the turn of the year, the System's holdings of government securities were at their prewar level. Further sales of about $300 million were made from June to December 1940; thereafter, the System's holdings of government securities were kept rigid until the United States entered the war. The System thus largely continued the policy with respect to open market operations and gold inflows that it had followed since 1933.

During the period of neutrality, the Treasury, like the Reserve System, undertook no operations to offset the gold inflow. Its weekly balances in cash and Federal Reserve deposits fluctuated considerably, from a minimum of about $2.4 billion to a maximum of about $3.4 billion. The billion-dollar range was nearly half again as wide as the range in Federal Reserve credit outstanding, so that Treasury operations were a more important factor affecting the money stock than Federal Reserve open market operations. But the fluctuations in Treasury balances were not undertaken for reasons of monetary policy and show no systematic connection with monetary factors. They were simply a largely unintended result of fluctuations in expenditures and tax receipts and of the flotation and retirement of securities.

In response to the rapid rise in prices and the stock of money, the Federal Reserve took two actions in addition to the open market sales in the latter half of 1940. Both were taken near the end of the period of neutrality and both, in line with the general policy of the thirties, involved use of new instruments of control.

On September 1, 1941, under authority of the President's executive order of August 9, 1941, the Board imposed controls on consumer credit, prescribing in Regulation W minimum down payments and maximum maturities applicable to consumer credit extended through instalment sales of certain listed articles. Because consumer durable goods shortly

---

since their object was not to affect the volume of member bank reserves and indebtedness. The operations were justified on two grounds: (1) their influence directly on the prices and yields of government obligations and indirectly on the prices and yields of corporate bonds, and hence on general economic recovery; (2) the importance of safeguarding the enlarged member bank portfolio of government securities from "unnecessarily wide and violent fluctuations in price" (Board of Governors of the Federal Reserve System, *Annual Report*, 1939, pp. 5–6). The first reference to maintaining "orderly market conditions" was made in the *Annual Report*, 1937, pp. 6–7, concerning Federal Reserve purchases in Apr. 1937, though, as pointed out in Chap. 9, concern with maintaining an "orderly market" dated from not later than 1935. Two important differences between the early enunciation of the policy of maintaining an orderly market for government securities and its later wartime character are evident: (1) in 1939, the professed aims were to protect member bank portfolios, not Treasury interests as a borrower, and to assure an orderly capital market as a condition of general economic recovery; (2) in 1939, a rigid system of support prices was not yet contemplated, but only the degree of support that would prevent wide fluctuations in the prices of government securities.

CHART 47

High-Powered Money, by Assets and Liabilities of the Treasury and Federal Reserve Banks, 1939–48

A. Liabilities

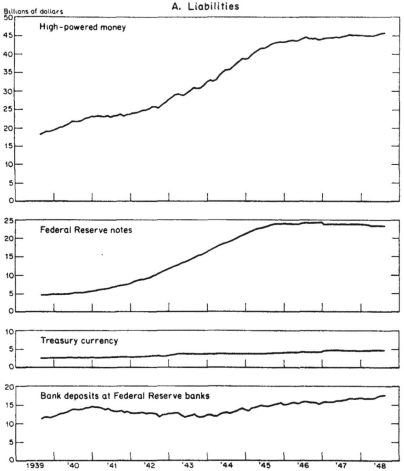

NOTE: Federal Reserve notes and Treasury currency are outside the Treasury and Federal Reserve Banks. Between $40 million and $65 million of gold certificates recalled but not turned in are included in high-powered money but not shown in its components viewed as liabilities.

SOURCE: Chart 39 was extended, using *Federal Reserve Bulletin* for Federal Reserve credit outstanding and monetary gold stock, and *Annual Report* of the Secretary of the Treasury, 1942–49, for the devaluation profit.

CHART 47 (Concluded)

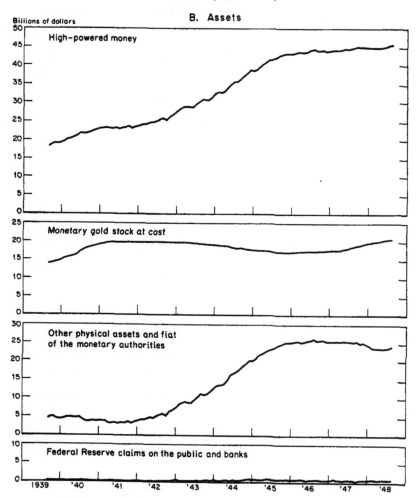

became unavailable for the duration of the war, the volume of consumer credit fell rapidly after Pearl Harbor. Consumer credit control was, in consequence, of little significance during the war. It is worth note, first, because it represented an extension to a new area of the principle, initially applied to security loans, of controlling specific types of credit, and second, because it was destined to play a somewhat more important role after the war.

The Board's other measure was to raise reserve requirements on November 1, 1941, to the maximum limit permitted by law, thereby rescinding the reduction made in April 1938. That measure converted $1.2 billion of the then extant $4.7 billion of excess reserves into required reserves.[5] A sign of the changed attitudes of banks is that they made no attempt to rebuild their excess reserves, as they had after the reserve increases of 1936 and 1937, but rather proceeded to continue to reduce their remaining excess reserves. The effect of the reserve requirement increase shows up only in a slackened rate of rise of the deposit-reserve ratio from October—immediately following the announcement on September 23 of the forthcoming rise—to roughly April 1942, when the Federal Reserve announced that it would peg the rate on Treasury bills. The ratio then started to rise at an even faster rate than before the reserve requirement increase. It is ironic that the increase, presumably intended to "tighten" monetary conditions and to restrain the expansion of bank liabilities, did so only to a minor extent, whereas the earlier increase, intended as a precautionary move and designed to have no immediate impact, had exercised a sharp restraining influence.

2. *Period of Wartime Deficits, December 1941–January 1946*

The expanded defense program initiated in 1940 and lend-lease initiated in early 1941 produced a substantial increase in government expenditures. These were offset for a time by a rise in tax rates and tax revenues. By early 1941, however, the deficit had begun to rise sharply. For calendar 1941, cash operating outgo exceeded cash operating income by $10 billion or nearly half of total expenditures.[6] Pearl Harbor brought a sharp intensification of these tendencies. Government expenditures nearly tripled from calendar 1941 to calendar 1942, and rose a further 50 per cent from 1942 to 1943, reaching a peak of nearly $95 billion in 1944. Tax re-

[5] Concern over the volume of excess reserves was expressed in a special report to the Congress dated Dec. 31, 1940, made jointly by the Board of Governors, the presidents of the Federal Reserve Banks, and the Federal Advisory Council (*Federal Reserve Bulletin*, Jan. 1941, pp. 1–2). Among other points in the program it presented, the report requested the Congress to increase the minimum statutory reserve requirements to the maximum defined in the Banking Act of 1935 and to permit the Federal Open Market Committee (not the Board of Governors) to increase requirements to double the new minimum.

The reader is reminded that, for the period after 1940, we have not had access to internal documents of the Federal Reserve System like those in the Harrison Papers, or to an insider's running account like the Hamlin Diary. Hence, our discussion of Federal Reserve policy is less informed in detail than for earlier years and it is not as well documented. The Reserve System could perform a service to students of the period by making such documents available.

[6] The cash deficit or surplus differs from the budget deficit or surplus in consolidating the accounts of the social security and other trust funds with those of other government agencies. It therefore gives a more satisfactory index for our purposes of the impact of government operations on the rest of the economy.

ceipts also rose but more slowly and in no greater ratio. As a result, the cash deficit rose to levels without precedent, either in absolute amount or as a percentage of national income: to nearly $40 billion in calendar 1942, over $50 billion in 1943, over $45 billion in 1944, and over $35 billion in 1945—sums averaging nearly 30 per cent of the contemporary net national product. Government expenditures fell rapidly after the end of hostilities while tax revenues remained high. As in World War I, within six months after the end of the war the government was taking in more than it was paying out, so that the period of wartime deficits came to an end about January 1946.

As in World War I, those changes involved a continuation and inten-sification of trends already in process. The transfer of economic resources from peace to war production had been going on apace since early 1940. On the physical side, intensification of trends was undoubtedly much sharper in World War II than in World War I. The period of neutrality was longer in World War I than in World War II and that of active hos-tilities shorter; and World War II saw a far more complete conversion to a "total war" economy than World War I did. On the financial side, the situation was reversed. Thanks to lend-lease, active war meant less of a change in the source of finance for war activity in World War II than it had in World War I.

PRICE MOVEMENTS

As in World War I, also, our entry into active war was rather sur-prisingly accompanied by a slowing down of the rate of rise in the available price indexes, while the termination of wartime deficits was accompanied by a sharp speeding up. As Table 23 shows, the wholesale price index rose at the rate of 4 per cent a year during the period of war-time deficits, compared with 9 per cent in the prior period and 16 per cent in the succeeding period. These figures are less reliable indicators of the behavior of prices in World War II than the corresponding figures are for World War I. General price control was instituted in early 1942 and suspended in mid-1946. During the period of price control, there was a strong tendency for price increases to take a concealed form, such as a change in quality or in the services rendered along with the sale of a com-modity or the elimination of discounts on sales or the concentration of production on lines that happened to have relatively favorable price ceil-ings. Moreover, where price control was effective, "shortages" developed, in some cases—such as gasoline, meats, and a few other foods—ac-companied by explicit government rationing. The resulting pressure on consumers to substitute less desirable but available qualities and items for more desirable but unavailable qualities and items was equivalent to a price increase not recorded in the indexes. Finally, there was undoubtedly much legal avoidance and illegal evasion of the price controls through a variety of devices of which the explicit "black market" was perhaps the least important. The result was that "prices," in any economically meaningful sense, rose by decidedly more than the "price index" during the period of price control. The jump in the price index on the elimination of price control in 1946 did not involve any corresponding jump in "prices"; rather, it reflected largely the unveiling of price increases that had occurred earlier. Allowance for the defects in the price index as a measure of price change would undoubtedly yield a decidedly higher rate of price rise during the war and a decidedly lower rate after the war than those recorded in Table 23, and hence a substantially smaller difference between the rate of price rise during the war and before and after. It seems unlikely, however, that allowance for these defects would reverse the qualitative conclusion that prices rose more slowly during the war than before or after.

In World War I, differences in the rate of price change were accompanied by corresponding differences in the rate of change of the stock of money: the stock of money also rose less rapidly during the war than before or after. In World War II, the reverse occurred: the stock of money rose much more rapidly during the war than before or after. This is the counterpart of the decline in velocity, 1942–46, and its subsequent rise—just the opposite of the behavior of velocity in 1917–18 and after.

BEHAVIOR OF VELOCITY

It is by no means clear what factors explain the behavior of velocity in World War II. Velocity rose by a fifth from 1940 to 1942—or slightly less than from 1915 to 1918—then declined by over a third to 1946. From 1946 to 1948 it rose by 13 per cent, to a level still much lower than in 1939 (see Chart 45). Quarterly data on national income and monthly data on personal income suggest that velocity reached its peak in the fourth quarter of 1942 and its trough in the final quarter of 1945 or the first quarter of 1946.

The initial rise in velocity is not surprising. Velocity, as measured, generally rises during economic expansions and falls during economic contractions. The expansion from 1940 to 1942 was vigorous and after mid-1940 was accompanied by sharp price increases which might be expected to discourage the holding of assets in the form of money.

What needs explanation is the decline in velocity after 1942. Price control inhibited increases in prices after early 1942 and kept many increases that did occur from showing up in the price index. It might be argued that the cessation of the rise in the index removed the incentive, provided by the prior price increase, to economize on the holding of money. But even if it were granted that the price index properly recorded the price movements that determined the amount of money balances the community desired to hold relative to its income, the cessation of the price rise could hardly account for more than a return of velocity to, say, the 1940 level. It could not account for the fall of velocity well below that level. Even to regard it as responsible for reducing velocity to the 1940 level would grossly overestimate its effect, since that would assume full adjustment of velocity to the prior rate of rise of prices, whereas the evidence of earlier chapters suggests that the adjustment of velocity to changes in the rate of change in prices is slow and tardy.

It seems likely that any direct effect of price control was less important than the unavailability to consumers of automobiles and other consumer durable goods, after wartime cessation of their production in 1942,[7] and than the restrictions imposed on construction and on private capital formation. Both consumers and business enterprises were prevented from using their funds to purchase kinds of goods they regard as increasing their wealth, which ordinarily absorb a large fraction of increases in income and an especially large fraction of transitory increases. The blocking of these channels of spending induced consumers and business enterprises to increase the stock of other assets—in particular, as it turned out, money and government securities—to a much higher level than otherwise, relative to income.

The counterpart on income account of the accumulation of liquid assets was an unprecedentedly high level of personal saving. Personal saving would have been large in any event because of the abnormally high level of income associated with full employment and the war boom. But saving was much larger than can readily be accounted for by income alone. One important reason is that consumers accumulated in the form of liquid assets funds that they would otherwise have spent or have tried to spend on automobiles, other durable goods, and residential construction. The recurrent bond campaigns with their appeal to patriotism may have contributed also to the high rate of saving, but we are inclined to be skeptical that they had much effect on the amount of saving. If they had any effect, it was probably on the form in which savings were held—more in government securities relative to other assets. Insofar as one of the alternatives was money, the bond campaigns tended to make the decline in velocity less than it otherwise would have been.[8]

---

[7] Limitation (L-) orders were first issued in the summer of 1941 by the Supply, Priority, and Allocations Board, a predecessor of the War Production Board, restricting the output of finished products and eventually prohibiting production for civilian use of automobiles, trucks, refrigerators, washing machines, electric appliances, etc. Prohibition of nonmilitary automobile production took effect Feb. 1, 1942, and of many other consumer durables by Sept. 1942.

[8] To avoid misunderstanding, it should perhaps be noted that the statements in the text are not intended to be a full analysis of the factors accounting for the high level of wartime savings. Numerous other factors doubtless played a role. See "A

Both money and government securities, of course, were fixed in value in nominal terms and so would have been poor forms in which to hold wealth if their holders had expected them to depreciate sharply in their command over real goods. Two points are relevant in this connection. First, the assets were being held to exercise command at a later time over particular kinds of goods—on the interpretation suggested above, especially over durable goods not currently available. It was entirely reasonable for the public to expect the prices of these goods to decline—in a formal sense, they had to, since their current prices were effectively infinite. And that expectation was reinforced by the sharp rise in the price of second-hand items of this kind. With respect to these goods, money holdings could be expected to be worth more after the war. Second, almost certainly the most widely-held expectation at the time was that prices would go down after the war—if this expectation seems unreasonable to us, it is only by hindsight. Memory of the sharp price decline after World War I was reinforced by the climate of opinion formed by the depressed 1930's and both were further strengthened by much-publicized predictions of "experts" that war's end would be followed by a major economic collapse.

These expectations about the postwar period were important not only because of their implications for the form in which savings were held but also because expectations of great instability in the near future enhanced the importance attached to accumulating money and other liquid assets. The expected price change meant that those assets would yield more than they would otherwise; the expected instability, that they were more desirable for any given yield. Both, therefore, worked in the direction of reducing velocity and hence also the price rise associated with any given increase in the stock of money. (See Chapter 12 for a fuller analysis of velocity and of the role of expectations about the degree of future economic instability.)

World War I differed markedly from World War II with respect to both the availability of goods and expectations about the postwar behavior of prices and income. "Shortages" and "controls" in World War I were nowhere nearly so sweeping as in World War II, and no major branch of civilian production suspended output entirely. World War I came after nearly two decades of generally rising prices, when the climate of opinion was characterized by belief in unlimited future potentialities rather than by fear of secular stagnation.

Once the war was over in 1945 and durable goods gradually became

National Survey of Liquid Assets Distribution According to Income," *Federal Reserve Bulletin*, July 1946, pp. 716–722; Michael Sapir, "Review of Economic Forecasts for the Transition Period," *Studies in Income and Wealth*, Vol. 11, New York, National Bureau of Economic Research, 1949, pp. 312–314; Lenore A. Epstein, "Consumers' Taxable Assets," *ibid.*, Vol. 12, 1950, pp. 440–453.

available again, holders of the accumulated assets tried to use them to purchase such goods. The attempt to use the accumulated assets tended to raise prices and incomes and to reduce the ratio of such assets to income. It is therefore entirely consistent with the preceding analysis that velocity should have started to rise in early 1946. What is perhaps surprising is that initially it rose so little and then subsequently rose for so long a period, but these puzzles we shall leave for later (section 3, below, and Chapter 12).

The decline in velocity and of course also the accompanying rise in output explain why prices rose so much more slowly than the stock of money during the period of wartime deficits. We turn now to the factors accounting for the rise in the stock of money.

PROXIMATE DETERMINANTS OF THE RISE IN THE MONEY STOCK

As Table 23 shows, the rise in the stock of money during the war was predominantly accounted for—in an arithmetic sense—by the concurrent rise in high-powered money, just as it had been in the period of neutrality. But, precisely paralleling World War I, there was a major difference in the source of the rise in high-powered money. In both war periods, Federal Reserve credit outstanding rather than gold accounted for the rise in high-powered money. The Federal Reserve System again became essentially the bond-selling window of the Treasury and used its monetary powers almost entirely for that purpose.

The Reserve System performed the same role somewhat differently in the two wars. In World War I, the System increased its private claims by discounting member bank bills mostly secured by government obligations; its own holdings of government securities were small throughout. In World War II, discounts were small throughout, and the Federal Reserve increased its credit outstanding by buying government securities. In our terminology, there was an increase in the fiat of the monetary authorities. The common effect was an increase in high-powered money which was distributed between currency and bank reserves—about equally in World War I, about six-sevenths to currency, one-seventh to reserves in World War II. The increment in bank reserves, of course, permitted a multiple expansion of bank deposits. The corresponding growth of commercial bank assets largely took the form of an increase in loans in World War I; of an increase in holdings of government securities in World War II.[9] But again the difference was largely formal. Perhaps half the World War I increase in loans to customers was secured by government obligations; in World War II, the banks purchased the securities directly. Dissatis-

---

[9] From June 1941 to June 1945, the increase in commercial bank holdings of U.S. government obligations was $64 billion, or 90 per cent of the increase in commercial bank assets over the period. From June 1917 to June 1919 the increase in total loans extended by commercial banks was $4.2 billion, or 44 per cent of the increase in commercial bank assets over the period.

faction with World War I experience led to a shunning of the earlier forms. Similar political and economic pressures led to the adoption of the same substance. Some idea of the magnitudes of those operations is given by the following figures: from November 1941 to January 1946, the government debt outside the U.S. government and the Federal Reserve System grew by $178 billion, of which some $69 billion was acquired by commercial banks; currency held by the public grew by $17 billion; commercial bank deposits, by $52 billion; and Federal Reserve credit outstanding, by $22 billion.

In April 1942, the Federal Open Market Committee announced that it would keep the rate on Treasury bills,[10] mostly 90-day maturities, fixed at $\frac{3}{8}$ of one per cent per year by buying or selling any amount offered or demanded at that rate.[11] That rate was kept fixed until the middle of 1947. No such rigid commitment was made for other government securities but an effective pattern was established for them as well—ranging from roughly $\frac{7}{8}$ of one per cent for certificates to 0.9 per cent for 13-month notes, 1.5 per cent for $4\frac{1}{2}$-year notes, and 2.5 per cent for long-term bonds.[12] The System bought whatever amount of these securities was

[10] Treasury bills are obligations issued on a discount basis with varying maturities up to 12 months. During the war they were issued weekly, usually for a term of 3 months in denominations from $1,000 to $1,000,000 at maturity.

[11] On Aug. 7, 1942, the Federal Open Market Committee directed the Federal Reserve Banks to give the seller a repurchase option at the same rate for an equal amount of bills of the same maturity, and extended the privilege of sale and repurchase to dealers in securities, corporations, and other holders of liquid funds.

[12] Certificates of indebtedness are Treasury obligations limited by law to a maturity of one year. They are sold at par plus any accrued interest, and interest on them is paid at the time of their maturity. They were offered by the Treasury in Apr. 1942 for the first time since 1934. The term of issue during the period of war deficits was usually 11 to 12 months. As many as ten issues a year were offered, usually as of the first of the month, in denominations from $1,000 to $1,000,000, at a rate, from Nov. 1942 on, of $\frac{7}{8}$ of one per cent. Maturing issues were usually refunded into new issues of certificates of indebtedness or occasionally into 13-month notes to prevent two issues from maturing on the same date.

Treasury notes are obligations with maturity of more than one year and not over 5 years. They are sold at par plus any accrued interest. Interest rates on them during the war ranged from about 0.90 per cent on 13-month maturities to 1.25 per cent on those maturing in about 3 years, and to 1.5 per cent on those maturing in $4\frac{1}{2}$ years. During the period of war deficits there were seven issues of Treasury notes exclusive of 13-month notes, which the market treats like certificates.

Treasury marketable bonds have maturities of more than 5 years. Maturities of most bonds offered during the war ranged from 10 to 25 years. They were sold at par plus any accrued interest, the interest rate varying with their maturity as shown in the tabulation.

Maturity of Bonds (years)	Callable by Treasury	Coupon Rate (per cent)
10	8	2
15	12	$2\frac{1}{4}$
25	20	$2\frac{1}{2}$

necessary to prevent their yields from rising but did not commit itself to sell them freely in order to prevent yields from falling. The relatively fixed pattern of rates on government securities was the counterpart in World War II of the relatively fixed discount rate in World War I.

The support program converted all securities into the equivalent of money. Since the pattern of rates was carried over from the late thirties and reflected an abnormally high valuation of liquidity, the Reserve Banks tended to acquire bills and, to a smaller extent, certificates and, to a still smaller extent, notes, rather than bonds; and banks to acquire bonds, notes, and certificates, rather than bills. So long as the bill rate was kept absolutely fixed, the pattern of rates for other issues could be maintained only if (1) the Treasury adjusted its issues to provide only the relatively small amount of bills holders desired at those rates; or (2) the Federal Reserve System changed the initial composition of debt instruments issued by the Treasury to the composition holders desired, by buying bills and other securities as they approached a comparable maturity, and by selling bonds. The Treasury was not averse to a decline in long rates and, as the System's bond portfolio declined (by the end of the war, bonds constituted only $1 billion of the System's total government security holdings of $23 billion; see Chart 48), attempts by other holders to get out of short-term securities and into long-term—"playing the pattern of rates," as it was termed—produced a decline in yields on long-term securities beginning in 1944.

In late 1942, the discount rate was lowered to $\frac{1}{2}$ of one per cent on advances secured by short-term government securities (Chart 49). However, that change was of little significance since, if banks held such securities, it was generally cheaper for them to acquire any needed reserves by selling bills yielding $\frac{3}{8}$ of one per cent rather than by using them as collateral to borrow at $\frac{1}{2}$ of one per cent. In 1942 also, the System lowered reserve requirements for central reserve city banks.[13]

With government security prices supported, there was no incentive for banks to hold excess reserves. They could satisfy liquidity needs instead by holding income-yielding securities. The reduction in excess reserves, together with the reduction just noted in required reserves, produced a continued increase in the ratio of bank deposits to bank reserves, from not quite 4 to 1 in November 1941 to over 6 to 1 by January 1946. Had there been no change in the deposit-currency ratio, the increase in the deposit-reserve ratio would have made the percentage increase in the stock of money about $1\frac{3}{4}$ times the percentage increase in high-powered

[13] The initial grant of authority in the Banking Act of 1935 to vary reserve requirements specified a uniform increase or decrease for all central reserve and reserve city banks and a uniform increase or decrease for all country banks. The authority to vary requirements for the central reserve city class separately was granted in July 1942.

CHART 48
Government Securities Held by Federal Reserve Banks,
March 1941–August 1948

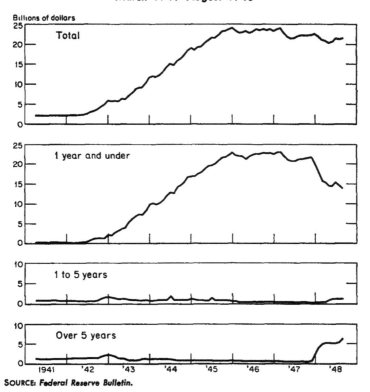

SOURCE: *Federal Reserve Bulletin.*

money. However, about half the excess of that 1¾ over unity was offset by a continued decline in the deposit-currency ratio from 6 to 1 in November 1941 to 4 to 1 in January 1946. In his detailed analysis of the deposit-currency ratio, Cagan has attributed its decline during the war in part to increased use of currency in preference to deposits as a means of avoiding increased income tax levies, in part to black market activities, expansion of the armed forces, and greater mobility of the civilian population.[14]

The direction of movement of both deposit ratios was the same in

[14] See Phillip Cagan's forthcoming volume on determinants and effects of changes in the U.S. money stock, 1875–1955, a National Bureau study.

CHART 49
Use of Tools by Federal Reserve System, August 1939–August 1948

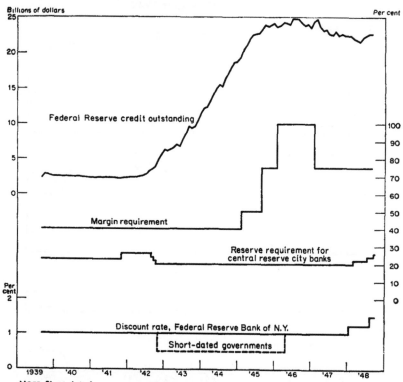

NOTE: Short-dated government securities, for which discount rate is shown, are due or callable in one year or less.

SOURCE: Same as for Chart 41, except that FRB is source for 1942–48 data.

World War II as in World War I. However, the relative importance of the changes differed sharply. In World War I, the decline in the deposit-currency ratio was some two to three times as important in its effect on the stock of money as the rise in the deposit-reserve ratio; in World War II, the relative importance was reversed.

The bond drives of World War II placed much emphasis on avoiding the sale of securities to commercial banks on the ground that purchases by banks were "inflationary" in a sense in which purchases by others were not. Certain issues were made ineligible for bank purchase and attempts were made to "tailor" other issues to particular classes of purchasers. At the same time, however, contradictory policies were also followed. The Federal Reserve System encouraged banks to purchase government securities by assurance that it would make reserves available. As stated in its 1942 *Annual Report,* " . . . the Federal Reserve authorities endeavored to induce banks to make more complete use of their existing reserves and also supplied them with such reserve funds as they needed from time to time to purchase the Government securities offered to them."[15] The Treasury, moreover, offered a large percentage of its securities at rates unattractive to nonbank investors.[16]

The attempts to avoid sales to commercial banks—which, partly because of the contradictory policies followed, did not succeed—rested on a misconception based on a failure to distinguish between sales to Reserve Banks and sales to commercial banks. Sales to Reserve Banks created high-powered money. For given deposit-reserve and deposit-currency ratios, each additional dollar of high-powered money meant an increment of several additional dollars of money—the famous multiple expansion. However, for a given level of high-powered money, the identity of the purchasers of securities and, in particular, their identity as commercial banks or others could affect the stock of money only if it affected one of the deposit ratios, and it is hard to see why it should have any appreciable effect on either.[17]

Still more basically, it is necessary to distinguish here, as it was in earlier chapters, between the arithmetic of changes in the money supply, just outlined, and the economics of the changes. Given the monetary policy of supporting a nearly fixed pattern of rates on government securities, the Federal Reserve System had no effective control over the quantity of high-powered money. It had to create whatever quantity was necessary to keep rates at that level. Though it is convenient to describe the process as running from an increase in high-powered money to an increase in the stock of money through deposit-currency and deposit-reserve ratios, the chain of influence in fact ran in the opposite direction —from the increase in the stock of money consistent with the specified pattern of rates and other economic conditions to the increment in high-powered money required to produce that increase. It is an elementary economic truism, applicable to the money market as elsewhere, that one cannot simultaneously control both the price and the quantity of a good without some explicit rationing mechanism. If the price is fixed, the

[15] Board of Governors of the Federal Reserve System, *Annual Report,* 1942, p. 9.
[16] See Clark Warburton, "Monetary Policy in the United States in World War II," *American Journal of Economics and Sociology,* Apr. 1945, pp. 377–389; *idem,* "A Hedge Against Inflation," *Political Science Quarterly,* Mar. 1952, pp. 5–8.
[17] See Friedman, *A Program for Monetary Stability,* New York, Fordham University Press, 1960, pp. 53–55 and 107, footnote 1, for further discussion of the monetary effects of sales of government securities to commercial banks.

quantity must be permitted to be whatever is consistent with that price, and conversely.

Success in avoiding sales to commercial banks could have been achieved by making the securities more attractive to nonbank purchasers by offering them higher returns. That would have involved a change in the pattern of rates pegged and could therefore have had a significant influence. A smaller increase in the total stock of money, and hence in high-powered money, would have been necessary to support the alternative higher pattern of rates than the actual pattern, since the higher rates would have made holding bonds more attractive relative to holding money. One consequence would also have been a higher velocity.

BASIC DETERMINANTS OF THE RISE IN THE MONEY STOCK

Given the pattern of rates supported, what determined the amount of increase in the stock of money? It is difficult enough to answer the question in abstract terms. It is far more difficult to fill in the details or to explain why the magnitudes involved were what they were, and we shall not attempt to do so at all exhaustively. For our purposes, we may regard the physical quantity of resources to be used by government as fixed by other considerations—though, of course, still more basically, the quantity might well have been revised, if it had been associated with a very different level of inflationary pressure. The quantity of resources used by government had to be matched by a corresponding release of resources by the members of the community. They received incomes corresponding to essentially the whole of resources employed, and they had to be persuaded or induced or forced to refrain from exercising command over a fraction of those resources corresponding to the fraction employed by the government. The financial counterpart of the release of resources was the payment of taxes, or the accumulation of claims against the government in the form of either interest-bearing government securities or noninterest-bearing debt of the government, the three together being equal over any period to the expenditures of the government. The increase in the stock of money had to be whatever was necessary to render the sum of the three items equal to the expenditures of the government. Part of the increase in the stock of money took the form of government issue of money, part took the form of whatever increase in privately created money (in that period, bank deposits not matched by an increment in reserves) was necessary to provide the public with the ratio of deposits to currency it desired and the banks with the ratio of deposits to reserves they desired.

It should be emphasized that all these items were being simultaneously determined. What we have taken as fixed was the physical quantity of resources to be used by government, not government expenditures. If prices (needless to say, as "correctly" measured, not as recorded in a necessarily imperfect index number) were constant during the process, any issue of money would correspond to "voluntary saving." It would mean that the public wished to add that amount to its real assets in the form of the noninterest-bearing obligations we call money.[18] And conversely, prices could remain constant only if the public did wish to add to its real assets in the form of interest- and noninterest-bearing obligations an amount equal to the excess of government expenditures at those prices over tax receipts at those prices. If prices rose during the process, the issue of money would correspond partly to "voluntary saving"—insofar as the real and not only the nominal value of the money stock rose—and partly to a tax on money balances. The nominal increment in the money stock required to keep its real value unchanged can be regarded as vouchers recording the payment of this tax on money balances.[19] In any event, the government could acquire real resources only through either taxation—consisting in part of explicit taxes, in part of an implicit tax on money balances—or borrowing, consisting in part of borrowing in a noninterest-bearing form. The distribution between taxes and borrowing was determined in part by the level of taxes imposed by legislation, in part by the preferences of the public with respect to "voluntary saving."[20]

The major government actions affecting the amount by which the money stock increased were therefore the decisions about how much real resources to devote to the war effort, the level of tax rates enacted, measures affecting voluntary saving, and measures affecting the fraction of their savings individuals wished to use to add to their holdings of money. For the period of war or wartime deficits, over 45 per cent of total federal expenditures were financed by explicit taxes. This was an impressive performance in comparison with that in World War I, but it left a much larger deficit compared with national income because of the

[18] Insofar as the issue of money was in the form of privately created money, the government was in essence sharing its monopoly of the issuance of noninterest-bearing securities with the commercial banks. From the government's point of view, it issued interest-bearing obligations corresponding to that part of the hypothetical "voluntary saving."

[19] Insofar as the issue of money was in the form of privately issued money, the government was in effect sharing the proceeds of the tax on money balances with commercial banks (see Friedman, "Price, Income, and Monetary Changes," pp. 619–625).

[20] For a fuller analysis, see Friedman, "Discussion of the Inflationary Gap," in *Essays in Positive Economics*, University of Chicago Press, 1955, pp. 251–262; also Martin Bailey, "The Welfare Cost of Inflationary Finance," *Journal of Political Economy*, Apr. 1956, pp. 93–110; Armen A. Alchian and Reuben A. Kessel, "Redistribution of Wealth through Inflation," *Science*, Sept. 4, 1959, pp. 537–539; Ralph Turvey, "Inflation as a Tax in World War II," *Journal of Political Economy*, Feb. 1961, pp. 72–73; and Friedman, "Price, Income, and Monetary Changes," *loc. cit.* See also above, Chap. 2, footnote 64, and Chap. 5, footnote 35.

larger magnitude of the war effort. We have already noted that the cessation of production of certain durable goods had the effect of raising voluntary saving. The rationing of other goods and the limited availability of still others may have had a similar effect. Aside from government measures, the widespread fear of a postwar depression worked in the same direction. The pattern of interest rates fixed on government obligations also affected the level of voluntary saving—a higher level of interest rates would have given a greater inducement to save, a lower level, a lesser inducement—but probably had its main effect on the form savings took. It seems not unlikely that the much higher level of rates paid on government securities in World War I than in World War II is one reason the nonbank public increased its holdings of government securities by about three dollars for every one dollar increase in its money stock in World War I and by only half that amount in World War II.

By comparison with World War I, the impressive difference is that despite a much larger war effort, longer continued deficits, and larger deficits relative to national income, prices rose more slowly during World War II than during World War I, both during the whole of the period from the start of the war to the postwar price peak, and apparently also during the period of wartime deficits. There appear to be two main reasons for the difference, neither having much to do with the design of government policy. The first is the much greater increase in willingness to save in World War II, the monetary counterpart of which was the decline in velocity during the war, discussed above. The second is that the tax on money balances implicit in inflationary money creation was a much more productive tax in World War II than in World War I, because of the lower velocity prevailing during World War II than during World War I (Table 24, line 3). Money balances averaged 45 per cent of one year's national income in 1914–20, 69 per cent in 1939–48. A 1 per cent tax on money balances—if we ignore the reflex influence of the tax on the amount of money balances held—therefore yielded 0.45 per cent of a year's national income in World War I, 0.69 per cent, or about 1½ times as much, in World War II.

This is the computation needed to judge the importance of the increase in the public's money stock. An additional problem is the fraction of the increase in the money stock created directly by the government and the fraction created by the banks or, to put it differently, the sharing of the tax yield between the government and the banks. The implicit sharing arrangement determines how much money the government can issue per dollar increase in the total money stock; or, alternatively, how much of its deficit it can finance by issuing money, how much by bonds, and how much of the bonds directly or indirectly must go to banks. In this respect, too, there was a substantial difference between the wars. In the World

War I inflation (1914–20), the total money stock increased $6.92 for every dollar of government-created money (high-powered money minus the gold stock), in the World War II inflation (1939–48), $4.74. The main reason for the difference was the change in the ratio of deposits to reserves. During the World War I inflation, banks added $14.16 to their deposits for every dollar increase in reserves; during the World War II

TABLE 24
COMPARISON OF MONEY CREATION IN TWO WORLD WAR PERIODS OF INFLATION

| | Period of Inflation | |
	World War I 1914–20	World War II 1939–48
Money created by government as a fraction of average annual net national product		
1. Total	0.050	0.146
2. Per year	0.008	0.016
Average velocity		
3. Average NNP ÷ average stock of money	2.205	1.445
Money created by government as a fraction of average stock of money		
4. Total	0.110	0.211
5. Per year	0.018	0.023
Expansion ratio of monetary system		
6. Increase in high-powered money per dollar increase in government-created money	1.377	1.357
7. Increase in stock of money per dollar increase in high-powered money	5.027	3.492
Increase in stock of money as a fraction of average stock		
8. Total	0.762	0.998
9. Per year	0.127	0.111
Increase in stock of money as a fraction of average annual NNP		
10. Total	0.346	0.690
11. Per year	0.058	0.077

NOTE: Figures for money stock, high-powered money, and gold stock are annual averages centered on June 30. Averages for each war period weight the initial and terminal years each as one-half year.

Government-created money equals high-powered money minus the gold stock.

inflation, $10.47. A subsidiary reason was a change in the relation between deposit and currency expansion—in World War I, the public added $6.91 to its deposits per dollar increase in currency; in World War II only $3.89.

For the war inflations as a whole, the effects of these differences are summarized in Table 24. As this table shows, the combined effect of the changes in the level of velocity and in the expansion ratio of the monetary system was that the government was able to acquire twice as large a fraction of average annual income (1.6 instead of 0.8 per cent, line 2) by direct money creation, yet produce only seven-eighths as large an increase in the total money stock per year (11.1 per cent instead of 12.7 per cent, line 9). This smaller increase in the total money stock was in its turn equivalent to a decidedly larger fraction of average annual income (7.7 per cent instead of 5.8 per cent, line 11) so that both directly and indirectly money creation was a more effective device for acquiring resources for government purposes.

In terms of federal government expenditures during the period of wartime deficits, 48 per cent was financed by explicit taxes; 7 per cent by direct government money creation; 14 per cent by private money issue, which can be regarded as the indirect effect of government money creation but had as its nominal counterpart interest-bearing rather than non-interest-bearing government debt; and 31 per cent by interest-bearing government securities not matched by money creation. If the wholesale price index is regarded as correctly measuring the price changes during the war, then about one-fifth of the money creation can be regarded as a tax on money balances, four-fifths as voluntary saving embodied in the form of noninterest-bearing monetary assets.[21] This would mean that, in all, slightly over half of expenditures was financed by taxes, and that about one-tenth of the taxes took the form of a tax on money balances. The defects of the price index mean that these figures probably underestimate the importance of taxes as a fraction of expenditures and of the tax on money balances as a fraction of total taxes.

EFFECT OF WAR LOAN DRIVES

One detail of the behavior of the money stock merits attention before we leave the period. In Chart 46 it will be noted that the money stock behaved in a much more irregular fashion during 1943, in particular, but also in 1944 and 1945, than it did before or after. The reason was the flotation of government securities through a series of bond drives—seven War Loan drives and a concluding Victory Loan—about five months apart, November 1942–December 1945. As it happened, three of the bond drives came in the final months of the year and two in the middle,

[21] Wholesale prices rose 14 per cent from Dec. 1941 to Dec. 1945 (roughly the initial and terminal dates of the calendar years included in our estimate of federal government expenditures during the period of wartime deficits). The nominal amount of money that would have been required to keep money balances at their initial real level was 13 per cent of the actual increase from Dec. 1941 to Dec. 1945. The amount that would have been required to maintain money balances at their terminal real level was 24 per cent of the actual increase. The correct figure, assuming the price rise to be correct, is between these two, and we have approximated it as 20 per cent.

For simplicity, we have combined direct and indirect money creation, and have neglected the assignment of part of what we have called the tax proceeds to the commercial banks. For a more refined analysis, see Ralph Turvey, "Inflation as a Tax in World War II," *Journal of Political Economy*, Feb. 1961, pp. 72–73.

CHART 50

Member Bank Deposits During War Bond Drives, With and Without U.S. Government War Loan Deposits, Monthly and Semimonthly Averages, Unadjusted for Seasonal Changes, 1942–45

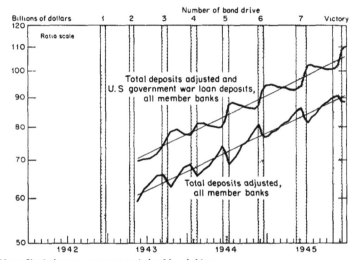

NOTE: Shaded areas represent periods of bond drives.

SOURCE: Data are monthly or semimonthly averages of daily figures, seasonally unadjusted, from FRB. Total deposits adjusted are demand deposits adjusted plus time deposits. Dates of bond drives, from *Annual Report* of the Secretary of the Treasury, 1946, p. 507.

which meant that they had some of the repetitive effects characteristic of a seasonal movement. As a result, their effects have been to some extent eliminated from the seasonally adjusted series plotted in Chart 46. That is mainly why the irregularity produced by the bond drives in our money series is much greater for 1943 than for 1944 and 1945.

Chart 50 is designed to enable us to study in some detail the effects of the bond drives. It is restricted to deposits, since the bond drives had no noticeable effects on currency, and to member banks only, because for that period we have monthly or semimonthly averages of daily figures for them but not for all commercial banks. It plots figures unadjusted for seasonal variations to avoid inadvertent elimination of any bond drive effects. The bottom line in the chart is for demand and time deposits owned by the public and thus excludes U.S. government deposits. The top line is the same total plus U.S. government deposits. The shaded areas in the chart are the periods of the bond drives.

On the occasion of each bond drive, purchasers of securities transferred deposits to war loan accounts maintained by the Treasury at commercial banks. As the government transferred its deposits from war loan accounts to Federal Reserve Banks, and thence to the public to pay for its expenditures, government deposits were transferred back to private accounts. This process is clearly marked in the chart. On the occasion of each bond drive, the upper line rises and the lower falls. Between drives, the reverse occurs.

After April 1943, the war loan accounts maintained by the Treasury were exempt from reserve requirements, so any transfer of funds to those accounts in the first instance reduced required reserves. If reserves held had risen steadily and if banks had taken full advantage of the released reserves, so that required reserves had risen during bond drives as they did between drives, the banks could have kept the lower line in Chart 50 free from any effects of the bond drives. On the occasion of each drive, they could have expanded their total earning assets to the amount of the deposits transferred to war loan accounts and subsequently could have reduced their earning assets as the war loan accounts were reduced. Under these hypothetical circumstances, our money stock figures, like the lower line of the chart, would have been unaffected by the bond drives. The whole of the effect would have been recorded in the upper line.

Conversely, if reserves held had risen steadily and if banks had taken no advantage of the reserves released by the transfer of deposits, so that required reserves had fallen during bond drives and risen between drives, the banks could have kept the upper line of Chart 50 free from any effects of the bond drives; the full effect would have been recorded in the lower line.

The actual situation was roughly midway between these extremes, as can be seen by noting that the fluctuations about the straight lines we have drawn to indicate the trends in the two series are not much different in amplitude for the upper than for the lower series.

There are three reasons the actual situation did not correspond to the first extreme. (1) The actual behavior of reserves was not that assumed above. During some of the drives, specifically the second through the fifth (April to May 1943–July to August 1944), the Reserve System offset some of the effect of the transfer of deposits by reducing its credit outstanding. To some extent, therefore, the declines in the lower line of Chart 50 reflect changes in available reserves. (2) The full use of the released reserves would have involved substantial transaction costs, since it implied first acquiring and then disposing of assets as government war loan accounts first increased and then decreased. (3) No doubt, it took time for banks to realize the possibilities of taking measures to increase deposits in advance or coincidentally with the drive itself, rather than subsequently when its effect was manifest in excess reserves. As time went on, the banks adjusted more fully to the bond drives. Visual evidence is provided by the chart, in which the fluctuations of the upper curve about its straight-line trend become wider, if anything, in amplitude, whereas fluctuations of the lower curve become a trifle narrower. And some rough calculations confirm this visual impression.[22]

3. From the End of the War to the Price Peak, August 1945–August 1948

Economic activity reached its wartime peak early in 1945 when it became clear that the end of the war was approaching. The National Bureau dates the reference peak in February 1945. Demobilization began after V-E Day (May 8, 1945), continued at an accelerated pace after V-J Day (September 2, 1945), and was accompanied by a sharp decrease in government expenditures and a rapid decline in industrial production. Nevertheless, the contraction was brief and relatively mild and the heavy unemployment that was widely feared did not develop. The trough, which the National Bureau dates in October 1945, was followed by a vigorous expansion. A decline in government purchases of goods and services from $83 billion in 1945 to $30 billion in 1946 was offset by rapid conversion from wartime to peacetime production. Seasonally adjusted unemployment in 1945 never reached 2.5 million and remained below that level thereafter until beyond the end of the expansion in November 1948.

After a brief pause in the third quarter of 1945, the wholesale price index continued rising and, as we have already noted, jumped sharply in mid-1946 when price control was dropped. The 16.4 per cent per year rate of rise in the wholesale price index from January 1946 to August

---

[22] For example, the ratio of the rise in the upper curve to the decline in the lower curve during the successive bond drives is shown in the tabulation.

Bond Drive	Ratio of Rise in Upper Curve to Decline in Lower Curve
3	1.30
4	1.28
5	1.46
6	1.68
7	1.55
8	3.51

For a more sophisticated calculation, allowance should be made for point 1 in the text. Such a more sophisticated calculation and, in general, a more detailed study of the effects of the bond drives than we have made would be of considerable interest. It might, for example, provide additional evidence on the time required for adjustment by the banking system to changes in circumstances.

We are indebted to George Morrison for pointing out to us that the use of seasonally adjusted figures in an earlier version had led us to erroneous conclusions about the reactions of banks to the bond drives.

1948 overstates substantially the rate of rise in prices during the period. Nonetheless, there was clearly a price rise of considerable magnitude. The rise in prices and in income reflected mostly the rise in velocity referred to earlier, rather than a growth of the money stock. The money stock grew only 14 per cent from the end of the war to August 1948 and only 11 per cent, or at the rate of only a little over 4 per cent per year, from January 1946 to August 1948.[23]

The rise in the money stock itself from January 1946 to August 1948 was attributable, in an arithmetic sense, mostly to growth of high-powered money. In sharp contrast with the corresponding period after World War I (when the gold stock fell and the increase in high-powered money came from a rapid expansion in Federal Reserve claims on the public and the banks), this time the increase in high-powered money was produced by a rise in the gold stock, about a third of which was offset by a decline in the fiat of the monetary authorities (see Tables 23 and 10). The gold inflow occurred despite U.S. participation in UNRRA —which was authorized even before the termination of lend-lease—the subsequent loan to Britain, and the Marshall Plan. Though these unilateral transfers satisfied many of the pressing demands of war-devastated countries, the residual demands, as well as the demands of neutral countries desiring goods not available during the war, led to a gold inflow.

A rise in the ratio of deposits to currency was as important as the increase in high-powered money in accounting for the increase in the stock of money. With the end of the war, the wartime factors affecting the demand for currency lost their influence, and the public increased its deposits relative to currency holdings. However, a minor part of the rise in the deposit-currency ratio was offset by a slight decline in the deposit-reserve ratio.

This description of postwar monetary changes needs to be supplemented by some account of events within the period. The slight decline in the deposit-reserve ratio was the net result of a rise from January 1946 to May 1947, which was more than offset by the subsequent decline to August 1948. A shift of deposits away from reserve and central reserve city banks, with higher reserve requirements, toward country banks mainly accounted for the movement in the deposit-reserve ratio from

---

[23] The coverage of the money stock series in 1948 is not strictly comparable to that of the series in 1945 and 1946 (see Appendix A). Currency held by the public in 1948 includes vault cash in banks in territories and the possessions, as well as in U.S. mutual savings banks; such vault cash is excluded in the earlier years. Likewise, demand balances of mutual savings banks at U.S. commercial banks are included in adjusted deposits in 1948, excluded in the earlier years. The percentage change figures in the text would not, however, be altered by revision of the 1945–46 money stock estimates to make them comparable to the later one. The excluded items totaled $165–$170 million in 1945–46, or slightly more than one-tenth of 1 per cent of the money stock excluding them.

August 1945 to April 1947; we do not know what accounts for the initial fall thereafter, but the noticeable acceleration of the fall after February 1948 clearly reflects three increases in reserve requirements imposed over the following seven months.

The expansion in high-powered money was concentrated within the 11 months from August 1945 to July 1946 ($1.9 billion) and the 15 months from May 1947 to August 1948 ($1.1 billion; see Chart 46). High-powered money was $3.1 billion higher at the end of August 1948 than at the end of August 1945, but only $1.2 billion higher than at the end of July 1946. From July 1946 to May 1947, the decline in the fiat of the monetary authorities just about offset the rise in the gold stock, so that high-powered money was roughly unchanged (see Chart 47B).

The initial and terminal expansions in high-powered money played quite different monetary roles. The first was a source of monetary expansion. The second was not; it was rather a reaction to other monetary measures.

Most of the terminal $1.1 billion increase in high-powered money from May 1947 to August 1948 was a reaction to changes in reserve requirements (Chart 49). Reserve requirements for member banks in central reserve cities were raised $1 billion by an increase of 4 points in the percentage they were required to maintain against demand deposits. The increase was imposed in two equal steps on February 27 and June 11, 1948. To acquire the added reserves, banks sold government securities which, under the support program, the Reserve System was committed to buy. Those security purchases thereby added to Reserve credit outstanding. (In September, a third increase affecting all member banks, and time as well as demand deposits, raised reserve requirements a further $2 billion. As a result, member banks sold government securities to the Federal Reserve, and Reserve Bank credit showed another increase—see the next chapter.)

In contrast, the initial increase in high-powered money from August 1945 to July 1946 provided the banks with a net addition to their reserves in excess of requirements. The money stock rose vigorously, by $11.1 billion, as compared with $5.3 billion in the period of stationary high-powered money from July 1946 to May 1947 and $1.8 billion in the terminal period of increase in high-powered money.[24] The money stock therefore grew decidedly more in the first 11 months of the three-year period than in the next 25 months. The money stock reached an absolute peak in January 1948 and declined mildly for the next 12 months, foreshadowing the approaching price peak and the recession of 1948 to 1949. This is another example of the previously observed tendency of monetary changes to precede changes in economic conditions.

[24] See footnote 23, above.

The foremost monetary puzzle of the immediate postwar period is why the money stock did not grow at a very much more rapid pace. The sharp difference from its behavior after World War I, when the most rapid rate of increase in the stock of money came after the end of the wartime deficits, does not reflect any fundamental difference in monetary policy. After both wars, the Reserve System continued the wartime policy of providing all the high-powered money demanded at a fixed rate: in World War I, through maintaining an unchanged discount rate; in World War II, through supporting the price of government securities at unchanged levels. And the reversal of the gold flows, from an outflow after World War I to an inflow after World War II, should have fostered a more rapid rate of monetary expansion after the later war.

Federal Reserve pronouncements were full of expressions of concern about the inflationary danger of the large stock of money, and about the necessity to avoid further expansion. Yet, until the middle of 1947, action was limited to requests for additional powers;[25] changes in discount rates which were of no significance (because the System continued its wartime support of the bill rate at ⅜ of 1 per cent and the certificate rate at ⅞ of 1 per cent, so that it continued to be cheaper for banks to meet reserve needs by selling such securities of which they held substantial amounts rather than by discounting);[26] and an increase in margin requirements on security purchases to 100 per cent in January 1946 followed by a reduction to 75 per cent in February 1947 (see Chart 49). Consumer credit controls were continued until November 1, 1947, when the Congress terminated the authority of the Board of Governors to regulate such credit. With the expansion of production of consumer durable goods, the controls became relevant as they had not been during the war. They may have limited the growth of this type of credit some-

[25] The Board of Governors suggested (*Annual Report*, 1945, pp. 7–8) that three additional powers be granted the System:

1. To limit the amount of long-term securities which any commercial bank could hold in relation to its net demand deposits
2. To require all commercial banks to maintain secondary reserves of Treasury bills and certificates in addition to their high-powered money reserves against net demand deposits
3. To raise reserve requirements, within some specified limit, against net demand deposits of any commercial bank

[26] By the end of Apr. 1946, the preferential discount rate of 1 per cent on advances to nonmember banks secured by direct obligations of the U.S. was eliminated at all Reserve Banks. Thereafter the rate in effect on loans to individuals, partnerships, and corporations (the rate ranged from 2½ to 2¾ per cent by the end of 1948) applied to advances to nonmember banks. In Apr. and May 1946 all the Reserve Banks discontinued the preferential discount rate of 0.5 per cent on advances to member banks secured by government obligations maturing or callable within a year, and the prevailing discount rate of 1 per cent became applicable to advances secured by all maturities of government obligations.

what but it is doubtful that they could have been a major factor affecting the growth of the money stock as a whole.

Yet from mid-1946 on, the rate of growth of the money stock fell sharply. The announced readiness of the Federal Reserve Banks to support the price of government securities led to no extensive monetization of the debt; on the contrary, Federal Reserve credit outstanding remained roughly constant during 1946 and then fell sharply in the spring of 1947. Yields on long-term government debt were below support levels throughout 1946 and the first part of 1947, so that the System could have sold long-term securities without violating its support policy. It did not do so, however, and indeed could not have gone far on its own in this direction, since it held less than $1 billion of such securities. Its holdings were in bills and certificates, and there was little demand for these at the support rates (see Chart 48).

During the war, the 2½ per cent interest rate on long-term securities which the Federal Reserve was committed to protect was below the level consistent with no change in the stock of money and required for its maintenance the continuous creation of high-powered money—as was the 3 to 4 per cent discount rate in the active phase of World War I, and the same or a higher rate for some eighteen months thereafter. By contrast, less than a year after the active phase of World War II, the same 2½ per cent rate was *above* the level consistent with no change in the stock of money and would have required for its rigid maintenance the destruction of high-powered money.

During the immediate postwar period and for some time thereafter, the Federal Reserve System did not question, at least officially, the desirability of supporting the price of government obligations.[27] But it did favor raising the bill and certificate support rates. On July 10, 1947, the posted ⅜ of 1 per cent buying rate on Treasury bills and the repurchase option granted to sellers of bills were terminated, though the pegged rate of ⅞ of 1 per cent on certificates was maintained. It has been reported that the Treasury, which had been reluctant to see any change in the pattern of rates, consented to the rise in the interest costs on its short-term debt because of the offset created by the adoption on April 23, 1947, by the Federal Reserve System of a policy of paying into the Treasury approximately 90 per cent of the net earnings of the Federal Reserve Banks.[28]

[27] See statements in *Annual Report*, 1945, p. 7; 1946, p. 6; 1947, p. 8; 1948, pp. 2, 4, 20; 1949, pp. 7–8; 1950, p. 2; 1951, pp. 3, 4, 95, 98.
[28] This was accomplished under the authority granted to the Board (sect. 16 of the Federal Reserve Act) to levy an interest charge on Federal Reserve notes not covered by gold certificates. Before 1933, each Federal Reserve Bank had to pay a franchise tax to the government equal to 90 per cent of its net earnings, after it had accumulated a surplus equal to its capital. That provision was repealed by

On August 8, 1947, the Federal Open Market Committee took the next step in the program of raising the support rates somewhat, by discontinuing the ⅞ per cent buying rate on certificates. The Treasury progressively raised the rate on newly issued certificates until it reached 1⅛ per cent in December 1947. At the same time, the bill rate moved up to 1 per cent. Not until the fourth quarter of 1948, after the price peak, did the Treasury increase the certificate rate to 1¼ per cent and the rate on bills to about 1⅛ per cent.

In addition to these measures, the Treasury changed the composition of the debt by increasing the amount of long-term debt relative to short, thereby achieving the same effect as the Federal Reserve could have by selling long-term securities and buying short-term, if it had had the long-term securities to sell.[29] Yields firmed, rising from 2.26 per cent in mid-October 1947 to 2.37 in mid-November. At that point the Federal Reserve and Treasury stepped in to prevent a further increase in yields, which is to say, decline in the price of bonds. The System bought $2 billion in government bonds in November and December, and Treasury investment accounts bought over $900 million. On December 24, the Federal Open Market Committee established a new lower support level for the price of government bonds and yields rose to 2.45 per cent. This was the level at which prices of long-term governments were maintained through 1948, the System buying an additional $3 billion through March 1948.

The sharp narrowing of the differential between short and long rates as a result of the rise in the rates on bills and certificates made short-term securities relatively more attractive to holders, led them to shift the composition of their portfolios, and thereby produced a reverse shift in the

---

the amendment to the Federal Reserve Act, contained in the Banking Act of 1933, providing for the establishment of the FDIC. The Congress required each Reserve Bank to subscribe to the capital stock of the FDIC an amount equal to one-half of its surplus on Jan. 1, 1933. Because of the reduction in their surplus as a result of the subscription, the Reserve Banks were relieved of the franchise tax. Earnings over the period ending 1944 were sufficient to restore the surplus only to less than 75 per cent of the Banks' subscribed capital. In 1945 and 1946, however, earnings were large enough to increase the surplus above the combined capital of the Banks.

The relationship between the action on earnings and the elimination of the posted ⅜ of 1 per cent buying rate is implied in the record of the Federal Open Market Committee, which reports discussions with representatives of the Treasury including those items on the agenda (Board of Governors of the Federal Reserve System, *Annual Report*, 1947, pp. 90–92). See *Commercial and Financial Chronicle*, July 10, 1947, p. 20 (124), for the suggestion that the transfer of Federal Reserve earnings to the Treasury was the *quid pro quo* for Treasury acquiescence in the rise in interest costs.

[29] From Apr. to Oct. 1947, the Treasury sold $1.8 billion of bonds held in its own investment accounts, and in Oct. issued a new nonmarketable 2½ per cent bond.

Federal Reserve System's portfolio (Chart 48). That shift rather than any net monetization of debt accounted for the Federal Reserve purchases just listed. The purchase of $5 billion of bonds from November 1947 through March 1948 was accompanied by a reduction of some $6 billion in the System's holdings of short-term government securities, so that Federal Reserve credit outstanding was more than $1 billion lower at the end of March 1948 than at the end of October 1947. The announced pattern of rates taken as a whole, therefore, continued to be above rather than below the level consistent with no change in the money stock. Since the pattern was then made effective, whereas before that actual rates had been below the announced rates, monetary contraction was, as we have seen, actually produced during calendar 1948.

The situation was not recognized at the time. Concern continued to focus on inflation even though, in retrospect, it is clear inflationary pressure was rapidly waning and the seeds of a contraction were being sown. In November 1947, the System tried its by now almost traditional confession of impotence—resort to moral suasion. A joint statement by bank supervisory authorities was issued to banks urging them to avoid making nonessential loans. In January 1948, discount rates at all Reserve Banks were raised to 1.25 per cent, and in August, to 1.5 per cent but, since in both cases market yields on bills and certificates were lower, neither rate was effective. More significantly, as already noted, reserve requirements were raised. Since country and reserve city bank requirements were at their prior legal maximums, the final rise—which occurred in September 1948, a month after the price peak—was applicable to all banks only because an act of Congress passed in the preceding month had authorized a temporary increase in the legal maximums, which were to revert to their former level in June 1949.[30] In August 1948, Congress also restored Federal Reserve control over consumer credit until June 1949, when control was once again permitted to terminate.

A counterpart of the relatively small rise in the money stock during the period from 1946 to 1948 was the relatively small rise in velocity. As we have seen, velocity fell by more than a third between 1942 and 1946. The rise from 1946 to 1948 offset less than a quarter of this decline, leaving velocity in 1948 at less than three-quarters its level in 1942 and at only seven-eighths its level in 1939, which itself was low by historical standards. Yet one might have expected both the attempt to "use" the wartime accumulation of liquid assets and the rising prices that rendered it costly to hold money balances to produce a sharp rise in velocity, which

[30] The new maximums against net demand deposits were 30 per cent at central reserve city banks, 24 per cent at reserve city banks, and 18 per cent at country banks, and against time deposits, 7½ per cent at all banks. The requirement imposed in September was 26, 22, 16, and 7½ per cent, respectively.

would, of course, have further intensified the price rise. To put the matter in terms of liquid asset holdings: in 1939, the year the war broke out in Europe, the public held money balances amounting to about 8 months' income, and mutual and postal savings deposits plus savings and loan association shares plus government securities amounting to an additional 5 months' income; so the total of those liquid assets amounted to 13 months' income. By 1946, money balances amounted to over 10 months of a much higher income and the broader total of liquid assets to 21 months' income. In the next two years, the public—despite its pent-up demand for goods unavailable earlier and despite vigorous economic expansion—reduced those balances only moderately: money to 9 months' income, about half-way between the prewar and immediate postwar levels; and the broader total of liquid assets to 18 months' income, or only three-eighths of the way back to the prewar level.

The connection between the changes in velocity and the public's willingness to hold liquid assets fixed in nominal amount perhaps helps to make clear why the low rate of increase in the money stock and the small rise in velocity are different aspects of essentially the same phenomenon. Both reflect a willingness on the part of the public to hold relatively large amounts of money and government securities at fairly low rates of interest. Paradoxical though it may seem, the low rate of increase in the money stock reflected the public's willingness to hold much money, as part of its willingness to hold much of its assets in liquid form. Had the public desired to dispose of more of its liquid assets, the attempt to do so would have tended to drive down prices of government securities and raise their yields, which, in turn, would have led the Federal Reserve, in pursuance of its support program, to buy government securities, thereby raising high-powered money and the total stock of money.

How was it that an interest rate of 2½ per cent on long-term government securities was above the level consistent with a stable money stock in a period of expansion and rising prices; or, equivalently, that at this rate, the public was willing to hold an abnormally high quantity of nominal dollar assets relative to its income?

One factor was the large surplus of the government in the calendar years 1946 through 1948: in 1946, which was a transitional year with respect to the money stock as well, the cash surplus was a nominal $0.04 billion; in 1947, $5.7 billion; and in 1948, $8.0 billion. The effect of the associated debt requirement on the technical monetary position has already been taken into account implicitly in our discussion of the arithmetic of the change in the money stock.[31] In any event, given the support policy of the

---

[31] In 1946, the Treasury used its unusually large General Fund balance, derived from overborrowing in the Victory Loan, to retire debt. That was a bookkeeping operation involving the simultaneous reduction of deposits in war loan accounts

Reserve System, the money stock during that period, as during the war, had to be whatever was consistent with the supported pattern of rates, and one or another of the proximate determinants—in practice primarily high-powered money—had to adapt to produce that stock. Hence, the important effects of the surplus are to be found elsewhere. Just as, during the war, any excess of federal expenditures over tax receipts had to be matched by an accumulation of government obligations—noninterest-bearing or interest-bearing—by the public at large, so after the war, an excess of federal receipts had to be matched by a reduction of government obligations. Put differently, during the war, the federal government spent more than it received in taxes, so the members of the public had to spend less than they received as income. The rise in prices was one factor inducing them to do so, and the rise in the stock of money was one form in which they accumulated their unspent receipts. After the war, the federal government took in more in taxes than it spent, so the members of the public had to spend more than they received as income. The failure of prices to rise more than they did was necessary to

---

requiring no reserves—a debt of the banks to the government—and of securities held by the banks—a debt of the government to the banks. (The exemption of war loan accounts from member bank reserve requirements expired on June 30, 1947, as a result of the Presidential proclamation, issued Dec. 31, 1946, terminating the period of hostilities of World War II.)

There has been much discussion of the monetary impact of the use of surplus revenues to retire debt, particularly of the effect of retiring debt held by different holders. This was a continuation of the wartime confusion assigning special importance to commercial bank-held debt. *Other things being the same*, retirement of Federal Reserve-held debt through the transfer of Treasury deposits at commercial banks involved a reduction in high-powered money, and therefore a contracting influence on the money stock. Retirement of debt held by commercial banks through the transfer of Treasury deposits at commercial banks requiring reserves involved initially a reduction of the same amount in deposits requiring reserves and in bank assets in the form of government securities. Given fractional reserves, the retirement released excess reserves that would tend to be used to restore the initial level of deposits and assets, and so it was neutral in its monetary effects. Retirement of nonbank-held debt with Treasury deposits requiring reserves involved simply a transfer of ownership of deposits with no direct effects on either deposits or reserves.

But other things were not the same. Given the support program, both the amount and distribution of the debt were effectively determined by the holders. Both had to be whatever was required to make the pattern of rates conform to the one being supported. For example, if the Treasury used the surplus to retire long-term securities held by the public, when, at the fixed rates, the public wished to retain the long terms and dispose of its short terms, the result would be a tendency of short-term rates to rise and long-term rates to fall. This would lead in turn to sales of long terms and purchases of short terms by the Federal Reserve in order to maintain the rate pattern, so leading to precisely the same result as if the Treasury had initially retired short-term securities. And similarly for any other pattern of Treasury operations and public preferences. Treasury operations only determined whether a particular holder acquired his securities from or disposed of them to the Treasury or the Federal Reserve or other holders.

induce them to do so, while the slow rise in the stock of money reflected the effect of the excess spending by the public.

Had the federal government not run a surplus, the public, with its accumulated liquid assets and pent-up demand, would have *tried* to spend more in the postwar period than it received—an impossibility, since one man's expenditures are another's receipts. The process of trying, however, would have tended to raise prices and incomes and so would have reduced the level of liquid assets relative to income by this inflationary route. Moreover, the process would doubtless have tended to raise interest rates and so would have produced a monetization of the debt and a still larger rise in prices. As it was, the federal surplus enabled some reduction of liquid assets relative to income to be achieved without inflation. To put the matter still differently: in terms of the market for loanable funds, the Treasury surplus constituted an increase in the supply of loanable funds and thereby reduced the interest rate that would clear the market at any given price level, just as the Treasury deficit during the war constituted an increase in the demand for loanable funds and so tended to raise the interest rate. The shift in the direction of the Treasury's influence helps explain why roughly the same level of supported interest rates was below the level consistent with no change in the money stock during the war, and above that level after 1946 or 1947.

The Treasury surplus explains how the public could reduce the ratio of its money and its liquid assets relative to its income, to a limited extent, without producing either inflationary pressure on prices or monetary expansion under the support program. It does not explain why the public sought to reduce the ratios only slightly more than by that limited extent. It is here that the second factor we believe to be important enters. That factor was a continued fear of a major contraction and a continued belief that prices were destined to fall. A rise in prices can have diametrically opposite effects on desired money balances depending on its effect on expectations. If it is interpreted as the harbinger of further rises, it raises the anticipated cost of holding money and leads people to desire lower balances relative to income than they otherwise would. In our view, that was the effect of price rises in 1950 and again in 1955 to 1957. On the other hand, if a rise in prices is interpreted as a temporary rise due to be reversed, as a harbinger of a likely subsequent decline, it lowers the anticipated cost of holding money and leads people to desire higher balances relative to income than they otherwise would. In our view, that was the effect of the price rises in 1946 to 1948. An important piece of evidence in support of this view is the behavior of yields on common stocks by comparison with bond yields. A shift in widely-held expectations toward a belief that prices are destined to rise more rapidly will tend to produce a *fall* in stock yields relative to bond yields because of the hedge which stocks provide against inflation. That was precisely what happened from 1950 to 1951 and again from 1955 to 1957. A shift in widely-held expectations toward a belief that prices are destined to fall instead of rise or to fall more sharply will tend to have the opposite effect—which is precisely what happened from 1946 to 1948.[32]

Despite the extent to which the public and government officials were exercised about inflation, the public acted from 1946 to 1948 as if it expected deflation. There is no real conflict. The major source of concern about inflation at that time was not the evils of inflation per se—though no doubt these played a role—but the widespread belief that what goes up must come down and that the higher the price rise now the larger the subsequent price fall. In our view, this fear or expectation of a subsequent contraction and price decline reconciled the public to only a mild reduction in its liquid asset holdings relative to its income and induced it to hold larger real money balances than it otherwise would have been willing to. In this way, it made the postwar rise more moderate. The situation at the close of the two world wars was therefore quite different. The situation after World War II, unlike that after World War I, as noted, was one of widespread expectation of a price decline.

To avoid misunderstanding: our belief that the most puzzling feature of experience during the early postwar years is why, *given the monetary*

---

[32] We are indebted to David Meiselman for calling this piece of evidence to our attention. The data follow.

Quarter	Yield on Baa Corporate Bonds	Yield on 125 Industrial Common Stocks		Corporate Bond Yield Minus Yield on 125 Industrial Common Stocks	
		Dividend	Earnings	Dividend	Earnings
		FALLING PRICE EXPECTATIONS			
I 1946	2.97	3.46	2.64	−0.49	0.33
IV 1948	3.52	6.56	15.18	−3.04	−11.66
		RISING PRICE EXPECTATIONS			
III 1950	3.25	6.49	15.93	−3 24	−12.68
III 1951	3.50	6.13	8 75	−2.63	−5.25
I 1955	3.47	4.14	8.25	−0.67	−4.78
IV 1957	5.04	4.46	6.78	0.58	−1.74

SOURCE: Bond and dividend yields are quarterly averages of monthly data; no seasonal movement was discernible. Earnings yield is earnings per share divided by a quarterly average of price per share and adjusted for seasonal by us. Data are from *Business Statistics;* primary source is Moody's Investors Service.

To make the risk roughly alike as between bonds and stocks, we used Baa bonds. The use of Aaa bonds would not, however, alter the direction of change in the yield differences for the three periods. Aaa bond yield minus dividend yield is −0.96, −3.74; −3.86, −3.24; −1.16, −0.46 (next to the last col.). Aaa bond yield minus earnings yield is −0.14, −12.36; −13.30, −5.86; −5.27, −2.78 (last col.).

policies followed, prices and the money stock rose so little does not imply either approval of those policies or belief that a higher rise in prices and the money stock would have been desirable. The relatively small rise in the money stock was not a product of monetary policy designed to achieve that result but, on the contrary, the policy followed involved surrender of any possibility of explicitly controlling the money stock. The relatively small rise was a product primarily of Treasury surpluses and of widespread expectations that a severe price decline was in the offing. Those expectations were partly a product of the severe 1929–33 contraction, which fostered a belief that severe contractions were the peacetime danger if not indeed the norm; and partly a product of the 1920–21 price collapse, which fostered a belief that major wars were followed by deflation and depression. Of course, had those factors not made the monetary policy actually followed consistent with a small rise in the money stock, the policy might have been changed, as it was subsequently under the impact of the Korean War experience.

In retrospect, an even lower rate of increase in prices and the money stock would have been preferable during 1946 and 1947. A different monetary policy permitting or forcing a rise in the interest rates on government securities could have contributed to this result, though whether without an overreaction like that of 1920 is harder to say. Hindsight is far better than foresight, and the possibility of understanding the course of events after the fact is no evidence that authorities at the time could have produced precisely the "right" pattern of changes in the money stock.

4. *The Balance of Payments*

World War II, like World War I, was characterized by levels of capital export (in World War II, including unilateral transfers) unmatched in any peacetime periods either in absolute magnitude or as percentages of national income. The pattern of the capital exports is fairly similar in the two wars (see Chart 51). A very sharp increase from 1914 to 1917 matches an even sharper increase from 1940 to 1944 (these appear as decreases in the chart, which plots capital inflows and hence shows outflows as a negative item). There was then a four-year decline in the World War I period, a one-year decline in World War II. The extension of aid in one form or another to the war-devastated countries of the world after the second war resulted in an increase for two years followed by a three-year fall to a level around which capital exports fluctuated for some years thereafter. After World War I, the decline which began in 1918 continued through 1923, with capital exports subsequently varying around a rather constant level until 1933.

The peak level of capital exports, expressed as a fraction of net national

CHART 51

U.S. Net International Capital Movement as a Ratio to National
Income, and Purchasing-Power Parity, 1914–60

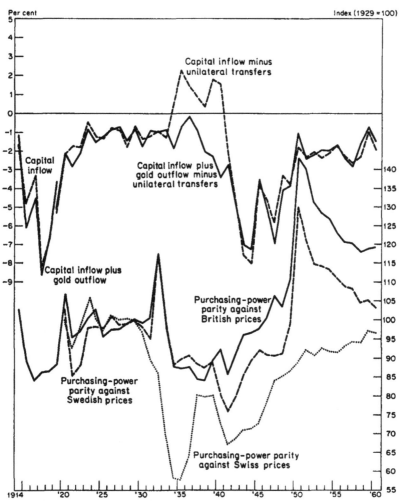

NOTE: Capital inflow, minus unilateral transfers, is plotted as plus. Gold outflow is plotted
as plus.

SOURCE: Table A-4.

product, was about the same in World War II as in World War I—8.0 per cent in 1944 compared to 8.2 per cent in 1917—but the period of abnormally high capital exports was somewhat more prolonged in the later period, nine years compared to six. The similarity in level of peak capital exports is surprising in view of the greater war effort involved in World War II; the difference in the length of the period of abnormally high capital exports reflects the longer duration of the second war.

After both wars, the new level attained when capital exports had receded was higher than the prevailing level under earlier peacetime conditions. From 1907 to 1914, the United States was in approximate balance, neither importing nor exporting capital; from 1923 to 1932, the United States exported capital on balance at the rate of about 1 per cent of net national product; and from 1950 to 1960, at about 2 per cent of net national product. The source of the shift was, however, different in the two postwar periods. The higher level of capital exports plus unilateral transfers after the first World War reflected private foreign lending; the higher level after the second World War reflected government loans and grants—the British loan, Marshall Plan, and other foreign aid expenditures, and loans through the Export-Import Bank, the World Bank, and other similar agencies.

The exchange rate between the dollar and the pound sterling behaved in one respect quite differently in World War II than it did in World War I. In World War I, the pound appreciated sharply on the outbreak of war, only subsequently returning to its prewar parity and being pegged during the rest of the war at near its prewar parity; in the second war, the pound depreciated sharply on the outbreak of the war. From the time Britain left gold in 1931, the pound had no official parity. It first depreciated sharply to a monthly low of $3.28 at the end of 1932, then apreciated to a high of $5.15 in early 1934 after the United States revalued gold. From 1934 to mid-1938, the pound fluctuated around a level slightly below $5.00. Munich and the stepped-up capital outflow from Europe brought a decline to slightly over $4.60 in August 1939. On the outbreak of the war, the pound fell precipitously, first, to under $4.00, then, to as low as $3.27 after the fall of France.

From that point on, the World War I pattern was repeated. Britain fixed the pound officially at $4.035, imposed exchange controls much more extensive and detailed than in World War I, and requisitioned foreign securities and exchange holdings of British nationals. The official rate was made effective by the autumn of 1940 and maintained thereafter. After lend-lease was enacted in 1941, most of the current pressure on the pound was removed, just as it was in World War I after the United States entered the war and assumed responsibility for financing the dollar purchases of its allies.

Whereas the curve in Chart 51 recording capital exports shows the same pattern in the two wars, the curve recording relative prices in the United States and in Britain, adjusted for changes in exchange rates, does not. In World War I, U.S. prices fell sharply relative to British prices along with the sharp increase in U.S. capital exports, and the price ratio rose along with the decrease in capital exports. As we saw in Chapter 5, the relationship between price movements and capital movements in World War I seemed roughly in line with the relationships displayed in the prewar period. In World War II, the price curve in the figure displays almost the reverse relationship; it rises markedly from 1941 to 1947, with no clear response to rises or falls in capital exports.

What explains this failure of the capital movements to be reflected in relative prices, as they had been in general throughout the preceding 70 years? One factor which immediately suggests itself is the system of exchange controls which Britain adopted in World War II, much more extensive than that in World War I. However, this factor works in the wrong direction. As we pointed out in Chapter 5, the effect of foreign exchange controls was to enable Britain, for any given exchange rate, to maintain a higher price level at home than she otherwise could or, alternatively, for given price levels at home and abroad, to maintain a higher dollar price of the pound sterling than she otherwise could. But either alternative means that foreign exchange controls would make the price ratio plotted in Chart 51 lower than otherwise, since this ratio is adjusted for the exchange rate. Yet the puzzle is why this ratio is so high. Foreign exchange controls could provide an explanation only if the United States had imposed such controls to a very much greater extent than in World War I, but it did not.

The only explanation we can offer is that the abnormal behavior of the price ratio reflects not exchange controls but internal price controls, which made the price-index numbers used to compute the ratio seriously defective as measures of "prices" in some more meaningful sense. Price control and rationing were far more extensive in Britain than in the United States, and hence the British index number might be expected to deviate even more from an ideal measure of prices than the U.S. index number.[33]

[33] In judging the relationship between price and capital movements in Chart 51, it should be noted that the capital movement figures have had a secular downward trend relative to the price ratio ever since the beginning of the series in 1871. This means that a given level of capital imports into the United States has tended to be consistent over time with an ever higher price level in the U.S. relative to Britain; or, alternatively, that a given ratio of prices has been consistent with an ever lower level of capital imports (or higher level of capital exports). The obvious explanation of this result is a growing comparative advantage of the United States relative to Britain, a consequence that might be expected to follow from a more rapid rate of technological growth and capital accumulation in the U.S. Such a growing comparative advantage was one of the most popular

Some evidence bearing on this explanation is furnished by the comparisons with Swiss and Swedish prices plotted in Chart 51. Though prices were controlled in Switzerland and Sweden to a considerable extent during the war, the controls were less extensive than those in Britain or the United States. In addition, both countries were probably subject to less inflationary pressure. A comparison of U.S. prices with Swiss and Swedish prices should therefore, if anything, be biased by price control in the opposite direction from the comparison of U.S. with British prices.[34]

As we saw in Table 20, British depreciation in 1931 produced a sharp dispersion in the international structure of prices, largely eliminated by the 1936 devaluations of the gold-bloc countries. Just before the war, from 1937 to 1939, the curves for the British, Swedish, and Swiss price ratios were closer together than they had been since 1930, so those years provide a fairly uniform starting point. The only other official change in exchange rates in years close to the war years is the appreciation of the Swedish krona by about 16 per cent in the summer of 1946, which accounts for the decline in the Swedish curve in that year.

---

explanations adduced for the alleged "dollar shortage" after the war (see John R. Hicks, "An Inaugural Lecture," *Oxford Economic Papers*, June 1953, pp. 121–135).

[34] A recent study of Swedish experience during World War II provides Swedish monetary and price data for a comparison with wartime changes in similar U.S. data.

Percentage change, II 1939–II 1945, in:	*Sweden*	*United States*
1. Currency plus adjusted demand deposits	110	203
2. Money stock (item 1, plus time deposits in commercial banks)	93	163
3. Consumer price index	49	30
4. Wholesale price index	80	39

The much smaller rise in Swedish than in U.S. monetary magnitudes suggests lesser inflationary pressure in Sweden, though, for two reasons, it is not decisive evidence. (1) The wartime disruptions of trade probably had a more serious effect on the productive potential of Sweden than of the United States. (2) Sweden had a smaller fraction of its productive potential unemployed in 1939 than did the United States.

The much larger rise in Swedish than U.S. price index numbers, despite the smaller rise in monetary magnitudes, seems reasonably clear evidence of a lesser suppression of price rises by price control. However, from the third quarter of 1942 to the second quarter of 1945, a period in which price controls tightened, there was no rise in Swedish prices, yet monetary totals rose a further 30 per cent. Perhaps that is why the discrepancy between the price ratios of U.S. against British and Swedish prices narrows after 1942, whereas the discrepancy between the price ratios of U.S. against British and Swiss prices continues to widen to 1945.

For Swedish figures, see Daniel J. Edwards, "Process of Economic Adaptation in a World War II-Neutral Country: A Case Study of Sweden," unpublished Ph.D. dissertation, University of Virginia, 1961, pp. 144–145, 163–164. We are indebted to Edwards for making his dissertation available to us.

For the war years proper, the Swiss and Swedish comparisons both yield results to be expected from the earlier relationships between capital movements and unilateral transfers, on the one hand, and relative prices, on the other. U.S. prices fell relative to prices in both countries from 1939 to 1941, rose from then to 1950 for Swedish prices, to 1951 for Swiss prices. The initial fall roughly coincides with a period when U.S. capital exports and transfers were increasing, and the subsequent rise with a period of generally declining U.S. capital exports and transfers. Moreover, the magnitude of the fall and of the rise in U.S. purchasing-power parity bore roughly the same relation to the magnitude of the changes in capital exports and transfers as it did in earlier periods.[35]

[35] Disruptions of transportation and financial arrangements were so great during World War II that it may seem pointless to seek to find a continuation of peacetime relations between capital movements and relative prices. And, of course, it is not impossible that these relations might be so thoroughly distorted by the wartime effects as to alter fundamentally the peacetime relations. However, our experience in World War I, when the relationships were little affected, should give pause.

Wartime or peacetime, any discrepancy between the amount of foreign currency Americans want to acquire to spend or invest or give away or hold and the amount non-Americans want to give up to acquire dollars for corresponding purposes will have to be eliminated, since ex post the sums acquired and disposed of are equal. The differences between wartime and peacetime are two: (1) the amounts that the parties desire to acquire or dispose of are altered (demand and supply curves for foreign exchange are shifted); (2) direct controls are used much more extensively to eliminate ex ante discrepancies. Regarding (1), it is not clear what the net effect of the shifts is. One might expect that for neutral nations both demand for and supply of foreign exchange would have been reduced by the increased hazards of trade (which, as it were, increased the average price of imports and simultaneously reduced the average proceeds from exports). Regarding (2), if the exchange rates prevailing could be maintained without extensive controls, it must have been because relative prices adjusted for exchange rates were not far out of line with those required to maintain equilibrium.

What was the mechanism that maintained the relationship between relative prices and capital outflows? Part of the answer may be that during World War II capital outflows adjusted to relative prices to a greater extent than they had during peacetime. Suppose, for example, citizens of a neutral country were tending to accumulate dollar balances. In peacetime, the attempt to dispose of these actual or potential balances would set in motion forces bringing relative prices, adjusted for exchange rates, into line with desired capital movements. In wartime, this attempt may have been short-circuited, partly because neutrals might have been willing to hold more dollar balances, just as U.S. citizens were, in anticipation of being able to acquire, after the war, goods currently unavailable; partly because foreign-exchange controls by either the neutral nation or the U.S. might freeze the balances temporarily. In either case, the accumulation of dollar balances, whether desired or undesired, would constitute a capital inflow offsetting the autonomous U.S. capital outflows to its allies. But insofar as that occurred, it meant the capital outflow was adjusting to relative prices, since high relative prices in the U.S. would tend toward a large offsetting capital inflow, low relative prices, toward a small offsetting inflow.

But this is only part of the story. As neutrals accumulated dollar balances in excess of desired amounts, they sought to acquire local currency, and government agencies fixing exchange rates were required to provide them with such currency,

These comparisons with Swiss and Swedish prices therefore offer some support for the hypothesis that internal price controls and consequent defects in price index numbers account for the failure of the British price ratio to show the same relation to price movements during and after World War II as it had earlier.[86]

---

thus producing the kinds of effects internally that gold flows would have produced. The mechanism was essentially the same as that during peacetime.

Finally, changes in exchange rates were always waiting in the wings if needed. As already noted, insofar as they were not needed, it meant that the prior adjustment mechanisms were adequate.

[86] A more decisive test of this hypothesis would require computation of the Swiss and Swedish price ratios for a longer period, and an examination for the earlier periods of the quantitative relation between movements in capital and in such alternative price ratios.

9 780691 615646